What people are saying about *From Chaos to Coherence* . . .

"These are very turbulent times for global businesses . . . with high shareholder expectations, high customer expectations, and high employee expectations. *From Chaos to Coherence* is clearly designed to help an organization excel rather than fall apart under these pressures. . . . Addresses individual health as well as organization health."

—Susan Mandl, President and Chief Executive Officer,
Newcourt Communications Finance

". . . Brings an apparent irrefutable scientific underpinning to what our hearts have always told us about leadership and organizational development: intuition, support for individuals, clarity, balance, and management of the emotional environment all add up to organizations that are productive . . . and to lives that are fulfilled."

—James A. Autry, author, *Real Power: Business Lessons from the Tao Te Ching*

"This book is a manual for anyone who wants to enhance their competitive edge through intuitive intelligence . . . and to adapt to more challenging times with effectiveness and ease."

—Vivian Wright, Strategic Change Services, Hewlett-Packard

". . . A book of profound operating intelligence."

—Allan Cox, author, *Straight Talk for Monday Morning,*
Redefining Corporate Soul

"A 'platinum-plus' effort to expand the impact of HeartMath within the business and government communities, in fact within all organizations coping with stress today! Its greatest contribution is that it speaks equally well to the leaders of large organizations as it does to people in all walks of life, encouraging them to use innate heart intelligence in dealing with the rapid pace of change during a very hectic time in our history."

—Colonel Susan Goodrich, United States Air Force

"The background physiology and the scientific underpinning of this technique are absolutely sound."

—Graham Bridgewood, M.D., Chief Medical Officer,
Shell International, United Kingdom

"Most corporate transformation efforts focus on factors such as creating a vision, an innovative strategy, developing a high-performance climate, cross-functional teamwork, implementing processes for continuous improvement, etc. However, these important factors are environmental. That is, they are all 'external' to the people who must always be at the heart of any organizational transformation. To create true and lasting behavioral change, an internal change within the people involved is the most critical and yet most often overlooked aspect for creating enduring improvement in business effectiveness. . . . HeartMath's Inner Quality Management system [has] provided ideal and simple tools for the internal transformation within our people. The results speak for themselves."

—Peter Buecking, Director, Sales and Marketing,
Cathay Pacific Airways Ltd., Hong Kong

"HeartMath is making significant progress in developing the research underpinnings that explain the powerful benefits of IQM for the person and the organization."

—**Tim Stone**, Vice President, General Manager,
Broadband Wireless Systems, Motorola

"From Chaos to Coherence offers proven techniques for organizations undergoing radical changes in chaotic times. . . . Doc Childre and Bruce Cryer provide us with the techniques required to deal with this real-time revolution so that individuals and companies can thrive in the coming millennium."

—**William M. Ulrich**, Information Strategist, consultant,
and author, *The Year 2000 Software Crisis*

"Being at the vortex of the high-tech industry is very stressful. Using the techniques outlined in this book have literally added ten years to my life!"

—**Patricia B. Seybold**, CEO, the Patricia Seybold Group, and author,
Customers.com: How to Create a Profitable Business Strategy for the Internet and Beyond

"When 100+ CEOs from top companies from around the world are on the wait list, that is 'stress!' So anything a manager can do to help one's collegues is a must to survive."

—**Wolfgang Hultner**, General Manager, Mandarin Oriental Hotel, San Francisco

". . . Exciting and life-changing . . . this book is a must for survival."

—**Fred Verhey**, Vice President of Sales, Western Region, Decker Communications, Inc.

"I am very impressed with the HeartMath technology. . . . I highly recommend learning this material."

—**Jannie Tay**, Managing Director, The Hour Glass, Ltd., Singapore

"From Chaos to Coherence offers powerful tools, research, and case studies [for] individuals and organizations seeking to make better decisions, create cohesive teams, and achieve sustainable results. [For] anyone who wants to improve their leadership effectiveness as well as create a caring, balanced, and productive working environment for themselves and others."

—**Kristine Dale**, General Manager, Entex Information Services

". . . Essential ingredients for business success."

—**Nancy Katz**, Vice President, Sales and Marketing,
LifeScan (a Johnson & Johnson company)

"[Identifies] the true forms of leadership that produce lasting results in corporations today: emotional intelligence, intuitive leadership, and balance."

—**Michael K. Takagawa**, President, Corporate Edge,
Executive Coaching and Consulting

". . . A wonderful, effective path to serenity for crazy, busy executives. The program not only works as a 'problem fixer,' but more importantly it enriches one's life. . . . Equips you to cope not only with all the stress in life, but then goes way beyond in introducing positive, lasting changes."

—**Bob Morgan**, President, Council of Growing Companies

"Challenging, insightful, provocative, practical, inspiring . . . a new and exciting perspective on how to improve . . . performance."
—**Warner Woodley**, Chairman and CEO, Mainstream Access Corp, Canada

"As the millennium approaches with increasing uncertainty about the future of the world as we know it, this work offers great promise for the healthy evolution of our species."
—**Richard Perl**, Attorney and businessman, New York City

". . . Masterfully weaves patterns of recent breakthroughs and chaos and complexity research, heart sciences, and organizational change work, into a rich tapestry of information, insights, and inspiration."
—**George Por**, Founder and Senior Consultant,
Community Intelligence Labs

". . . HeartMath's core approach and its related programs . . . yield remarkable results."
—**Lucius C. Tripp**, M.D., MPH, Division Head, Occupational Medicine,
Henry Ford Health Systems; former Regional Medical Director,
General Motors; and Principal, Wellness Group, Inc.

". . . Begin[s] with coping with chaos and stress but ultimately it leads us to a universal source of inner peace and clarity. . . . consistent with the leadership at HeartMath."
—**James E. Warren**, Jr., CFP, President,
Warren Financial Review, Inc.

"There are two notable breakthroughs for Childre and Cryer in this book. They take the complex and make it simple, and the abstract and make it real. A must read for anyone who wants to lead, support, or be a part of a high-performance team."
—**W. R. "Max" Carey, Jr.**, Chairman and CEO,
Corporate Resource Development

"The book reveals sophisticated medical research about heart intelligence that is understood by nonmedical minds. . . . [It] provides meaningful data and information marinated with practical tools on how to simplify solutions to life's challenges."
—**Tim McGarvey**, President/CEO Eclipse 2000, Inc.

"Provocative and highly practical approach at the heart of business and personal success in the next millennium. . . . Describes the powerful, innovative Inner Quality Management process—a potent combination of biomedical and research validation with heart-based technology. A must-read for any businessperson or executive wanting to measure and sustain organizational improvement."
—**Ken Blanchard**, co-author, *The One-Minute Manager* and *Gung Ho!*

"The fact that the very effective techniques outlined in the book require only one or two minutes of concentration will be cause for rejoicing to any busy executive. . . . Simple methods which, when used consistently, begin to grow, seemingly on their own, into a sturdy platform for substantial dynamic personal and professional accomplishment."
—**James Grove**, Vice President, Salomon SmithBarney

"[As] a professor of management and motivation for more than thirty years, and I am quite sincere in saying that in all the books, texts and papers that I have read concerning effective management none has had the positive impact on me that this book has had. . . . Every aspect of effectively managing any organization is covered with special emphasis on dealing with chaos. . . . Pioneering, enlightening, and highly readable."

—**Jack H. Holland**, Ph.D., DSD, Emeritus Professor
of Management, San Jose State University

" . . . HeartMath . . . has the added benefit of providing tools and techniques that improve the quality of our existence—at work or at home. . . . The changes they enable are utterly profound."

—**Edie Heilman**, Vice President, Voice Technology Solutions,
Charles Schwab & Co., Inc.

"No kidding . . . this book will change your life at work and home. *From Chaos to Coherence* offers a powerful, yet practical, life-enriching process. For years I've recommended going to HeartMath's training programs. Today I highly recommend reading this book for yourself, and giving it to your partners."

—**Heather Shea**, CEO, Inspiritrix, Inc.; former President of Tom Peters Group/
Learning Systems; and co-author *Dance Lessons: Six Steps to Great Partnerships
in Business and Life*

" . . . HeartMath gives organizations the courage to transform costly chaos into coherence. They provide the blueprint no one else can put their finger on, and they have the data to prove it . . . CHANGE is PERSONAL."

—**Dr. Natalie L. Petouhoff**, Change Management Consultant,
PricewaterhouseCoopers

" . . . A great commentary on one of the most controversial issues—how to view management analytically as well as with a heart (emotion and sincerity), and how to motivate people as well as earn their commitment and trust while driving to great results."

—**Zur Feldman**, Executive Vice President, Packard Bell NEC, Inc.

"If there is hope for a real transformation from the information age to the knowledge age—and what lies beyond—the concepts presented here are central to it. The 'silk threads that connect the brain and the heart' are made visible, and the case for realizing their potential in business is compelling."

—**Claudia Welss**, Director, Berkeley Center for Executive Development,
Haas School of Business, University of California, Berkeley

"HeartMath takes the mystery out of boosting organizational performance. Expect to elevate not only your business but your own personal existence as well. This book will profoundly and significantly change your life."

—**Debbie Reichenbach**, Manager, Employee Development, Tellabs

From Chaos to Coherence

From Chaos to Coherence

Advancing Emotional and Organizational
Intelligence Through Inner Quality Management

Doc Childre and Bruce Cryer

BUTTERWORTH
HEINEMANN

Boston   Oxford   Johannesburg   Melbourne   New Delhi   Singapore

Butterworth–Heinemann supports the efforts of American Forests and the Global ReLeaf program in its campaign for the betterment of trees, forests, and our environment.

Library of Congress Cataloging-in-Publication Data

Childre, Doc Lew, 1945–
    From chaos to coherence : advancing emotional and organizational
    intelligence through inner quality management / Doc Childre and
    Bruce Cryer.
       p.   cm.
    Includes bibliographical references and index.
    ISBN 0-7506-7007-X (alk. paper)
    1. Organizational behavior. 2. Psychology, Industrial. 3. Work—
    Psychological aspects. 4. Quality of work life. I. Cryer, Bruce.
    II. Title.
    HD58.7.C486 1998
    158—DC21   98-29911
                                                        CIP

British Library Cataloguing-in-Publication Data
A catalogue record for this book is available from the British Library.

The publisher offers special discounts on bulk orders of this book.
For information, please contact:
    Manager of Special Sales
    Butterworth–Heinemann
    225 Wildwood Avenue
    Woburn, MA 01801–2041
    Tel: 781-904-2500
    Fax: 781-904-2620

For information on all Butterworth–Heinemann publications available, contact our World Wide Web home page at: http://www.bh.com

10 9 8 7 6 5 4 3 2 1

Printed in the United States of America

HeartMath, Freeze-Frame, Inner Quality Management, IQM, Heart Lock-In, Emotional Virus, and HeartMapping are registered trademarks of the Institute of HeartMath.

Contents

Foreword by Scott Shuster   *xv*
Preface and Acknowledgments   *xix*

Chapter 1   Achieving Coherence Out of Chaos: The Inner
Quality Management Model   1
The Four Dynamics of IQM   *3*

Chapter 2   Why Organizations Need Coherence   8
Entrainment   *10*
A Case Study in Enhancing Organizational Coherence   *12*
*Improvements in Productivity, Teamwork, Health, and
  Empowerment*   *12*
The Changing Face of Organizations   *15*
The Impact of Change   *15*
Stress   *16*
The Globalization of Stress   *16*
"Only the Dead Have Done Enough"   *17*

DYNAMIC 1   **Internal Self-Management**   **21**

Chapter 3   A New Model of Human Intelligence   23
Distributed Intelligence   *24*
Intelligence Throughout   *25*
The Brain in the Heart   *26*
The Geography of Emotion   *27*
Resilience   *27*
Emotional Intelligence   *28*
Evolution, Intelligence, and Stress   *30*
Perception and Stress   *32*

Emotional Stress and the Brain   33
The Physiology of Stress   33
The Biology of Heart-Brain Communication   36
With Every Beat of Your Heart   36
Cardiac Coherence   37
Learning and the Amygdala   38
Coherence and Learning   39
Emotional Buying   41
Heart Intelligence   41
Frequencies of Intelligence   42
Intuitive Intelligence   44
Self-Care   45

Chapter 4   Stress and Adaptability: What It's Like Growing
Up in the Hudson River   49
Maladaptation   50
Hormonal Maladaptation   52
Emotion and Immune Health   53
Burnout Hits the Wall Street Journal   54
Emotion and Stress Affect Heart Survival   54
Stopping Emotional Drain   55
Accumulate, Do Not Waste, Your Energy   56

Chapter 5   Freeze-Frame: One-Minute Self-Management   58
Freeze-Frame Steps   59
Why Does Freeze-Frame Work?   60
Neutral   61
The Power of Becoming Neutral   63
Stress Prevention   63
Button Pushers   64
Energy Efficiency   64
The Asset-Deficit Balance Sheet   65
Business and Well-Being Improvements   66

Chapter 6   Time, Expectations, and Other Things Difficult
to Manage   70
Time Experts   72
Time Convenience   73
Expectations   73
Sales Expectations and "Ratios"   75
Judgment   76
Dynamic Balance   77

DYNAMIC 2   **Coherent Communication   79**

Chapter 7   Authentic Communication   81
Electric Communication   83
The Electricity of Touch   83
Deep Listening   85
Barriers to Effective Communication   86
Intuitive Listening   87
Organizational Applications   91

Chapter 8   Technology, Inner Technology, and the Measure of Human Capital   94
A Heart Intelligent Response to Information Technology   98
Enhancing Human Productivity with Heart and Information Technology   100
The Heart and Human Capital   101
Using Intuitive Intelligence to Enhance Information Sharing   103
Freeze-Frame and Inner Technology   104
A Creative Vision of the Future of Information Technology   104

DYNAMIC 3   **Boosting the Organizational Climate   109**

Chapter 9   Organizational Climate and the Emotional Virus   111
The Brown and Leigh Study   112
Ignoring the Climate   114
Tracking and Taming the Emotional Virus   115
What Is the Virus?   117
Who Is to Blame?   118
How to Strengthen the Organizational Immune System   119
How to Spot the Emotional Virus   120
Assessing Organizational Coherence: The Organizational Coherence Survey   122
Content   123

Chapter 10   Core Values: The Foundation of Sustainability   126
Core Values as a Foundation   126
Adaptability Revisited   127

The Role of Significance   128
Care   129
Reviving the Corporate Heart   130
Sincere Care   131
The Drain of Overcare   132
Identifying Overcare   133
Self-Care Revisited   135
The Heart Lock-In   136

Chapter 11   Male-Female Balance   139

The Biology of Gender   139
Male and Female Brains   140
Language Differences Between Men and Women   141
Emotions and Gender   141
Hormonal Zones   142
Emotional Intelligence in Women and Men   143
Communication Styles   144
Male-Female Differences: A Global Perspective   144
What Women Can Do   145
Heart Balance   147
A Heart Stand   147
Inner Male-Female Balance   148
Diminishing Male-Female Competitiveness   149
Next Steps   150

DYNAMIC 4   **Strategic Processes and Renewal   153**

Chapter 12   Managing a Coherent Organization   155

The Service-Profit Chain   156
Management Skill   158
Energizing Teams   161
Appreciation   162
Big Picture and Little Picture   163
Overachieving?   163
Service Straight from the Heart   164
Coaching   165
Military Coherence   167
HeartMapping®   168
HeartMapping Improved Teamwork   169
HeartMapping Applications   171

Chapter 13   Creating a Quantum Future   175
Creating the Future   175
Quantum Management   177
Creating Your Plan   179
Presence   180
Einstein's Vulnerability   181

Appendix   Organizational Case Studies   183
Global Oil Company (European Senior
* Management Team)   183*
Global Technology Company   186
California State Agency #1   187
California State Agency #2   189
Government Consulting Firm   192
Organizational Coherence Survey Data
* for a Large U.S. Government Agency   195*

Glossary   199
Selected Reading   207
Index   211

Foreword

Scott Shuster
Founding Director, Executive Programs, *Business Week*

The world is an internally created phenomenon. We take the inputs received through our senses and process that sensory data through our mentality and emotions to create what each of us experiences as "the world."

Every person's world is necessarily different from everyone else's.

The quality of your individual world depends on your skill in managing and using the data that pours into you: The better you are at operating your body's data processing systems, the more accurate your understanding of the world. And the more accurate your impressions of the world around and within you, the better chance you have of responding to the world in the manner most effective for you and those with whom you associate.

But what are your internal systems? How do they work? Where are the levers of control within us and how do we reach those levers? Such mysteries of human design and response have been the work of Doc Childre for over 25 years. In the early 1970s, Doc discovered that the human heart, an organ that appears to be principally a pump, in fact plays a demonstrable role in human emotional response and intelligence. Hardly a surprise to lovers, songwriters, poets, or parents. But Doc proved it, developing a thoroughgoing set of mental and physical practices that harness the emotional power of the heart muscle and direct that power toward the reduction of stress, improved group interaction, and other positive effects. He called it *HeartMath*.

Doc and his collaborators—Sara Paddison, Rollin McCraty, Howard Martin, Deborah Rozman, Bruce Cryer, and others—learned that the linearity of human thought and the pace at which the body and mind tend to move from one momentary experience to another were additional tools that could lever the basic discovery concerning the role of the heart muscle. They also learned that the HeartMath practice is especially effective when conducted in the presence of others—coworkers, for example.

Through the work of the not-for-profit Institute of HeartMath and more recently through the development of IQM (inner quality management) techniques, Doc's HeartMath tools for the enhancement of personal experience have been turned to the sphere of team development and the improvement of organizations. HeartMath and IQM today are being fielded to the corporate, government, and military sectors. Repeat buyers of the training include Motorola, Hewlett-Packard, Canadian Imperial Bank of Commerce, Royal Dutch Shell (UK), and Cathay Pacific Airways (Hong Kong), as well as many state, federal, and provincial government agencies throughout North America. IQM is so hot that Doc, Bruce, and the management team of his newly formed for-profit training and consulting company, HeartMath LLC, are rapidly expanding to meet the worldwide corporate demand for their training courses.

On an afternoon in 1992, Bruce Cryer first appeared in front of my desk at Business Week Executive Programs, 36 floors up in Rockefeller Center in the heart of midtown Manhattan. His task was to impart an awareness of what at first appears to be pop psychology to a frankly skeptical editor interested only in information of practical application to the needs of large corporations. Bruce had no corporate clients at all: only a few prisons, a juvenile delinquency program, some school districts, and a U.S. Army base.

But the technology of HeartMath proves itself to any skeptic in seconds: Focus your thinking on the pump beating in your chest. Immediately the body warms and frame of mind is loosened and changed. This was Doc Childre's remarkable discovery, a naturally occurring transformative technology of the human body that had somehow gone undiscovered or at least undeveloped, unrecorded, and untransmitted for centuries. It was as though Bruce had brought me the first report of the wheel, the telephone, or the semiconductor. I could see that this was a new and dramatically useful technology.

HeartMath is significant both as a discovery and as a definition: Thanks to this book by Doc and Bruce, and to several of Doc's past volumes, *Self-Empowerment* (1992), *Freeze-Frame* (1994), and *A Parenting Manual* (1995), this remarkable internal technology of the human body is unlikely to again be forgotten. As news of the techniques spreads, HeartMath will become part of the lexicon of human behavior, part of everyone's life.

There is no limit to the potential of HeartMath because at root it is a simple, physical act: a mental formation, a thought with physical effects. It is neither philosophy, faith, nor belief. The essentially physical character of the practice enables its easy application across all the barriers that customarily divide humanity. There is nothing culturally "American" about Heart-Math. It will not transgress any religious or cultural precept. It will work as well in India, Iran, China, or Nigeria as it works in California, New York, the United Kingdom, or Sweden.

Within this potential universality lies HeartMath's immense promise: If everybody did this, what a wonderful world.

Preface and Acknowledgments

I founded the Institute of HeartMath in 1991 as a nonprofit research and educational think tank specializing in innovative approaches to stress relief, quality, creativity, and effectiveness. My initial focus on creating a system (the HeartMath system) that included and emphasized practical tools for the individual was intentional. I always have believed that concepts and theories needed to be grounded in practicality if they were to have meaning and value throughout society. My earlier books describe how *individuals*— parents, teens, women, people in all walks of life—can grow in self-empowerment through learning and applying scientifically researched tools to develop what I call *heart intelligence*. I also designed the HeartMath system to be effectively utilized to improve organizations. HeartMath now has been applied successfully in hundreds of organizations that have participated in inner quality management (IQM) training initiatives. Many people have asked me to write a book about IQM, so it is now my pleasure to present this work on how HeartMath technology can accelerate organizational change.

Everyone is in an organization of some kind whether the person is aware of it or not. It is also true that we are influenced by and dependent on any number of organizations. You simply cannot escape involvement with organizations, whether you need to work in one to make a living, buy products from one, or get your driver's license renewed. Organizations are what organize life.

It also is true that organizations are made up of people. Organizations have names and specific functions, but the people working in these organizations make them what they are. Because of this simple truth, organizational change has to take place first and foremost within the individuals who make up the organization. There is no way around it. As people in an organization develop new levels of mental and emotional self-management, organizations will become more productive, integral, caring, and creative. Without creating an environment that fosters mental and emotional balance and providing the information and motivation needed to help people develop new self-management skills, organizations cannot expect to see long-term sustainable growth in today's business world.

Whether you are in a giant multinational corporation or a small start-up firm, I believe if you want to grow and stay profitable you eventually will have to consider placing as much emphasis on the well-being and development of the employees as you do on annual profits. If you work in a government agency, the same principles hold true, although profits are not an intended outcome. Many organizations have started to realize this, and I applaud them. They will be the survivors that grow and prosper in the new millennium. Now, and especially in the near future, organizations will rise and fall based on the collective inner quality of their people. Society is changing, and people are changing. No longer will old-school business philosophy sustain organizations. This is not a far-fetched prediction. If you look around, you will see that many government agencies, large corporations, and even some of the younger, fast-growth, technology-based companies are starting to fall apart at the seams. Old management styles, rigid policies, new policies implemented without care, unrealistic workloads, and an inordinate preoccupation with "Lord Dollar" are taking their toll. Twenty years ago, if you worked hard, you could make a good living and have a career that offered opportunity and security. Today, you can work hard, be asked to work harder and then harder, which you do, and then get laid off or fired with very little warning because the company is failing or has simply changed priorities. Times have changed. Many people no longer feel supported or cared for by the organization they work for; they lack the skills to deal with the increasing complexities of life and, as a result, the future of many organizations is in jeopardy.

One basic principle for business growth and success these days is very simple. If you drive employees into the ground without balanced care and concern for them, in due time the company will experience steadily decreasing profits (or increasing bureaucratic gridlock) and fade into obscurity. However, if you do all you can to help your people develop new skills to meet the challenges of modern life, both personally and professionally, you will have a workforce that is more enthusiastic, resilient, innovative, and flexible. This translates into an organization that grows, profits, and succeeds for years and years.

The inner quality management process provides the conceptual understanding, tools and techniques, and empirical data needed to advance an organization by improving the individual at the mental and emotional levels. The key to accomplishing this lies not in the mechanics of just reshaping an organizational model from the outside, looking in, but rather in activating the natural intelligence of the heart found within all people. Let me explain.

For centuries philosophers, writers, and spiritual leaders have referred to the heart as something special. They have called it the source of courage, of wisdom, of strength, of intuition. Books abound asking us to regain soul, heart, passion, but in many cases these concepts have been looked at as out of place in business. In truth, I do not blame business people for feeling that way. Why? Because, more often than not, too much of this discussion has remained up in the *sky*, for people with enough time on their hands to even consider such questions. Little of it makes it to the *street*, where concepts become reality through the process of actualization. HeartMath is an intelligent bridge between sky and street. It is about *heart*, a heart that has been taken out of the philosophical, sweet, or sentimental contexts into science, common sense, and direct application. It is a nuts-and-bolts system for efficient living—personally and organizationally. It is about a business deal between the head and the heart, between a person and himself or herself.

I believe this book's greatest value is its blend of organizational *and* individual application. My coauthor, Bruce Cryer, has been key in creating many of the successes where we have introduced HeartMath technology into the business world. We have worked together closely for the past ten years, and now as vice president for global business development for HeartMath LLC, Bruce brings broad-based corporate experience with HeartMath to this work. *From Chaos to Coherence* represents the collective insights of HeartMath, Bruce, and me into emotional and organizational intelligence. Because Bruce has been central to the integration of HeartMath into organizations around the world, often you hear his voice in the stories and case studies that follow.

I originally established the institute to bring together the fields of science, health, psychology, and business. It grew very quickly; so in 1998, we launched HeartMath LLC to provide training and consulting services globally in all the markets formerly served by the institute. The institute continues as a leading-edge not-for-profit research organization. Many people within these two organizations and our associates at Planetary LLC, as well as clients and colleagues, played key roles in helping bring this book into existence. Sara Paddison's editing help was central to the book's coherence. Rollin McCraty was an invaluable research advisor, and Tom Beckman has scoured the Internet and World Wide Web for the last several years in search of data related to the issues of workplace productivity, health care, stress, and corporate efficiency. A special thanks to Dr. Karl Pribram for his contributions to the chapter on human intelligence. Tricia Hoffman, Christiana Bramlet, Jennifer Barr, Dana Tomasino, and Veronica Yousoofian added tremendously to this research effort, while Brandi Barchi and Sherye Woodley were essential in keeping the pieces organized and clear. J. J. McCraty was invaluable in producing the illustrations, and Joseph Sundram's perspective was a tremendous asset to the final chapter, as was Sibyl Cryer's throughout the process. As executive vice president of HeartMath LLC, Deborah Rozman helped guide every phase of HeartMath's development. Howard Martin, president of Planetary LLC, also made many valuable contributions to this work as well as assistance and direction in the entire publication process. A special thanks to Karen Speerstra of Butterworth-Heinemann, who approached us enthusiastically with the invitation to write this book.

We also want to thank Nancy Katz of LifeScan; Chris Sawicki and Dr. Alan Watkins of Hunter-Kane Ltd.; David Pendleton, Jenny King, Phil Smith, and Sharon Lloyd of Edgecumbe Consulting; Vivian Wright of Hewlett-Packard; Susan Mandl of Lucent Technologies; Torrey Byles of Granada Research; Cassandra Pulig of Silicon Graphics; Peter Buecking of Cathay Pacific Airways; Jim Warren of the Warren Financial Group; and Wolfgang Hultner of the Mandarin Oriental Hotel in San Francisco, all of whom offered encouragement and valued input.

Enjoy!

1

Achieving Coherence Out of Chaos: The Inner Quality Management Model

The conductor strode to the podium confidently, plainly comfortable in his role despite the odd khaki safari outfit he was wearing. The orchestra, dressed in evening wear, seemed pleased to meet him, although many in the audience of 1,000 CEOs[1] and spouses were perplexed at the apparent unfamiliarity between orchestra and conductor. The conductor placed his baton on the podium and invited the orchestra to play the first movement of a Beethoven symphony—without him. Startled but professional, the concertmaster (first violinist) raised his bow and with a nod of his head the orchestra began, playing flawlessly—leaderless, in sync, harmonious. Whatever nervousness they may have had about the conductorless performance quickly dissolved in the coherence of their effort.

The conductor then turned with a challenge to the CEOs. "How many of you have such faith in the professionalism and skill of your people? Do you really appreciate their talents and creativity?" He was not done.

The conductor then demonstrated how, with the caring application of intelligence, even greater potential could be realized in the orchestra. He rehearsed each section of the orchestra (a group of professional musicians who had been assembled for one night only) through the same symphony, singing passages where subtle nuances would bring the symphony to life. He encouraged balance and coherence among the sections, orchestrating an entire performance with intelligence and passion. They performed it again, this time with even greater brilliance, grace, and poise. Thunderous applause greeted their final note.

Many in the audience were stunned by the transformation they had just witnessed. Entrepreneurial and driven, the CEOs were being asked to appreciate more, to care more, to go beyond "living life from the neck up." We all had witnessed a coherent organization take shape in front of our eyes. The CEOs now had a new challenge: how to translate this inspiring metaphor into practical application that recognizes the realities of business and organizational life.

From Chaos to Coherence was written for the future of organizations and the future potential of people. It proposes a new system of building organizations that respond to change, crises, and challenges with poise and balance. It highlights organizations built of people who know how to manage themselves mentally and emotionally, who care about the organizations they work in, and who are motivated to manifest their best qualities. This book proposes new ways to achieve such organizations, grounded in science, practicality, and the intelligence of the human heart and intellect. It is designed to educate, inspire, and stretch you into new understandings that can affect how you live your life and how you lead or influence your organization.

We start by facing up to what really is going on in the workplace for most people. It would startle most organizations to have a computer readout weekly—the "Noise Report"—showing the amount of work time people spent thinking and emoting over their problems. If a second computer readout showed the amount of negative hormones released into the body as a result of those thinking habits and the health consequences, in the name of smart business you might insist your people make some mental and emotional adjustments. Then, if you could trace a path of poor decisions and lost opportunities arising from the internal inefficiencies of your people, you would take action. Fortunately, computers cannot generate all that data yet, so we need not face the facts. Yet, the reality of organizational incoherence finds us—anyhow.

From Chaos to Coherence suggests a paradox: considerable chaos exists within many organizations and within society today and a new level of coherence is a potential outcome. Our view is that a new level of organizational efficiency, synchronization, and effectiveness is possible by studying and applying new information about the intelligence of the human system. Organizations will make only incremental improvements in effectiveness and sustainability until a more thorough and sensitive understanding of human processes resides at the core of how organizations function.

When Doc founded the Institute of HeartMath in 1991, he knew stress would dramatically increase during this decade and beyond. How could it not? Globalization in communication technology, markets, and increasing cultural diversity on all continents were just some areas where the rules of the game were changing faster than people could keep track. One of the most profound ironies is that, in the late 1990s, many of the world's technology-driven economies are enjoying unprecedented growth and expansion, yet personal fulfillment plummets and fear soars. The Year 2000 computer problem exemplifies the type of chaos facing us today. The resulting uncertainty and anxiety compels people to ask new questions of themselves and their organizations. Conveniently, new answers have arrived on the scene. Research during the last decade has profoundly affected our knowledge of human intelligence, opening up surprising new possibilities. The fact that intelligence is *distributed* throughout the human system and that *the heart is an intelligent system profoundly affecting brain processing* represents an exciting new model for helping organizational systems become more intelligent, more adaptive, and more humane.

Our team set out to build a coherent organization that would put both care and efficiency at the heart of all our activities: care for our clients and care for ourselves, efficient service for our customers, and internal efficiency for ourselves. Many of the 20 or so who formed the original core team here had worked in companies or public agencies mired in incoherence and ineffectiveness. Human values often were absent, and so was business efficiency. Early on, Doc recognized a link between the heart of a person and the heart of an organization. He knew organizations reflect the collective mind-sets and attitudes of the people who inhabit them. He also knew a new more coherent system that addressed personal needs and organizational vitality was the next step.

This work over several years has yielded tremendous insights, resulting from extensive research into human physiology and the consequences of stress, research into organizational effectiveness, our direct work with dozens of public and private sector organizations, and our experience growing three organizations. Through this process developed Inner Quality Management® (IQM), a set of scientifically based tools for bringing people and organizations into *coherence*.

THE FOUR DYNAMICS OF IQM

The four dynamics of inner quality management (see Figure 1–1) are integrated and operate in parallel in healthy organizations. They involve a thorough, research-based set of tools for

- Internal self-management
- Coherent communication

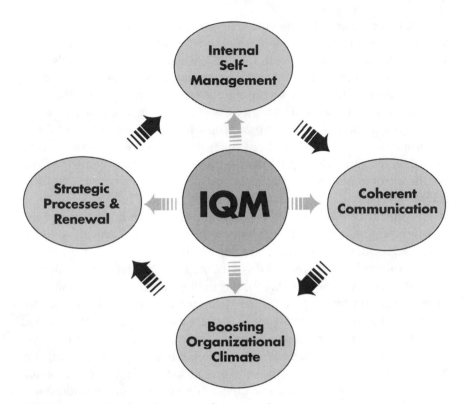

FIGURE 1-1   The four dynamics of inner quality management.

- Boosting the organizational climate
- Strategic processes and renewal

IQM starts with *internal self-management,* the bottom line of individual effectiveness and productivity. It recognizes the negative impact stress has on people while providing the science and tools for neutralizing the negative effects. Achieving *coherent communication* in an increasingly noisy world is the prime objective of the second dynamic; while a growing body of research is revealing the role *climate* plays in an organization's long-term health and performance, the objective of dynamic three. Dynamic four reminds us, through additional tools and case studies, of the ongoing need for *renewal* in the very processes organizations rely on. The objective of all this is increased coherence in all aspects of individual and organizational life. (Chapter 2 will introduce the four dynamics in greater depth.)

Consider that all organizations are living systems composed of people who think *and* feel. Each organization really is a large complex organism whose health and resilience depends on many of the same factors that determine an individual's health and balance. The IQM model is a dynamic process with full intelligence required to keep the various elements in balance and in focus. Smart organizations—like smart people—will recognize and seek to measure the elements that are working as well as those that are out of balance. Any number of factors can weaken and diminish the effectiveness of the others: change in market, change in leadership, change in government. Change of any kind increasingly affects an organization's resilience, its perspective, and its clarity of purpose. This is why the first dynamic in organizational coherence is *internal self-management*. It starts with the individual.

Dynamic 1. Internal Self-Management

Much has been done in organizations to improve quality, think strategically, outpace the competition, or keep the customer or constituent satisfied. A tremendous need exists in most organizations to maintain an external focus instead of being isolated and self-centered. However, more and more, organizations are realizing that without tools for increasing adaptability, creativity, and intelligence within the individual, the organization's effectiveness—let alone its long-term viability   is severely hampered. The military historically has focused on this much more than the private sector. Its number one objective must always be "force readiness."[2] There is no question, in the minds of military leaders, that the individual must be prepared mentally, emotionally, and physically to deal with anything, including life-and-death situations. Too often businesses forget this critical emphasis on sustaining, nurturing, and preparing the individual and, because of a basic emotional imbalance in most organizations, twist mundane problems into life-and-death dramas. People making the transition from military to business careers often are shocked by the craziness in for-profit organizations over issues "it ain't worth losing any sleep over." One of our clients, a veteran of the military and intelligence communities who interrogated Iraqi defectors during the Persian Gulf War, told us of his shock at the wasted energy he has seen in corporate America over mundane issues magnified beyond reason.

Internal self-management is based on several foundational themes, which will be explained in greater depth in the chapters to come.

1. Understand human processes—mental, emotional, and physical.
2. The pressure on the individual will increase in the years to come.
3. Identify and plug the leaks in your own personal system.
4. Increase the capacity for intelligence.

Dynamic 2. Coherent Communication

The success of internal self-management techniques is first tested in interactions with others; and in an increasingly connected world, communication is more prevalent and demanding than ever. Significant organizational and personal inefficiency compounds when the quality of communication is low, when the importance of it is ignored, or when we simply tell ourselves "other things are more pressing." Coherent communication is a model for effective information transfer between coworkers, with customers or constituents, and within oneself. Coherent communication is based on four key principles:

1. Achieve understanding first.
2. Listen nonjudgmentally.
3. Listen for the essence.
4. Be authentic.

Dynamic 3. Boosting the Organizational Climate

Significant research has demonstrated—and most people's personal experience confirms—the necessity of a positive workplace climate for effectiveness. This topic should not just be the domain of the human resources or personnel department, since everyone in the organization contributes to the climate, as do factors external to the workplace. This dynamic creates the internal environmental factors that support or, if ignored, undermine dynamics 1 and 2. The key principles here are

1. A healthy organizational climate includes supportive management, contribution, self-expression, recognition, clarity, and challenge.
2. An "emotional virus" is attacking many organizations today.
3. Human qualities such as adaptability, flexibility, care, and appreciation underlie sustainable organizational climates.
4. We must understand the distinction between knowledge and wisdom.

Dynamic 4. Strategic Processes and Renewal

Moving from theory, intelligent models, and case studies to practical application is essential for ongoing organizational coherence. This is the nitty-gritty of how the organization applies its learning. This also is the dynamic that allows the organization to renew itself at a strategic level, provided that the internal, communication, and climate dynamics are well balanced and positive. The principles of this dynamic are:

1. Teamwork and entrained systems.
2. Complex decision-making and project planning.
3. Coaching as an essential management skill.
4. Leadership, creativity, and innovation.

This book will provide specific tools for the intelligent orchestration of each of these dynamics. Weakness in any area strains the whole system and hinders performance. Progress in any area boosts overall efficiency and effectiveness. Intelligent organizations of the future will maintain a keen awareness of and *appreciation for* each dynamic, adding emphasis and focus as changing conditions necessitate.

NOTES

1. The event was the 1995 YPO (Young President's Organization) International University in Washington, DC. Bruce Cryer was presenting HeartMath technology in several workshops to the CEOs. Ben Zander, conductor of the Boston Philharmonic, was the conductor.
2. Because of HeartMath's extensive work in the military, we have had many conversations with military personnel from all four branches. Several bases, including McClellan AFB in Sacramento, have incorporated IQM programs in their training curricula.

2

Why Organizations Need Coherence

Scientists who study the behavior of light, as well as those who study biological systems, understand the concept of *coherence*. The difference between an ordinary household lightbulb and a laser illustrates the concept well. A standard lightbulb produces light waves or particles that spread out from the light source, bumping into each other and diluting the potency of the output. Scientists call this *incoherent* light. Not terribly efficient, but this is the inherent nature of an ordinary lightbulb. As a result, the light from such a bulb illuminates only a narrow field of view. The more powerful the bulb, the more far-reaching is its effect and the more energy is required to power it. But significant energy must go into a bulb for it to create significant light because of the incoherence—or inefficiency—of its light waves. It gets the job done but at a considerable energy expense. Most ordinary bulbs also burn out fairly quickly.

However, if these waves could be brought into coherence—in other words, made more focused and organized—a dramatically new level of power and effectiveness would be achieved. This is the underlying principle behind what makes lasers so powerful. A laser produces coherent light waves that are highly *efficient*. The energy is ordered; it is not wasted and dissipated bouncing into itself. As a result, commercial lasers need operate only on a tiny wattage because they are so efficient. They are incredibly precise in a growing array of surgical procedures and commercial applications because they are so focused, coherent, and penetrating. The shift from incoherence to coherence can bring dramatic effects: a 60-watt lightbulb whose light waves could be made coherent as a laser, would have the power to bore a hole through the sun—from 90 million miles away.[1]

We all have experienced moments of coherence, where things seemed in sync, we were in "the flow," our actions and intentions matched, and the outcomes were productive, efficient, and fulfilling. For many, how rare and random these moments can seem to be. Imagine if we could bring our lives and our organizations into a new level of coherence, focus, and clarity. We can, but we have to become more aware of what real coherence is. What if an organization is doing an admirable job, providing decent customer service, good products or services, just like a household lightbulb while, unbeknownst to itself, canceling out much of its effectiveness because of internal distortion, static, and stress? Lightbulbs burn out; so do people, and so do organizations.

If employees are constantly brooding over negative comments from coworkers or thinking about a problem at home, coherence within those individuals surely will be compromised. How could it not be? They may try to be attentive to their work, but the mental and emotional processes they are going through will drain them of vitality and dilute their effectiveness. Just as in the example of the household lightbulb, they would be producing randomly and it will take a lot of power to even keep the light burning. In the workplace, people somehow find this power through drawing on raw nerve energy or in some cases on the fear of not meeting management's expectations. If not checked, they burn out and productivity ceases.

Putting emphasis on learning how to deal effectively with workplace and personal problems will create more coherence in the individual. Attention span, mental clarity, and creativity naturally will increase. Coherence is efficiency in action. Coherent people thrive mentally, emotionally, and physically. Coherence is not a static, rigid state. When a system is coherent, virtually no energy is wasted because of the internal synchronization. Power is maximized—the power to adapt, flex, innovate. This coherent power results in a major leap in efficiency and effectiveness.

Coherence within people can be measured biomedically, with profound implications for productivity, mental clarity, and cardiovascular, immune system, and hormonal health as well as overall fulfillment. *Cardiac coherence* is a term used to describe one's cardiovascular system when the electrical and mechanical systems of the heart are beautifully synchronized and efficient.[2] Internal coherence can be measured by monitoring the electrical synchronization of brain and heart and determining whether the nervous system is full of noise or static free. The effect of increased individual coherence means we spend less energy to maintain health, we waste less energy through inefficient thoughts and reactions, and our body does not need to strain to keep us focused and productive.

Coherence is a progressive state—the more we build it, the more we have in reserve. The aim is to increase the ratio of time spent, personally and organizationally, in coherence. Increased personal coherence yields greater flexibility, adaptability, creativity, and perhaps most important, the self-security to regain hope. This is not just a clever theory or speculation of what the future might be. It is grounded in practical research and tools you can apply today to act, think, and feel better.

Organizations—being the sum total of the intelligence, creativity, self-management, and coherence of their people—operate the same way. As coherence increases within individuals and teams, a much higher level of organizational coherence and alignment is possible—coherence between the organization's mission, its vision, and its actions. Coherence is *consistency* between customer expectations and customer delivery. Coherence is *continuity* in every internal process and communication modality. Coherence is *balance* within the personal life of each stakeholder in the process. Does this imply or necessitate a static external environment? Hardly. It has long been our contention—now borne out in the research of many others—that the increasing chaos and incoherence in all segments of the planet require highly flexible, adaptive, coherent responses. *Coherence is the energy-efficient modality in a chaotic world.*

Organizational coherence also can be measured. There is no need anymore to guess, no need to merely theorize or provide appealing anecdotes that are difficult to translate to a unique organization and its ever-changing needs. Research conducted at the Institute of HeartMath labs,[3] as well as other researchers cited in this book, confirms what many organizational thinkers and businesspeople have known intuitively for years: Organizational systems must simultaneously address personal dynamics *and* organizational structures. This book will share stories of several organizations determined to understand clearly how they are doing.

ENTRAINMENT

Through our work with teams in many types of private and public sector organizations, it became clear that individuals first must learn tools for their own self-management. That is the foundation. Workshops and offsite seminars abound to address "team building" but most ignore the fundamental mental and emotional processes *within* the individual. We questioned how teams could ever be more effective until the individuals became more "in sync" with themselves. We began to see practical examples of a phenomenon known to scientists but quite lacking in most organizations, the phenomenon of entrainment. *Entrainment* is the scientific term for the synchronization of systems (see Figure 2–1). Flocks of birds, schools of fish, the pacemaker cells in the human heart—all are examples of entrainment. Teams that are

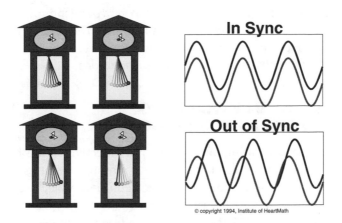

© copyright 1994, Institute of HeartMath

FIGURE 2–1   Entrainment. The concept of entrainment was first discovered in 1665 by the Dutch clock maker Christiaan Huyggens, who observed that pendulum clocks fell into synchronized rhythm if their pendulums were of the same length. Even after breaking their rhythm they fell back into synchronization. Numerous examples exist in the biological world of this innate tendency to conserve energy.

entrained function smoothly, capitalizing on the creativity and intelligence of the individual members with minimal distortion or static. To use Faith Popcorn's term, they are "clicking."[4] They are more coherent in everything they do. There is less distortion and internal conflict and greater resilience and flexibility in the face of challenge or crisis.

Coherent individuals are the prerequisite for entrained teams. Individuals who are coherent enjoy greater balance in their work and personal lives, finding decision making easier. For such people, the challenges of the mind and the desires of the heart are in greater balance, allowing the opportunity for more fulfillment and fun.

Numerous examples of entrainment and its lack are available—companies that grew too fast and became incredibly disjointed; athletes who performed "in the zone" only to lose it and grow despondent; music groups, sports teams, and dance troupes who achieved a high level of entrainment and moved effortlessly as one coherent whole without sacrificing individual excellence and uniqueness.

A common thread seemed always to be the heart. Was their "heart" in what they were doing? Were they operating from a deep intuitive intelligence or had personality differences overridden common goals, common values, and a common mission? Were love and appreciation guiding principles fueling their actions? Our professional careers have been extremely varied—manufacturing, music, business, biotech, publishing, and now personal and organizational effectiveness consulting. The high points always happened when our hearts were fully in what we were doing. That process always yielded creative insight and efficient solutions.

A CASE STUDY IN ENHANCING ORGANIZATIONAL COHERENCE

As a research organization, a fundamental objective of the Institute of HeartMath was to inform leaders in science and business of its discoveries and to leverage previous work into more extensive projects. Proving the institute's ideas of organizational coherence in a world-class organization was a high priority. In 1994, the director of emerging technologies for a Fortune 50 company approached Bruce about one of the firm's core objectives: enhancing the human performance of its people. The company already had a global reputation for product innovation and an unusually strong focus on people. It entered markets where it had no expertise and quickly dominated them. The company often credited the organizationwide focus on training as fundamental to its market leadership.[5]

But now the company's issues were changing. Technology advances in their key industries were becoming so rapid, leadership no longer was assured. Stress on people was increasing, partly due to the organization's size and challenge to sustain its healthy growth, partly due to societal and family issues unrelated to the organization. The HeartMath team was asked to design a series of programs for a wide range of staff members to address and measure multiple issues, such as productivity, teamwork, communication effectiveness, health and stress, creativity, and innovation.

Plans were drawn to recruit three teams of employees for the pilot programs, which would be held in two different locations in the United States. The pilot groups would consist of one group of executives, middle managers and administrative staff members; one intact software engineering team; and a team of assembly line workers. This was HeartMath's first significant research-based corporate intervention[6] and the first to test the validity of its concepts, so the project was mildly daunting.

IMPROVEMENTS IN PRODUCTIVITY, TEAMWORK, HEALTH, AND EMPOWERMENT

The study was conducted over a six-month period. Dramatic improvements in productivity were measured in the assembly line workers (see Figure 2–2):

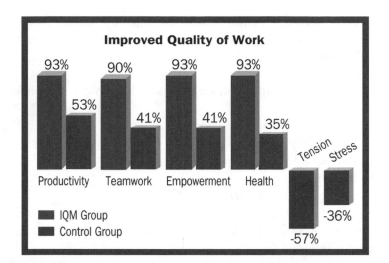

FIGURE 2-2 The graph shows changes in productivity, teamwork, empowerment, and health as compared to a control group of workers performing the same job.

- 93% had increased productivity.
- 90% had improved teamwork.
- 93% acknowledged an increased sense of empowerment.
- 93% felt healthier, including significant gains in energy and vitality, less tension, fewer physical problems, a reduced need for medication, and greater personal and professional fulfillment.
- Not only were they feeling better, but their input was being received: more than 20 recommendations made by the associates for improving productivity were implemented by the management team.

A key factor of concern to the company was cardiovascular health and efficiency. Of the adult working population in America, 28% have high blood pressure.[7] The figures are similar in Europe. High blood pressure (or hypertension) is the leading risk factor for heart disease and stroke[8] and can dramatically inhibit *performance* and *productivity*. While this intervention had not been positioned as a wellness program—the intent was *increasing business productivity*—our clients intuitively knew the relationship between individual health and productivity:

- 26% of the executive, administrative, and engineering teams were hypertensive at the start of the study, in line with the national average.

- After six months, all participants had regained normal blood pressure. They also had learned to lower blood pressure during highly stressful situations.

There were significant improvements in other productivity-affecting factors:

- 18% less anxiety
- 26% less burnout
- 20% less hostility
- 32% increase in contentment

There was a 36% reduction in overall stress symptoms, which included the following:

- 56% reduction in sleeplessness
- 31% decrease in rapid heartbeats
- 27% reduction in headaches
- 33% reduction in heartburn
- 30% reduction in trembling due to stress

Bruce also received many comments that showed greatly increased personal and team coherence.

- "More inventions were disclosed in the last six months."
- "Since my stress levels are now lower, I am more relaxed and able to think more clearly. My negotiation skills have improved."
- "My number of patents per month literally doubled."
- "I feel happier with myself. I perform better with my job. I communicate more—without being afraid."
- "I'm handling family life a lot better with less worries, and I've resolved a lot of prolonged issues. I can listen to others, be open-minded, willing to train coworkers, and come to work feeling happy and ready to work."

In corporate speak, we "hit a home run"—great data, great personal enthusiasm, plans to expand the implementation throughout at least one factory. The fact that the company was Motorola gave us enormous credibility and leverage to begin speaking with other organizations about the potential benefits of the institute's technology. We even were rewarded with a special prize at an internal competition held by the company.

At the end of a story like this, you might expect something downbeat, like "the program later collapsed because the bureaucracy was threatened that something so simple could be so effective." But there is no downbeat ending here. Now, more than 1,000 people have gone through the IQM program, coherence is increasing, and morale is up. The primary division where these tools were implemented has seen record growth and the corporate university is offering IQM at headquarters. So we offer this story as an example of what could be. In an age when organizational strain and uncertainty predominates, when our most productive hours and years remain dedicated to organizations that often show little or no loyalty to us, there are compelling reasons to do things differently. And they can result in measurable improvements that organizations—and people—require.

THE CHANGING FACE OF ORGANIZATIONS

This clearly is an era of unprecedented change. For corporations, increased customer awareness has resulted in greater expectations and demands. Increased competition has increased internal pressures while reducing profit margins. A more complex marketplace has required ever more sophisticated sales and marketing techniques. The rapid proliferation of information technology has created a mountain of information to manage and respond to. The public sector has faced many of these same profound changes with the added burden of an electorate deeply cynical about the relevance of governmental institutions and policies. *Gridlock* now is used to describe political impasses as often as freeway traffic. Downsizing, also known euphemistically as *right-sizing* and darkly as *capsizing*, has arrived in every segment of society, with numerous military base closures in the United States causing wrenching change in the communities grown dependent on them. Reengineering and outsourcing have been initiated to boost internal efficiency, while new skills to manage the changes have been required. Feeling tired yet?

THE IMPACT OF CHANGE

Many organizations have gotten flatter, and the reduction in bureaucratic layers has meant people have to be much more flexible, have multiple skills, and struggle with roles that often are less defined. Even the world of science has felt the pain and promise of change. In the United States, managed care has totally altered how disease is treated and dramatically affected already strained doctor-patient relationships. At the same time, the fragmentation of science into thousands of subspecialties is seeing a backlash into more integrated approaches that build on interdisciplinary strengths such as psychoneuroimmunology, the study of mind-body interactions.[9]

A U.S. Bureau of Labor Statistics study discovered that significant effects occur in employee productivity and actual behavior as a result of change.[10] As a direct consequence of organizational change—whether brought upon by changing market, downsizing, change in leadership, or simply a series of bad decisions,

- Productive work dropped from 4.8 hours per day to 1.2 hours per day, a loss of 75%.
- Social chat and gossip increased from 1.5 hours per day to 3.2 hours per day, an increase of more than 100%.
- Retraining time went from 0 hours to 1.8 hours, now occupying nearly 25% of the employee's time.

STRESS

According to the U.S. Department of Labor, the workplace is the greatest single source of stress, no matter what you do or how much you earn.[11] Stress may now account for 75–90% of all visits to physicians, according to the American Institute of Stress.[12] The price tag to American businesses for stress is at least $200 billion a year.[13] In one recent study (www.job-stresshelp.com, June 1998), 44% of the workers questioned believed their workload is excessive, 46% worried about layoffs, 55% worried about the company's future, and 50% felt their jobs were not secure. This equates to millions of people trying to work through worry and insecurity, on a daily basis. Another study found that 42% of Americans had looked for a new job because of the struggle to maintain work-personal life balance (International Survey Research LLC, Weekend Report [May 30, 1998], Chicago, IL).

THE GLOBALIZATION OF STRESS

America has no exclusive franchise on workplace stress. A recent *New York Times* article noted that the word *stress* has become so universal it does not need to be translated into the local languages.[14] Say "stress" in virtually any country of the world and the locals will know what you mean. A 1992 United Nations Report called job stress *"the* 20th-century disease."[15]

In the United Kingdom, as much as 10% of the GNP now goes to stress-related costs. A recent study in the UK[16] showed that 60% of managers work in excess of the normal workweek, and 52% claim to be suffering from too much work, up from 40% in 1993. Furthermore, 40% of male respondents felt they did not spend enough time at home. Over 50% cited the balance between home and work as stressful. This study also found that 47% of those interviewed found their workload had "increased greatly" during that year. In Canada, at least $12 billion is spent each year on trackable stress-related costs, and 46% of Canadian women and 36% of Canadian men cite "being too busy" as the main cause of work stress.[17]

Their colleagues in Japan, Hong Kong, and the developing economies of Asia have similar issues. In fact, Asian managers have mirrored many of the same stressed out behaviors and consequences of their European and North American counterparts.[18] In Japan, the word *karoshi* literally means dying at your desk and is considered a national health crisis affecting tens of thousands each year. According to the National Police Agency, suicides in Japan in 1996 totaled about 23,000, more than double the number of traffic fatalities. "The demise of the job-for-life system is especially tough for the Japanese salaryman, whose social rank is determined by his company and his position," reported *Time* magazine in a February 1998 cover story.[19] At least 200 lawsuits have been filed by families of people who dropped dead after too many all-nighters.[20]

These statistics amount to a mountain of inner turmoil and incoherence, around the world. How could this not affect productivity and fulfillment in the workplace?

Typically organizations attempt to answer these questions on organizational stress by rightly looking at systemic problems, blaming the "culture," the "way decisions get made," the management style of the board or senior management team. All these often are fundamental to the problems, but research at the institute suggests that until solutions and tools become individualized, there will be an acceleration of stress and noise in organizations. Too many management fads have addressed large-scale systems issues, but neglected the *core* of every human system—the individual.

"ONLY THE DEAD HAVE DONE ENOUGH"

There clearly is much that could be feared today. Incoherence reigns. There also is much that could be appreciated. Coherence emerges. Which is it? Where do we focus our attention? If we appreciate only what's good, will we not ignore the real problems and issues that cry out for attention? A recent high-level meeting of a global telecommunication company shifted course considerably when an exhausted manager stated, "Only the dead have done enough." This statement, cynical and desperate though it was, was met with complete understanding and sympathy from the other over-worked and underappreciated managers and executives in the room.

It is remarkable to see the ambivalence in organizations today. We hear the excited conversations about fantastic technological breakthroughs that promise unheard-of conveniences and instantaneous information transfer. And we see the stark reality of a workforce, at all levels of organizations, experiencing ever increasing levels of stress and personal imbalance. We experienced the dilemma in our own organization's need to keep pace and innovate technologically, while maintaining focus on how the *people* are doing.

Many are beginning to ask, as Margaret Wheatley does in her excellent book *Leadership and the New Science*: "How do we create organizational coherence, where activities correspond to purpose? How do we create structures that move with change, that are flexible and adaptive, even boundaryless, that enable rather than constrain? How do we simplify things without losing both control and differentiation? How do we resolve personal needs for freedom and autonomy with organizational needs for prediction and control? . . . Is there a magnetic force, a basin for activity, so attractive that it pulls all behavior toward it and creates coherence?"[21] To this we would answer yes. That force does exist. It can and must be tapped for the future of organizations and ourselves.

Perception—the lens through which we view life—is at the root of how we deal with all of it. As Victor Frankl, a Holocaust survivor and author, put it so eloquently, "everything can be taken away from a man but one thing: the last of the human freedoms—to choose one's attitude in any given set of circumstances, to choose one's own way."[22] Doc has spent years showing that it is one's attitudes that underlie every aspect of personal and organizational coherence. Too often it is the hand-me-down mind-sets, inherited from generations or managers before us, that reinforce organizational rigidity and inflexibility. By freeing ourselves from those attitudes, coherence becomes possible, especially in an age where all the rules have changed.[23] As Albert Einstein said, "The world we have created is a product of our way of thinking."[24] We need a new way of thinking. We need a new intelligence.

NOTES

1. William A. Tiller, *Science and Human Transformation: Subtle Energies, Intentionality and Consciousness* (Walnut Creek, CA: Pavior Publishing, 1997), p. 196.

2. William A. Tiller, Rollin McCraty, and Mike Atkinson, "Cardiac Coherence: A New Noninvasive Measure of Autonomic Nervous System Order," *Alternative Therapies* 2, no. 1 (January 1996).

3. The Institute of HeartMath has conducted numerous case studies with organizations applying IQM tools. A summary of several of these studies appears in the Appendix.

4. Faith Popcorn and Lys Marigold, *Clicking: Sixteen Trends to Future Fit Your Life, Your Work, and Your Business* (New York: HarperCollins, 1996).

5. Robert W. Galvin, *The Idea of Ideas* (Schaumburg, IL: Motorola University Press, 1991), pp. 109–111.

6. Bob Barrios-Choplin, Rollin McCraty, and Bruce Cryer, "An Inner Quality Approach to Reducing Stress and Improving Physical and Emotional Wellbeing at Work," *Stress Medicine* 13 (1997), pp. 193–201.

7. "Common Sense About Feeling Tense," *Heart at Work Program*, Dallas, TX: American Heart Association, 1995.

8. Ibid.

9. Alan Watkins, ed., *Mind-Body Medicine: A Clinician's Guide to Psychoneuroimmunology* (London: Churchill Livingstone, 1997). This is an excellent overview of the emerging field of mind-body medicine edited by Dr. Alan Watkins. Several references are made in this book to research conducted at the Institute of HeartMath.

10. U.S. Bureau of Labor Statistics, March 20, 1997.

11. "Taking the Stress Out of Being Stressed Out," *Business Week Health Wire* (March 20, 1997).

12. Paul J. Rosch, "Job Stress: America's Leading Adult Health Problem," *USA Magazine* (May 1991).

13. B. L. Seaward, *Stress Management* (Boston: Jones and Bartlett, National Safety Council, 1995).

14. Richard A. Shweder, "America's Latest Export: A Stressed-Out World," *New York Times* (January 25, 1997).

15. Cited in Seaward, *Stress Management*.

16. Karen Charlesworth, "Are Managers Under Stress? A Survey of Management Morale," *Institute of Management* [London] (September 1996).

17. Statistics Canada, Carleton University, and the Conference Board of Canada were the sources for these Canadian statistics.

18. In addition to two Reuters studies cited in Chapter Eight, our work in Asia, especially since the collapse of several Asian economies in late 1997, has revealed a significant level of despair and anxiety in many Asian managers. The collective cultures of many of these countries have left them unprepared for the precipitous economic downturn in that part of the world.

19. Irene M. Kunii, "Caving Under Pressure," *Time* (February 16, 1998).

20. Sandy Sugawara, "Japan Eases Its Killer Work Ethic," *Washington Post* (April 20, 1997).

21. Margaret Wheatley, *Leadership and the New Science: Learning about Organization from an Orderly Universe* (San Francisco: Berrett-Koehler, 1992), p. 8.

22. Victor Frankl, *Man's Search for Meaning* (New York: Simon and Schuster, 1970).

23. Several of Doc's earlier books discuss this theme in great detail. Of particular interest are *Self-Empowerment: The Heart Approach to Stress Management* and *Freeze-Frame: One-Minute Stress Management* (both Boulder Creek, CA: Planetary Publications).

24. Quoted in Joseph Jaworski, *Synchronicity: The Inner Path of Leadership* (San Francisco: Berrett-Koehler, 1996), p. 9.

INTERNAL SELF-MANAGEMENT

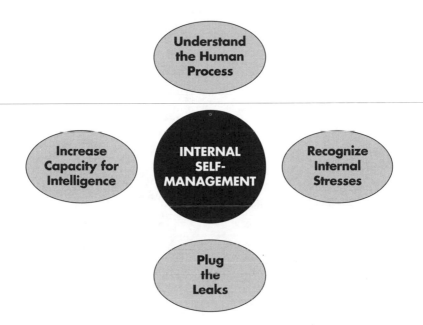

1. *Understanding human processes—mental, emotional and physical—is necessary* to create sustained organizational transformation. A new model of human intelligence provides clues.

2. The *pressure on the individual will increase* in the years to come as societal, family, and internal stresses mount and the pace of change accelerates.

3. As individuals learn to *identify and plug the leaks in their own personal systems*, they stop draining energy and effectiveness personally and organizationally.

4. Individuals can learn to *increase their capacity for intelligence*, resulting in more effective decisions, greater resilience, and a heightened sense of well-being. This provides enormous value to any organization.

3

A New Model of Human Intelligence

The human body is an incredible system—roughly 7 trillion cells with a mind-boggling level of physical and biochemical coordination necessary just to turn a page, cough, or drive a car. When you consider how little of it you have to think about, it becomes even more amazing. When was the last time you reminded your heart to beat, your lungs to expand and contract, or your digestive organs to secrete just the right chemicals at just the right time? These and a myriad of other processes are handled unconsciously for us every moment we live. Intelligence manages the whole system, much of it unconscious. But what also is becoming increasingly apparent is that the same processes are profoundly affected by what *we* consciously do: what we *think*, what we *feel*, how we *react*. Research is now clear that *the inability to manage oneself efficiently leads to premature aging, diminished mental clarity, and even blocked access to our innate intelligence.* The converse is also true: Increasing internal coherence leads to more efficiency in all physiological systems and greater creativity, adaptability, and flexibility.

This is the backdrop for the first theme in the internal self-management dynamic:

> Understanding human processes—mental, emotional and physical—is necessary to create sustained organizational transformation. A new model of human intelligence provides clues.

Science's view of intelligence itself has begun to change. Historically, *intelligence* has been defined simply as mental capacity. Some have even proposed that it is, therefore, fixed, finite, and genetically predetermined. Now it appears intelligence has other dimensions as well, physiologically and emotionally. We all have considerably more intelligence than we thought; we just have not learned to bring our capacity for intelligence into coherence.

The parallels between the development of computing and the evolution in our understanding of human intelligence are striking. Thirty years ago, mainframe computers and the human brain were considered the supreme source of all intelligence in their respective domains: smart computer, dumb terminal; intelligent gray matter, organs that simply follow commands. The explosion in computational power of the microprocessor meant smart desktops connecting with other desktops. Soon the network became the computer and connectivity meant increased intelligence, or at least increased access to information. Simultaneously, scientists began to discover that human information processing was far more distributed than previously thought. They discovered redundant systems in the brain ensuring a backup should certain functions be impaired. They discovered billions of neurons linked together in circuits that "remembered" how to speak, move, act, and so on. But perhaps most challenging to our notion of centralized intelligence was the discovery that intelligence is not confined to the gray matter within the human skull.

DISTRIBUTED INTELLIGENCE

Neural circuits are pathways in our brains that develop as we learn new behaviors and skills. They grow and develop as we do. At birth, 100 billion neurons exist in our brain.[1] How they connect with each other is determined largely by what we experience and by the human and social factors in our environment. Their connections with other neurons form the neural circuits—a grid—that greatly affect perception and learned behavior. They are the storehouse of memory. Yet, neural networks exist in other parts of the body as well, begging the question, Where else does intelligence exist?

Many scientists talk now of cellular intelligence, nervous system intelligence, immune system intelligence, and the inherent information processing capacity of DNA.[2] DNA is a complex molecule found in every cell in our body. It contains the genetic blueprint for the cells and how they will shape our bodies. The DNA in every cell is identical during development of the human fetus, yet somehow certain cells "know" to become skin cells, while other cells "know" to become heart cells. Some intelligent operating system is guiding this whole process, which is in operation long before brain cells have even developed. In terms of brain development, DNA has coded within it the basic patterns for the brain's structure. However, DNA does not determine the neuronal pathways (circuits) and connections that form nor the strength of those connections. These form through our repeated experiences and the influence of the environment in which we live and to which we adapt. Imagine a computer chip whose circuits formed through experience as the operator used the computer, not only through its intrinsic design. Every computer would be totally unique to its user.

The essence is that, while DNA gives us a basic structure for brain development, the patterns formed by the neurons and the strength of their connections develop as a result of the input and experience we each have. As young children our neurons are rapidly forming new circuits in response to learning a new skill, such as walking, physical coordination, or adapting to the environment. If children are often stressed, circuits develop that are hypersensitive to stress in later life, and their ability to adapt is limited. Puberty is characterized by the start of sex hormone production, resulting in a variety of physiological changes including a reduction of "plasticity" in the neural circuits. For example, learning a second language after puberty is considerably more difficult, neurologically speaking, than before. It takes much more focus and energy to reconfigure the neuronal circuits once a basic pattern has been set. This does not mean that the brain cannot be rewired or that we cannot learn a new language after puberty; it just requires more energy. Once a thought pattern is set firmly in place it becomes a "mind-set," meaning our perceptions and responses are bound by that pattern. This limits our range of possibilities and adaptability. If you ever wondered why changing mind-sets can seem to be such a daunting experience, have you ever tried to unhook a neuron?

The concept of intelligence has required some updating as this new information has been uncovered. The experience of being human transcends mere survival, so to limit our definition of intelligence to mental capacity could obstruct a new understanding of the entire human system as intelligent. If we see our system as one that absorbs, reacts, feeds back, and adapts, it could be that intelligence underlies everything we do. Intelligence itself has many dimensions.

INTELLIGENCE THROUGHOUT

It is now known that complex neuronal structures exist not only in the brain but also within the gut and the human heart. Neurochemicals, the carriers of nervous system information, are produced in vast quantities in these areas as well. The chemicals in turn affect brain processing and virtually every other organ in the body.

Have you ever felt "butterflies" in your stomach or a "knot" of worry? Of course, we all have. For several years researchers have studied the enteric nervous system, a complex set of nerves found in the intestinal tract. This elaborate network of neurons and neurochemicals is so sophisticated and profound in its impact, it is now being called the *gut brain*. Its activity is directly tied to brain function. This system appears to be heavily influenced by our emotions and may be the underlying cause of such conditions as colitis and gastrointestinal disorders. More neurons exist in the gut—about 100 million—than in the entire spinal column.[3]

The gut feeling many people trust has biological roots. "Considered a single entity, [the gut brain] is a network of neurons, neurotransmitters and proteins that zap messages between neurons, support cells like those found in the brain proper and a complex circuitry that enables it to act independently, learn, remember and, as the saying goes, produce gut feelings," according to an article in the *New York Times*.[4] In many martial arts traditions, this area of our anatomy, sometimes called the *solar plexus*, is viewed as a source of power and intelligence. Here, martial arts teachers tell us, is where to center yourself and gain power.[5]

THE BRAIN IN THE HEART

As a result of research that may totally restructure our views about intelligence, a sophisticated intrinsic nervous system is also now known to exist within the human heart. A key researcher working to understand its role and influence, research cardiologist J. A. Armour of Dalhousie University in Nova Scotia, calls this intrinsic nervous system of the heart the *little brain in the heart*.[6] It has powerful, highly sophisticated computational abilities and profoundly affects both heart and brain function. Neurochemicals such as norepinephrine and dopamine, formerly believed to be produced only in the brain and nervous system, also are produced within the heart, as well as hormones such as ANF. These appear to directly affect brain function.[7] Just as the gut brain's circuitry allows it to act independently, learn, remember, and produce "gut feelings," so does the existence of the heart's brain help explain the wide range of feelings associated with the heart. The information processing neurons in the heart are named after the neurons in the hippocampus, a region of the brain associated with memory and learning.

Research also indicates that heart function is closely linked to both emotion and intuition. Several new reports suggest that the heart plays a role in both personality and memory. Books such as *Change of Heart* by Claire Sylvia and William Novak[8] and *The Heart's Code* by Paul Pearsall[9] recount numerous stories of heart transplant recipients taking on distinctly different personality characteristics, as well as memories, from the donors. In one particularly dramatic story, a young girl who received the heart of someone who was murdered began to have dreams of the murder and led police successfully to the killer.[10] The heart clearly is a multitasking, multi-dimensional organ intricately tied to human intelligence and perception. The poets and philosophers were right.

So it appears at least three brains are networked together, influencing each other 24 hours a day, much of it below our conscious awareness. Stress and emotional mismanagement appear to negatively impact the coherent functioning among these three intelligent systems.

THE GEOGRAPHY OF EMOTION

In his book *Descartes' Error: Emotion, Reason and the Brain*, neuroscientist Antonio Damasio offers compelling evidence that emotions and intellectual functions are processed in different parts of the brain, which then are integrated in the prefrontal cortex.[11] The notion that intelligence is a purely cerebral, aloof activity uncontaminated and unaffected by emotions has been shown in this and many other recent research publications to be an outdated and misguided myth. Emotions play a primary role in the development and function of the mind. Emotions clearly play a role in day-to-day productivity. Think of the last bad decision made in your organization. Did mismanaged emotion play a part? Did someone overreact and create a policy based on knee-jerk reactions? Did reactive emotions in the organization play a key role in the hue and cry greeting the unfortunate decision? Probably so.

RESILIENCE

Consider for a moment the durability and resilience of the human body. Under extreme duress, humans have been known to live for more than an hour without air. The body shunts blood from the extremities to the vital organs—the heart, the brain. It closes down unnecessary activity so it can preserve life. Without water, humans have lasted about a week; without food, more than two months. In both cases, the body cannibalizes itself, feeding on the nonessential to preserve the essential.[12] Media reports boost our spirits with news of hikers being found after days of isolation or earthquake survivors being discovered alive days after the disaster.

The innate drive to sustain life is truly incredible. But without hope, no one can live fully. The positive emotional experience provided by hope creates sufficient internal coherence for life to sustain itself, even in the most dire of circumstances. Organizations with hope are resilient and buoyant. They continue to learn and grow and are able to healthfully adapt to crises or challenges within the environment. The biological roots of hope and despair are becoming more clear.

Child development specialist and author Joseph Chilton Pearce recounted research showing that, when we become "upset" for any reason, "all neural action, learning, memory, cognition, problem-solving, and so on, is adversely affected."[13] (How often does this happen in your organization?) Our emotional state is critical to what and how we learn and how well we can recall and apply what we learned. Sometimes called *state-specific learning*, feelings and learning are imbedded together in memory. An unhappy experience while learning something new can, in the future, bring up that same feeling as we recall the item we learned. Without conscious thought or choice, a person often avoids learning environments and challenges that give rise to the unpleasant feelings imbedded in neural tracks in our brain at an earlier time. Effective learning is state dependent.[14]

EMOTIONAL INTELLIGENCE

Daniel Goleman's work[15] on emotional intelligence confirms these findings. Goleman, a Harvard-trained Ph.D. and *New York Times* science writer, has popularized this concept in his book of the same name. He cites example after example of studies showing that emotional balance and self-awareness are essential to success in all aspects of life. He argues that we must begin to value emotional skills at least as highly as intellectual ones, since standard IQ is so rarely an accurate predictor of personal or professional effectiveness.

He summarizes what he means by *emotional intelligence* as the ability:

- To motivate oneself and persist in the face of frustrations.
- To control impulse and delay gratification.
- To regulate one's moods and keep distress from swamping the ability to think.
- To empathize.
- To hope.

If we are honest, our organizations and our lives could use a lot more of these characteristics than they currently exhibit. Because of this lack of emotional intelligence, we offer the following hypothesis: *In an age of chaos, organizations rise and fall more due to emotional management or mismanagement within the culture than mere product success or process improvements.* This is as true of start-up firms that experience rapid success but are unprepared for its operational realities as for the massive older organization or bureaucracy "in denial" about the emotional turmoil and malaise of its workforce.

Early on in our careers, we began to understand the consequences of organizational incoherence. One biotech company we were associated with worked hard to land major national media coverage on a key product, knowing that would catapult the company into the consumer mainstream and success would be assured. In fact it had become highly focused on this idea, and determined to achieve it. The firm was looking for the quick bang, instant recognition, the sizzle, the stimulus of the quick hit. (Deeper discussion on the operational and human consequences was absent.) The media story hit, and business grew 500% in one month. Needless to say, the company was ill-prepared for this kind of growth. Not only were all the essential systems not effectively in place, the human foundation had not been solidly built so the employees began a revolving door syndrome of coming and going that sapped the organization's effectiveness. Incoherence reigned. The company never again reached the sales level of that one rocket-ship month.

Emotion, not intellect, is the fuel that drives the engine of business. Mismanaged emotion drives it crazy. Intellect provides the direction, but not the fuel. In most organizations, this understanding has not been activated, so the fuel being used hardly is high octane but more like kerosene. We all pay the price. How a company reacts, how it prepares its people for change—the emotional "field" of a company—all have underlying emotional components organizations no longer can ignore. Truly intelligent organizations of the future will understand that learning to harness and manage coherent emotional intelligence will unleash tremendous power within that organization.

The mind is severely impaired when unmanaged emotions drain our energy or distort our perceptions. One of the great ironies and opportunities is that the mind becomes far more *effective*, *sharp*, and *clear* as the emotions become *balanced* and *understood*. The mind itself can tap into another dimension of intelligence when unmanaged emotions are not leaking all the fuel.

What biology underlies this concept of emotional intelligence? Built into the emotional-cognitive structures of the brain are many evolutionary functions that date back to our species struggle for survival and the mechanisms that evolved to cope with that stress. Brain structures like the amygdala in the "emotional" or limbic region of the brain can "hijack" intellectual processes when intense emotions are experienced in the system.[16] This is why even very smart people can make very foolish choices when under emotional stress. And, even scarier for organizations and people today is that millions of us have *maladapted* to the stress in our lives and have no idea we are under stress!

EVOLUTION, INTELLIGENCE, AND STRESS

A commonly held view in neuroscience is that different brain structures perform different functions that have evolved over time (see Figure 3–1). In a general sense, the human brain can be thought of as having three main structural regions, which are associated with differing levels of control and a variety of functions and basic drives. We call these the first, second, and third brains.

The first brain is comprised of the brain stem structures in the modern human brain processes, including hypothalamus, pons, medulla, and reticular formation. It governs reflex and instinct, and is responsible for many basic functions necessary for survival, including:

- approach/avoidance behavior
- hormonal control
- temperature control
- hunger/thirst control
- basic respiration and heart rate control
- reproductive drive

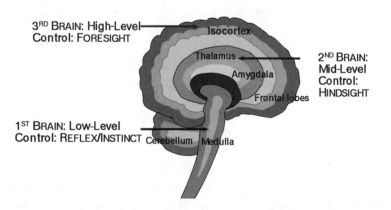

FIGURE 3–1   This diagram depicts the three generalized stages of brain evolution and the levels of control, functions, and behaviors that are associated with the three main structural regions of the modern human brain. Source: Institute of HeartMath.

The second brain consists of the subcortical (also called limbic) areas, including hippocampus, thalamus, amygdala, and pituitary. This region of the brain exhibits control over the first level and is capable of *hindsight*, the ability to see, after the event, what should have been done. This is an aspect of the development of memory, which is an important evolutionary addition. Its functions and basic drives include:

- territoriality
- fear, anger, attack
- maternal love
- anxiety
- hate
- jealousy

Emotional information appears to be processed in this brain region, yet it is not where we actually experience the physical manifestation of the feelings. Positive feelings, such as love or appreciation, are usually experienced around the heart area; negative emotions, such as fear or anger, are often experienced in the solar plexus, where the gut brain clues us in to things that do not feel right, and heartache is an experience felt by many in both the heart and solar plexus.

The third brain has the highest level of control and is capable of foresight and many other important functions, including:

- perception and differentiation of thought and emotion
- self-reflection
- discrimination of appropriate behavior
- problem resolution
- guilt
- goal satisfaction
- forgiving

The third brain, including the isocortex, frontal lobes, temporal lobes, parietal lobes, and occipital lobes, constitutes roughly 80% of the human brain. An organization hires you largely based on what it thinks it can squeeze out of this portion of your brain. Higher order human capabilities like language, creativity, self-reflection, complex problem solving, and the ability to choose what is appropriate behavior are believed to emerge from these structures. From our teen years onward, specialized circuitry continues to develop in the prefrontal lobes that helps us chart a moral course in life. We learn to manage and balance reaction and emotion in making the little and big choices in life through the development of the frontal lobes.[17]

Institute of HeartMath (IHM) research suggests that emotional reactiveness and stress, which we often experience as feelings of inner turmoil, can inhibit the cortical regions in the third brain.[18] With the cortical functions inhibited, problem-solving is hampered, reaction speeds and coordination are impaired, and we cannot think as clearly. Higher intelligence can be jammed by the reactions and pulls of the first and second brain regions. Our decisions are less effective, our listening skills impaired, our creativity obstructed. Fortunately, the reverse also is true. When we feel harmonious and balanced, cortical (higher brain) function is enhanced. We can see possibilities where previously we could perceive only dead-ends. (Many people intuitively know this to be true. It is fun to have the research catch up with intuition.)

PERCEPTION AND STRESS

Let us look deeper into the role of perception and stress. For many years, it was believed we consciously perceive an event prior to the awareness that it could be dangerous or a threat to our survival. However, in recent years, research has revealed the role of an almond-sized structure that profoundly influences both perception and behavior. Called the amygdala and located in the region of the second brain, one of its key roles is to compare incoming information with past experience, looking for a match (see Figure 3–2). It also is believed to be the storehouse of emotional memory, so the matches it is

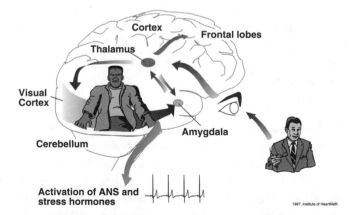

FIGURE 3–2   The amygdala is an almond-sized structure in the subcortical areas of the brain. It "eavesdrops" on information received through the thalamus, looking for an emotional match to previous experience. Working at high speed, if a match appears to be found, it communicates to the higher regions of the region affecting our behavior and decision making.

looking for are emotionally significant. The amygdala is not terribly precise, so if new information *appears* to match, messages are sent to the brain that in deed a match has been found. This can result in what has been called *emotional hijacking*, where we have an immediate emotional reaction to something based on past experience, whether or not that experience is relevant to the new situation. This emotional reaction not only bypasses the higher centers of the brain but also profoundly affects perception and ultimately behavior.

EMOTIONAL STRESS AND THE BRAIN

Stress is at epidemic levels in North America, Europe, and much of the world, especially among the underemployed, unemployed, inner city poor, and disenfranchised members of society. Feelings associated with stress like anger, anxiety, frustration, alienation, depression, victimization, self-judgment, intolerance, and so on activate this internal hijacking of cognitive function and lead to diminished capacity for learning and retention and a more rapid breakdown and aging within the body. Too often, chronic high levels of cortisol, a hormone produced by the adrenal glands in stressful situations, actually destroy brain cells in the hippocampus, the region associated with learning and memory.[19]

THE PHYSIOLOGY OF STRESS

Classic physiology says stress, which we believe to be primarily caused by inner emotional turmoil, is characterized by a state of high arousal or the fight or flight response, and the production of such hormones as adrenaline. When relaxed, other hormones such as acetylcholine are produced in greater amounts. Two branches of our autonomic nervous system (ANS) are primarily responsible for these effects: the sympathetic nervous system activates the fight or flight response, while the parasympathetic system activates the relaxation response (see Figure 3–3). Overdominance of the sympathetic drive can result in hypertension. Imbalance in these two branches underlies many chronic diseases.

Research carried out at the institute and many other centers around the world has identified an additional axis of human experience that profoundly influences the stress reaction: *emotion*. If negative emotions, such as fear, anger, worry, or anxiety are present, cortisol production is increased to the point that it can negatively impact health, productivity, immune function, sleep patterns, etc. (see Figure 3–4). When we are in a consistently positive emotional state, on the other hand, production of hormones such as

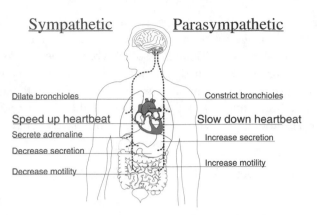

Sympathetic   Parasympathetic

Dilate bronchioles   Constrict bronchioles

Speed up heartbeat   Slow down heartbeat

Secrete adrenaline   Increase secretion

Decrease secretion   Increase motility

Decrease motility

FIGURE 3–3   Autonomic nervous system. The ANS consists of two branches, the sympathetic and parasympathetic systems. It regulates over 90% of the body's functions automatically. The heart, brain, immune, hormonal, respiration, and digestive systems—all are connected by this network of nerves.

FIGURE 3–4   The physiology of stress. The vertical axis represents the autonomic nervous system described in Figure 3–3. At the top is sympathetic activity, indicated as *high arousal/effort.* At the bottom is parasympathetic activity, indicated by *low arousal/relaxation/sleep.* The horizontal axis represents the emotional domain. Negative emotion on the right is associated with excessive levels of cortisol, while positive emotion leads to increased DHEA levels.

DHEA is increased, and the accompanying feelings are ones of well-being and success, as well as hardiness and resilience. Adrenaline and cortisol mobilize energy to deal with the perceived threat, but if our perception stays threatened, we stay in this negatively aroused state, causing long-term damage and unnecessary aging.[20] Traditional stress management techniques seek to bring down the level of arousal, but if the emotional state does not improve, boredom can be the outcome.

Positively transforming the internal emotional state effects a profound hormonal shift, such as increased production of DHEA[21] along with a reduction in cortisol levels. DHEA is an essential hormone, known as the *vitality hormone* because of its antiaging properties. If our emotional state is more positive and coherent, even difficult external factors do not destabilize us, so we are able to move between excitement and contentment more of the time.

Even though the normal stress reactions people process on a daily basis clearly produce negative short-term and long-term consequences, stress itself should be viewed not as negative but as a *wake-up call*, an opportunity to switch gears and find more productive perspectives and solutions.

It is important to remember that *we have control over this whole process*. Our *perceptions* and the underlying *reactions* we generate create a cascade of events either enhancing or limiting effectiveness. Perceptions generate thoughts and emotions, which in turn produce measurable effects in such physiological functions as heart rate, hormonal balance, immune system strength, and a host of other internal processes. These physiological effects, in turn, affect the neural circuits themselves, which affects our perception. This is a feedback system. When we are in a negative mood, for example, a distorted perception can generate negative thoughts and emotions, causing physiological imbalances in the heart, immune, and hormonal systems, which reinforce the circuitry, and the negative cycle continues.

"I had a really bad day" is a common complaint. However, people can intelligently manage this process, to a very large extent. Research has shown that the most successful people in life are the ones who have learned to manage their emotional reactiveness, neutralizing or transmuting negative emotions and in the process gaining a new richness of experience.[22] These people, even though they might have less formal education, often are the ones who move rapidly upward in organizations and are able to establish stable and happy lives. Despite their circumstances, these people have learned how to "live well." Emotional intelligence can be taught and learned. The human heart provides the key.

THE BIOLOGY OF HEART-BRAIN COMMUNICATION

It has become clear that the heart is central to a whole array of processes that affect brain function. The heart communicates to the brain through two sets of nerve pathways. It also radiates an electromagnetic signal that reaches every cell in your body, including your brain. We often speak of the importance of "heart" in getting things done, in having pride in our work, in having the courage to take risks or speak our truth. However, in North America and Europe over the past 50 years or so, the heart has been seen as a sign of weakness, irrational behavior or being "soft." It has been barred from most business discussions on the grounds of immaturity and over-emotionalism. Ironically, many organizations today act in remarkably immature, overemotional ways because of a *lack* of heart, understanding, and compassion. Meanwhile, heart disease has become the number 1 killer in much of the world.

WITH EVERY BEAT OF YOUR HEART

Many cultures have viewed the heart as the core of intelligence, the seat of wisdom, courage, intuition. In the Japanese language, two words describe the heart. *Shinzu* is the organ; *kokoro* is the mind of the heart. In the Chinese language, the modern pictogram for *listen* depicts an ear and a heart (see Figure 3–5). An ancient pictogram for *think* shows a brain and a heart. Research over the last two decades has revealed that emotional states profoundly affect the rhythmic beating of our hearts,[23] in turn causing measurable changes in our brains' ability to think and process information. Researchers in the 1960s found that the heart acted as if it had "a mind of its own."[24]

In the fetus, the heart starts to beat before the brain and nervous system have developed. The heart appears to have its own type of intelligence. The electrical energy in each heartbeat and *the information contained therein* is pulsed to every cell of the body. Research is revealing that the heart has specific information processing capabilities. It is a sensory organ designed to detect and transmit certain types of information and may have perceptual capacities as well. In fact, when the electrical patterns of the brain synchronize with the rhythmic patterns of the heart, people operate with greater physiological coherence, resulting in increased intelligent awareness. The ability to self-generate feelings such as care, appreciation, and compassion is key to greater brain efficiency, enhanced learning, and a more emotionally balanced life. This is one reason why *heart intelligence* is such a powerful concept for increasing personal and organizational effectiveness.

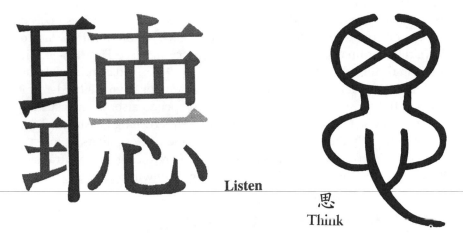

Listen

思
Think

FIGURE 3–5   The modern-day pictogram (left) for *listen* is composed of symbols for ear, king, eye, and heart. The meaning is to listen with the ear, giving respect as you would to a king, watching with the eye, and doing this with a full heart. The ancient pictogram for *think* (right) represents a baby's skull connected to the heart. The meaning is to that to think requires an open mind connected to the heart. An ancient dictionary definition describes the "silk threads" that connect brain and heart.

CARDIAC COHERENCE

Karl Pribram is one of the preeminent neuroscientists of the 20th century. His work at Stanford for many years created breakthroughs in understanding how learning occurs and how emotions are stored. According to Dr. Pribram and Deborah Rozman,[25] the coherence of the heart's rhythms can change the coherence of brain wave patterns (EEG). The heart continuously sends information about one's emotional state (as measured by coherence) to the cardiac center of the brain stem, which in turn feeds into the thalamus and to the amygdala, which is directly connected to the base of the frontal lobes. In addition, signals are sent to the rest of the cortex to help synchronize its activity. This is happening right now in your body as you read this page. A negative reaction to an unpleasant interruption, for example, would cause erratic rhythms in your heart, which in turn can inhibit cortical activity.[26] You have been jarred, focus is lost, and it requires an additional expenditure of energy to get back on track.

This understanding can serve as a focus for relating emotional to cognitive processes in early childhood development as well as later in life. In practical terms, it is now clear that *negative emotional states cause more erratic heart rhythms, so the information being sent to all these structures in the brain is less coherent.*[27] Desynchronization within the brain is a common result, leading to poor or shortsighted decisions, impulsive communication, lack of physical coordination, and other no-win outcomes (see Figure 3–6). The result in the brain, first discovered in the 1960s,[28] is called *cortical inhibition.* It manifests itself as less efficient decision making or having a harder time finding the right words. Physical reaction speeds also are measurably slowed at these times. Usually, it is when you are rushing or panicked that you accidentally knock a cup of coffee onto the pile of papers or into the keyboard. Internal self-management begins by reducing and neutralizing the internal reactive process, instead of being its unwitting victim.

LEARNING AND THE AMYGDALA

The amygdala, that storehouse of emotional memory, receives an input from baroreceptors, sensors that are part of the heart's intrinsic nervous system. The baroreceptor system has been shown to regulate a person's "openness" to external sensory input.[29] In other research, the amygdala has been shown to affect heart rate and blood pressure through the autonomic nervous system.[30] When such regulation is interfered with by removal or damage to the amygdala, rapid learning is impaired. The heart and blood pressure systems serve as a "booster" to such learning. A Russian scientist expressed this as follows: "an ounce of emotion is worth a pound of repetition."[31] To that we would add, a mere morsel of *coherent* emotion is worth a

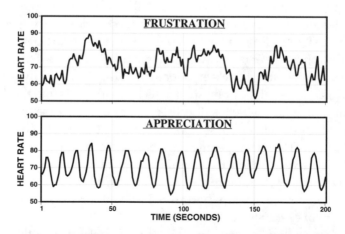

FIGURE 3–6   Your changing heart rhythms affect not only the heart but also the brain's ability to process information, including decision making, problem solving, and creativity. Jagged rhythms, shown at top, lead to *cortical inhibition*, while smoother rhythms, below, are associated with *cortical facilitation*.

pound of emotion. Perhaps the organizations of the future will study closely how learning happens at the biological level within all the players involved in an organization. (Another recent study has disclosed that the amygdala is the most active part of our brain during dreaming.)

COHERENCE AND LEARNING

This aspect of brain research has a direct correlation in the level of coherence or noise within the organization. The amygdala organizes what feels "familiar," whether coherent or incoherent.[32] If patterns generated by the heart and blood pressure control systems are disordered and incoherent, the body learns to expect disharmony as the familiar; thus, people come to feel "at home" or comfortable with incoherence, which will affect learning and adaptability. This incoherence also affects peer selection: People feel "comfortable" only with incoherence, that is, discomfort among peers.

It probably is fairly easy to imagine certain colleagues (perhaps, all of us to some extent) who must have adapted to significant levels of incoherence as children, resulting in nonproductive behavior they hang onto throughout adulthood. A Canadian executive, who had spoken French fluently as a child, recently found herself yelling at her granddaughter in French. Her husband asked her what she had said, only to find out they were the exact words her mother had scolded her with 40 years earlier. Such is the power of emotional memory.

Organizational incoherence—the accumulated noise, turmoil, pressure, and conflict—can increase the internal distortion people feel, strengthening or reinforcing the negative pattern. The good news is that a positive environment can play a significant role in coherence becoming more familiar and the negative patterns dissolved. (Organizational climate is discussed in Chapter Nine.) In our experience, even with people who have had lifelong patterns that are nonproductive or unhealthy, a core remains that yearns to be productive, be effective, and feel fulfilled. Increasing levels of stress in the world only amplify the contrast between the drive for coherence and the ever-present incoherence. As the gap widens between how people feel and how they *want* to feel, despair or resignation too often fills the gap. Biologically, this only makes matters worse and our effectiveness in dealing with the problems in our lives is weakened or distorted. Identifying the reactive patterns in oneself and understanding their consequences is the first step in reprogramming them. Research suggests that reprogramming inefficient thought and emotional processes indeed is possible.[33]

On the basis of what the amygdala recognizes as familiar, the prefrontal cortex makes decisions as to what is appropriate behavior in a given situation. Studies using EEG (electroencephalogram, a graph of brain waves) have shown that the frontal lobes of the brain mature rapidly in the early years, up to age 3, then not again until the ages 17–21.[34] Therefore, these early years are critical in the development of emotional maturity. Initially, there is an overgrowth of junctions in the brain, especially in the cortex. These junctions are pruned back as an infant grows. "Pruning" means literally a cutting back and shaping of developing patterns of brain connections.[35] For example, all children can learn all languages at an early age. But, as children grow older, certain language abilities get lost through this pruning process.

Thus, in the early years, the initial cognitive and emotional patterns are laid down and shaped through pruning. Frontal lobe controls are initiated at this early age; if there is separation from a loving primary caretaker, say, before age 3, problems in development can occur unless another loving caretaker can take his or her place. The degree of coherence—or love—a child receives during these early years profoundly influences that child's desires and attractions later in life. But, regardless of the incoherence a child receives early on in life, love still is the core attractive force for people.

Emotional states are contagious. Smile at a baby, and the baby smiles back. Treat a customer sincerely, and the customer appreciates you and rewards you with loyalty. You get upset, and the baby cries. Treat employees with anger and disrespect, and employees internalize their resentment and lose the motivation to do their best. You can sense an immediate shift in a baby's emotional state by virtue of muscle tone and the way it holds its whole body. Ever noticed the same shift in an uncomfortable staff meeting or customer interaction? Usually, this is much more subtle and covert than with babies, who have no social conditioning to edit their behavior. By adulthood many of us have perfected the "storefront," hiding our real feelings behind a facade of strained niceness while the internal engine of discontent revs furiously.

In adult learning, the quality of transference from the "teacher" or coach, which often is a supervisor or manager, has everything to do with the internal coherence of that teacher. The level of insecurity is so high in many organizations, interactions between supervisor and supervised are filled with the silent noise of uncertainty, fear of criticism, and resistance. The supervisor's warmth and coherence can do much to dissolve the hardness and tension; on the other hand, the manager's discomfort, frustration, or anger tends to reinforce the resistant attitude on the part of the employee.

EMOTIONAL BUYING

Let us take this discussion of internal emotional coherence to a very practical business situation: the sales call. The first impression within the buyer usually is an emotional one: feelings of discomfort and distrust or security and comfort with the salesperson. The emotional state of the salesperson sets the tone for the exchange that follows. When people are being "sold" they tend to observe more acutely and, rightly or wrongly, form opinions about the salesperson at high speed. People often buy from someone they like, and if a salesperson seems insincere, pushy or emotionally unstable, the buyer often has reservations about making a purchase. An old axiom in the sales profession is that nothing is as ineffective as a desperate salesperson. Conversely, increased coherence in the salesperson fosters greater respect and trust in the buyer, deeper, more effective listening, more understanding and clarity, and greater potential for a successful sale. Now we can see the biological and electromagnetic roots of that observation.

People actually can learn to rewire the maladapted neural tracks that inhibit the learning, growth, and emotional maturity necessary for success in any aspect of life. With practice, profound results can occur. These changes can be measured in cardiac rhythms,[36] spectral analysis of the ECG, in brain waves,[37] in the immune system,[38] and in hormonal balance.[39] These powerful effects are brought about through the application of techniques that foster the entrained state. Caring and appreciation, consciously applied, are perfect examples of how heart intelligence changes physiology. The impact for organizational coherence is highly significant.

HEART INTELLIGENCE

The term *heart intelligence* implies the notion that the heart is far more than a pump, mechanically beating at least 110,000 times a day. In fact, its electrical, magnetic, neuronal, and hormonal properties make it a truly remarkable part of the human system. Does it possess even more intelligence than those functions suggest? Yes.

It already has been said that the changes in heart rhythm, driven by a person's internal emotional changes, have far-reaching effects in the brain's processing capacity. Cultures around the world are full of expressions about the heart's "feeling" capacity—big-hearted, lion-hearted, a broken heart, cold-hearted, a heart of gold. Few of us think the fist-sized organ in the center of our chest is *producing* these feelings, yet nearly all of us have experienced emotional sensations in the physical area that surrounds our heart. We can *feel* the heartache, just as we can *feel* the warmth of sincere appreciation or the power that comes from an act of courage.

If you were asked to point to yourself, would you point to your heart and not your brain, elbow, or knee? We think of the heart as core to our very existence, and we use the word *heart* to describe anything that is core, central, or fundamental. As the West has believed in the supremacy of the intellect, the heart—viewed as a sentimental trap—has fallen out of favor. Viewing the heart as weak, emotional, and irrational is an old-fashioned mind-set that no longer serves our highest interests. These perspectives are not bad, just a simple misunderstanding. It is time for the heart to stop taking the blame for mismanaged emotions and be seen for what it is—the source of our core power and essential for accessing new intelligence.

The heart we are talking about is not synonymous with emotion. HeartMath research suggests that the heart possesses an intelligence beyond the emotional or analytical. The heart does indeed *sense* emotional information and is capable of transcending the traps of *unmanaged emotion*. Evidence is mounting that the heart's intelligence is a core operating system in the human being, capable of the coherent organization of mental, emotional, and cellular intelligence. A radical proposition? Perhaps. One worth exploring? We certainly believe so.

FREQUENCIES OF INTELLIGENCE

Our world is awash in a sea of frequencies. Light, sound, X-rays, gamma rays—all are examples of the types of frequencies we live with every day. Some of these, like sunlight, we can perceive consciously while others, like X-rays, we cannot. A frequency is a measure of a vibration rate, expressed in cycles per second. Ocean waves hit the beach about every 20 seconds; three waves a minute would be their frequency. Light waves vibrate trillions (10^{14}) of times per second; that is the frequency range of visible light. The light we can see is visible to us because our eyes are attuned to certain frequencies, or vibrations, of light.

Frequencies are not abstract mathematical concepts. We can *see* light frequencies, *hear* sound frequencies, and *sense* the varying frequencies of thought and emotion. Think of the eyes as receiving stations designed to pick up certain frequencies of light but not all. In the same way, our ears are designed to hear audible frequencies in a specific range. They cannot hear what a dog's ears are designed to hear, although the sounds a dog hears are just as real. Human ear technology is designed to operate on only certain frequencies necessary for our survival and enjoyment. An AM radio is designed to receive frequencies in the AM range of a radio dial; FM stations broadcast in another frequency range, which an FM radio is designed to pick up. Although the heart and brain each radiate electrical frequencies vibrating within yet another range, primarily 0–30 Hz, the heart's amplitude is 40–60 times stronger than that of the brain. At the same time, these intelligent organs also "receive" incoming information and can produce a host of biochemical and electrical changes in response to this sensory input.

Heart intelligence can be defined as *the intelligent flow of insight that arises once the mind and emotions are balanced and coherent*. Appreciation, caring, and compassion are examples of core "frequencies" within the bandwidth of heart intelligence. Each time you generate one of these frequencies, or positive emotions, your physiology shifts into a more efficient mode. Activation of heart feelings is an intelligent use of the body's feeling capacity and serves as the ignition key for intuitive intelligence. Often, in moments of peace, stillness, or appreciation, intuitional insights start to "flow." Even the most restless mind gains new perspective and understanding in the presence of a caring heart.

HeartMath defines *mental intelligence* as that range of human intelligence in which the brain can analyze, deduce, reason, and memorize. Emotions influence and perturb these processes, which are the most prominent part of human interaction. Similarly, HeartMath defines *heart intelligence* as that part of human intelligence that operates in a bandwidth embracing mental, emotional, and even cellular intelligence. As one's mental process comes under management by this heart intelligence and the fuel of emotion surrenders to the intelligence of wisdom, intuitive intelligence unfolds. New understanding about oneself, the organization, the market, or anything important is quicker to emerge.

Consider the link between a positive emotion such as compassion with intuition. Think about people you know who are particularly intuitive. Undoubtedly, they also possess a measure of emotional sensitivity. While people who possess this sensitivity are highly valued in organizations because of their compassion, understanding, and inner confidence, this capacity is innate in people and can be developed through regular focus on internal balance and the experience and self-generation of positive emotions.

Heart intelligence is to intuition as mental intelligence is to analysis. The management of one's emotional nature—and the freeing up of positive emotion inside oneself—provides the doorway for unleashing intuition. Without intuition active, life becomes rigid and inflexible, so we easily miss important cues on lessons to be learned or opportunities to be created.

INTUITIVE INTELLIGENCE

One of Doc's insights that shaped IHM's laboratory research was his suggestion that intuition is a bandwidth of intelligence central to the design of the human being. All people are born with the capacity for intuition. It is just as central to humans as the drive to survive or care for others. It can be blocked and obstructed, to be sure, but that makes it no less powerful in its potential to guide people's lives or the organizations in which they work. The roar of ambition and survival has drowned out the voice of intuition in our society. The good news is that it's still there. It just needs to be dusted off.

Consistently tapping into one's innate intuitive intelligence represents the most efficient method of internal self-management available. HeartMath research would suggest that the human system is preprogrammed to operate with a high level of operational intuitive intelligence and that the accelerated age we live in has created the perfect conditions to optimize it. With consistent practice, it becomes automatic instead of random.

We must understand, however, that intuition does not always appear as the ingenious breakthrough or something grandiose. Intuitive thoughts, feelings, and solutions often manifest themselves as good old common sense. Common sense is efficient. Although sometimes simple, common sense should be respected. Simplicity is complexity that has been tamed and reduced to something that easily can be applied. It is like a complex math equation that finally results in "equals." The equation can be quite long, but eventually it resolves itself and produces just a few very appropriate and accurate numbers. Intuition often leads to simplicity and common sense. How many situations do you face right now that you wish could be made simple and dealt with through common sense?

The educational system most of us were raised in has trained us well in the art and science of analysis, deduction, and reductionism. We learned to memorize facts. We know how to boil things down to their parts; we are less effective at seeing connections, relationships, and interdependencies. Yet, that perhaps is the greatest strength, and appeal, of intuition. You just *know*, without knowing exactly how you know. The bigger picture is far easier to see because you are not obsessed with the bits and pieces or "the furniture," as Doc sometimes calls it. You have clarity and you know it and feel it inside. Intelligence is optimized. The "default" mode in most of us would be to retain our usual mental learning styles until life backs us into a corner and requires or inspires new ways of thinking and feeling. That is why people finally go deep within themselves to try to reach a core intelligence that can provide security and answers in the face of turmoil and distortion. From the brain research presented here, it is clear these default patterns are the result of "frozen" neural circuits, with the amygdala playing its part of reminding us of what is "familiar" even in the face of new or unfamiliar information.

The kind of personal and organizational breakthroughs needed to move through the densities and inertia of the old ways will not come from analysis or reason based primarily on past experience. A new way of thinking—collaborative, compassionate, and creative—will be required for success and coherence in the future. Activating heart intelligence will be key.

SELF-CARE

So how does care for the physical body fit into this model of internal self-management? The last 20 years have seen an explosion of information on the role of diet and exercise and the consequences of ignoring them. Label reading is in style these days. Product labels and even restaurant menus now advise us of calorie and cholesterol intake, while gyms, personal trainers, and corporate wellness programs encourage (or scare) us into taking better care of ourselves. Many people today intelligently pay more attention to what goes in the mouth, and a balanced diet does help to boost energy levels and reduce disease risk.

Indeed, many people in the West probably do not eat enough grains or fresh vegetables, their lifestyle has become too sedentary, and imbalance has become the norm. Yet the "diet and exercise police" run the risk of adding considerably more stress, confusion, and anxiety to people's already burdened lives. Some people worry endlessly about what they are eating. They judge themselves for not eating right, and people who have decided to clean up their diets often judge people who do not eat the way they do. A friend of mine once confessed that, during his years of being a strict vegetarian, he constantly judged others who did not believe in his dietary principles. He got to a point where he realized that the potential benefits he was receiving physically from his diet were being severely compromised by the stress, strain, and toxicity produced by his negative, judgmental attitudes toward others.

No one diet or exercise program possibly could suit everyone or be fair to the demands of all lifestyles. But consistently activating intuitive intelligence—asking yourself what would be physical balance at this moment while balancing your "mental and emotional diet"—is a highly efficient way to begin your health program. By *mental and emotional diet*, we mean those daily thoughts and emotions you still chew on long after you inhaled the Big Mac or rushed your way through the sushi, affecting your physiology as deeply as they drain your energy. While blaming fast foods and overconsumption of stimulants is convenient and partially true, it misses the deeper message and the core power. Balance is key in everything, including your choice of diet and exercise programs.

In essence, heart intelligence is a core human operating system capable of balancing mental, emotional, and cellular intelligence. A mind (or organization) without heart is scattered, impulsive, and easily distracted. Emotions (and organizations) without the intelligent balance that comes from the heart create flash fires of instability and waste, causing people to stay locked in self-justified mental loops, missing a heart intelligent perspective that could offer deeper understanding. Cells operating only on instinct stay constrained in modalities that imprison the spirit and age us needlessly. The heart puts first things first, from the 7 trillion cells it nourishes to the life it sustains to the vitality it ensures—intuitive, intelligent, businesslike; core, fundamental; the first priority.

NOTES

1. Madeleine Nash, "Fertile Minds," *Time* (February 24, 1997).
2. Lila L. Gatlin, *Information Theory and the Living System* (New York: Columbia University Press, 1972).
3. Sandra Blakeslee, "Complex and Hidden Brain in Gut Makes Stomachaches and Butterflies," *The New York Times* (January 23, 1996).
4. Ibid.
5. Called *chi* or *qi* in the Chinese tradition, and *ki* in the Japanese tradition, the source of power is believed to emanate from the solar plexus region. Practitioners are taught to still the mind and focus attention in that area, so power is focused and balanced. In our view, this practice really is stilling emotional turmoil, thereby helping a person become more coherent. But our research also indicates the heart supersedes the solar plexus, electrically and biomechanically.
6. J. A. Armour, "Anatomy and Function of the Intrathoracic Neurons Regulating the Mammalian Heart," in I. H. Zucker and J. P. Gilmore, eds., *Reflex Control of the Circulation* (Boca Raton, FL: CRC Press, 1991).
7. M. Cantin and J. Genest, "The Heart as an Endocrine Gland," *Clinical and Investigative Medicine* 9, no. 4 (1986), pp. 319–27.
8. Claire Sylvia and William Novak, *A Change of Heart* (New York: Little, Brown and Company, 1997).
9. Paul Pearsall, *The Heart's Code* (New York: Broadway Books, 1998).
10. Paul Pearsall, "The Heart Remembers," *Natural Health* (March–April 1998).
11. Antonio Damasio, *Descartes' Error: Emotion, Reason and the Human Brain* (New York: Putnam, 1994).

12. Jim Taylor and Watts Wacker, with Howard Means, *The 500-Year Delta: What Happens After What Comes Next* (New York: HarperCollins, 1997), p. 141.

13. From Joseph Chilton Pearce's Introduction in Doc Childre's *Teaching Children to Love* (Boulder Creek, CA: Planetary Publications, 1996), p. 9.

14. Ibid., p. 10.

15. Daniel Goleman, *Emotional Intelligence: Why It Can Matter More than IQ* (New York: Bantam Books, 1995).

16. Ibid.

17. Karl H. Pribram, *Languages of the Brain* (New York: Brandon House, 1971).

18. R. McCraty, W. A. Tiller, M. Atkinson, "Head-Heart Entrainment: A Preliminary Survey." Proceedings of the Brain-Mind Applied Neurophysiology EEG Neuro-feedback Meeting, 1996. Key West, Florida (pp. 26–30).

19. Rollin McCraty, Bob Barrios-Choplin, and Deborah Rozman, "The Impact of a New Emotional Self-Management Program on Stress, Emotions, Heart Rate Variability, DHEA and Cortisol," *Integrative Physiological and Behavioral Science* (1998, in press). Also, D. S. Kerr, L. W. Campbell, and M. D. Applegate, "Chronic Stress-Induced Acceleration of Electrophysiologic and Morphometric Biomarkers of Hippocampal Aging," *Society of Neuroscience* 11, no. 5 (1991), pp. 1316–17.

20. Alan Watkins, *Mind-Body Medicine: A Clinician's Guide to Psychoneuroimmunology* (London: Churchill Livingstone, 1997).

21. McCraty, Barrios-Choplin, Rozman, "The Impact of a New Emotional Self-Management Program on Stress, Emotions, Heart Rate Variability, DHEA and Cortisol," *Integrative Physiological and Behavioral Science* (1998, in press).

22. Goleman, *Emotional Intelligence*.

23. Rollin McCraty, William A. Tiller, Mike Atkinson, et al., "The Effects of Emotions on Short Term Power Spectrum Analysis of Heart Rate Variability," *American Journal of Cardiology* 76, no. 14 (November 15, 1995), pp. 1088–93.

24. S. A. Rosenfeld, *Conversations Between Heart and Brain* (Rockville, MD: National Institute of Mental Health, 1977).

25. Karl H. Pribram and Deborah Rozman, "Early Childhood Development and Learning: What New Research on the Heart and Brain Tells Us About Our Youngest Children," presented at the White House Conference on Early Childhood Development and Learning, San Francisco, 1997.

26. William Tiller, Rollin McCraty, and Mike Atkinson, "Toward Cardiac Coherence: A New Non-Invasive Measure of Autonomic System Order," *Alternative Therapies* (1996).

27. Ibid.

28. Rosenfeld, *Conversations Between Heart and Brain*.

29. Ibid.

30. S. Oppenheimer and D. Hopkins, "Suprabulbar Neuronal Regulation of the Heart," in J. A. Armour and J. L. Ardell, eds., *Neurocardiology* (New York: Oxford University Press, 1994), pp. 309–41.

31. Cited in Pribram and Rozman, "Early Childhood Development."

32. Ibid.

33. McCraty et al., "The Impact of a New Emotional Self-Management Program."
34. Pribram and Rozman, "Early Childhood Development."
35. Ibid.
36. Tiller et al., "Toward Cardiac Coherence."
37. McCraty et al., "Head-Heart Entrainment: A Preliminary Survey."
38. Rollin McCraty, Mike Atkinson, and Glen Rein, "Music Enhances the Effect of Positive Emotional States on Salivary IgA and Heart Rate Variability," *Stress Medicine* 12 (1996), pp. 167–75.
39. McCraty et al., "The Impact of a New Emotional Self-Management Program."

4

Stress and Adaptability: What It's Like Growing Up in the Hudson River

Many years before I met Doc, I was an actor and appeared in about 700 performances of the New York run of *The Fantasticks*. Early on, the process of speaking the lines, singing the songs, and bounding around the stage became automatic; for an actor, the challenge in a long run is mechanicality, not memory. One night, about 400 performances into my run, I went totally blank. Time warped for a split second and I experienced total terror until, without my conscious mind knowing what I was saying, the words started coming out of my mouth, automatically. I was relieved and amazed words were being spoken with no apparent conscious input.

A portion of the brain—the medulla—helps us "bail out" of the conscious thought process because of what are called *stereotyped behaviors*. This is the part of the brain where we learn functions that soon can become automatic. With stereotyped behaviors, you often are unconscious you are doing them. People who commute to the same place daily often have no actual recollection of how they got to work, because they may be so preoccupied with business problems or personal issues. Yet your innate intelligence of the brain and muscular system handles it all automatically while your primary focus of attention lies elsewhere.

We do many things automatically, without really understanding the impact of the behavior or its cellular consequences. As a boy growing up in northern New Jersey in the 1950s and 1960s, long before I worked on Broadway, I made frequent trips into Manhattan.

Seeing the Hudson River in those days, I wondered how fish—or anything—could survive in such murky, oily, garbage-infested water. Later, in the context of what I had learned through HeartMath tools, I mused how a fish perceived life. Growing up in the Hudson River, the fish knew nothing else, had no other life experience to compare it to. Born and raised in that environment, fish were forced to adapt, no matter what the health consequences might have been. Indeed, we heard stories of diseased fish being caught on poles off the old docks in lower Manhattan. What if one of those poor Hudson River fish won a "dream vacation" to Lake Tahoe? That fish might at first be shocked by the purity and pristine nature of the lake but would quickly adapt and thrive and probably would find the casinos on the Nevada side especially intriguing.

Many people are so familiar with a certain level of anxiety, tension, or frustration in their organization or in their lives in general, they think that is the only alternative; another way of functioning seems a distant or cruel dream. Then, if they hit the jackpot, their company goes public, or they achieve a new status in life or move to a nicer neighborhood, how quickly they can "adapt" and take it for granted. The novelty, and the regenerative power of appreciation, has worn off.

One of the truly remarkable aspects of life on this planet is adaptability. The adaptive power of the human system is essential in accelerated times. Yet, people have a tendency to *maladapt* that needs transforming in order for new intelligence to be available.

MALADAPTATION

One morning over coffee, we discussed the challenges of maladapting. Doc explained it this way. *Maladaptation* means adapting in an unhealthy way to circumstances in ourselves and our environment. Maladapting to stressful events means we live unconscious of their consequences, thinking there is no alternative or, worse, that it is okay to act in certain ways, detrimental or not. Everyone around us is thinking and acting in a similar manner, so we fall into an unconscious sleep, allowing our behavior to slowly drain us. This results in the belief we are doing just fine, but in fact it could be taxing our bodies unnecessarily and have us operating with far less effectiveness and fulfillment than we actually could. The way in which many people respond to stressful situations provides a perfect scenario for this maladaptation process. For example, when management implements a new policy, many employees typically will complain about the change. It appears as if it is not only okay to moan and groan, but that is the appropriate response to the situation. The complaints spread like an infectious virus, and once on the rampage, it can seem as if a contest is going on to see who can come up with the most creative gripe. Whether the policy change is for the best or not makes no difference to our bodies. The stress created by negative, judgmental thoughts and feelings creates a hormonal imbalance, imbalances the nervous system, taxes the heart, and burns a lot of energy. Cortical inhibition results, and we think less clearly. We feel tired and do not know why but conveniently blame it on the pressures of the job. After all, isn't that what your coworkers are saying? Blame further amplifies the negative impact of the response to the required change, and people sink further into a quicksand of their own making while thinking they are responding appropriately.

How many in your organization *maladapt* to daily stress, rather than adapt healthfully? Even the positive benefits of regular exercise can mask the causes of stress—nonefficient perceptions—while treating only the symptoms, such as fatigue.

As stress mounts, most people internalize the strain and react—that is the extent of their adaptive process—so that a new level of tension and internal distortion seems normal. This process continues unchecked, but because it is so gradual, most cannot see its devastating effects. You could call this "death by a thousand paper cuts." Physiologically, maladaptation is blamed for contributing to certain chronic conditions such as high blood pressure. Our bodies maladapt to the external stress, without neutralizing its effects; and it comes with a big price tag. Now the bar has been raised, physiologically speaking, we have absorbed the noise instead of quieting it, and a new level of internal incoherence begins to seem normal.

This process is at the root of a primary theme of Internal Self-Management:

> The pressure on the individual will increase in the years to come as societal, family, and internal stresses mount and the pace of change accelerates.

The word *stress* has old roots in the Low Latin word *strictus* and ancient meanings like "afflict," "punish," and "pull asunder." Soon after World War II, the medical establishment began packaging a new concept of *stress*, the notion that the trials and tribulations of life trigger a physiological "stress response," resulting in measurable physical and mental illness.[1]

Hans Selye coined the modern use of the term *stress* and described it as "the rate of wear and tear on the body."[2] New research has found that what creates more stress than any other stressor measured is people having to shift concepts, shift intention and focus, to many different tasks, many times an hour. The stress is worse when you also feel worry, anxiety, insecurity, or feel that you have no control. Unlike 30 years ago, in the fast pace of life today, research suggests the average person in an organization is called on to shift concepts—or shift the focus of attention—dozens of times each hour. This number undoubtedly is increasing. E-mail, interruptions, faxes, phones ringing, people (including spouse and children) demanding attention while you are trying to get something else done—all are examples of concept shift demands. When you consider the number of people in fairly routine jobs with few interruptions, that means many people are dealing with *10 to 20 or more concept shifts per hour*. When you consider an 8–10-hour day, this concept shifting easily could translate into 80, 100, or even 150 shifts a day. At each of these shift points, you have a choice: react and let stress accumulate, or stay neutral and balanced with full access to your intelligence. Do you shift and grind the gears internally or, with more applied intelligence, could you shift through "neutral" before activating the next gear and save yourself a lot of wear and tear? This can sound abstract or idealistic, yet most of us know someone who seems to glide effortlessly from task to task, with feathers unruffled and productivity remaining remarkably high. These people are incredibly valuable to organizations.

Stressful reactions have an impact on our health, sleep patterns, communication effectiveness, health care costs, decision making—the list goes on. Clearly, the sheer volume of stressful reactions most people face—many of which are automatic and unconscious—represents the most serious challenge to health, productivity, and organizational coherence. It is nonstop.

Focusing on internal self-management of your mental and emotional habits and processes begins by identifying when an individual is stressed or operating below par, then neutralizing the dozens of internal reactions to increase his or her internal coherence. *Recognizing* whether the individual has adapted or maladapted, however, can be especially challenging, since many people are like the fish in the Hudson River with automatic, programmed reactions to the environment and no apparent alternative. More than once, HeartMath facilitators have heard workshop attendees describe how they have no stress in their lives and are wondering why the facilitator is spending so much time talking about it. Then, when asked, the participants explain that they do not get along with their coworkers, hate their boss, and have few friends, but fortunately, no stress!

HORMONAL MALADAPTATION

Maladaptation results in increased levels of the stress hormone cortisol and depressed levels of the vitality hormone DHEA. DHEA and cortisol have very different effects on human cells. When the ratio between these two powerful hormones is imbalanced, the body responds in several ways: Insulin drops; bone density goes down; muscle mass is decreased; fat accumulation around the waist and hips goes up; and skin repair, tissue healing, and immune activity slow down—all leading to accelerated aging. This is because, biochemically, the body is in "survival mode" as a result of the unseen maladaptation. If these reactions continue, the hypothalamus in the brain is reset to higher cortisol levels. This eventually destroys brain cells in the hippocampus, a part of the brain that causes memory, while spatial and other learning abilities diminish. REM sleep is impaired, resulting in sleeplessness or waking up depressed. Increased cortisol and decreased DHEA levels are a predisposing factor to many age-related diseases, including obesity, osteoporosis, arthritis, Alzheimer's disease, arteriosclerosis (hardening of arteries), and some forms of cancer.

Recent studies on aging by the MacArthur Foundation reported that, "The way people age—whether they end up sick, demented or sexless in their 70s or 80s or vigorous, sharp and libidinous—is mostly a matter of how they live. Only about 30% of the characteristics of aging are genetically based; the rest—70%— is not." Genetics play the greatest role in health characteristics early in life. But, by age 80, for many characteristics, hardly any genetic influence is left. According to John Rowe, gerontologist and president of Mount Sinai Medical Center in New York, "People are largely responsible for their own old age."[3]

"This job is killing me" may make literal sense, according to a pair of reports in the *British Medical Journal*.[4] According to the researchers, men who showed large increases in blood pressure as they anticipated an exercise test and who reported high job demands had 10–40% greater carotid artery thickness than men whose *perceived* job demands were low. These findings were strongest among men who showed at least 20% carotid artery thickening on their baseline ultrasound exams. Moreover, in this subgroup, men with high job demands and whose blood pressure went up "had more than 46% greater progression of atherosclerosis than the others."[5] Perception rears its head again. An important axiom here is that *flexible attitudes build flexible physiology*.

EMOTION AND IMMUNE HEALTH

A study conducted at the Institute of HeartMath[6] demonstrated a link between emotion and immune function. Groups of volunteers were asked to focus on two different emotions—anger and care—while a key immune system antibody, secretory IgA, was being measured. IgA (immunoglobulin A) is widespread in the immune system, acting as a protective coating for the cells against invading bacteria or viruses. Stress is known to decrease IgA levels, leaving us more vulnerable to respiratory problems such as colds or flus. The study found that a five-minute period of recalling an angry experience caused a six-hour suppression of IgA levels. Five minutes of sincerely feeling care or compassion, on the other hand, boosted IgA levels for six hours.

You come out of a staff meeting feeling annoyed and angry at how your proposal was dismissed. You replay the scene in your mind, scripting the perfect defense, anger simmering the whole time. (You are lucky if you spend only five minutes doing this; many people spend hours.) More effectively than most environmental factors could do, you have suppressed a key part of your immune function—for hours. Chronic replaying of negative emotions has dramatic health consequences and easily can lead to an increasingly common state—burnout.

BURNOUT HITS THE *WALL STREET JOURNAL*

The malaise hitting the workplace clearly is not an isolated instance. A respected writer for the *Wall Street Journal* covered such issues for years, then felt compelled to come clean about her own challenges:

> Though I've written about burnout as a workplace issue, I secretly believed it was a malady suffered by others. Studies have said as much as 25% of the work force is at risk of burnout. Nevertheless, I thought of the term as a pop-culture label for fatigue, or a scapegoat for bad work habits. With a flexible job I enjoy, I thought I was immune. That's what I thought. And with that attitude I ran my life—straight into the ground.[7]

EMOTION AND STRESS AFFECT HEART SURVIVAL

More and more studies are demonstrating a link between one's emotional state and long-term health. A study conducted at the Georgetown University School of Nursing in Washington, DC, shows that psychosocial factors can contribute to heart survival even more than the person's physiological status. In an article published in the *American Journal of Critical Care*,[8] Dr. Sue A. Thomas, lead researcher in the study, said:

> Patients who suffer serious cardiovascular disease are at higher risk if they have changes in their emotional status, too. We can't just treat one and neg-

lect the other and expect that people are going to get well. We can't just treat the physical. We have to treat the whole person, the mind and the body. . . . The pattern of higher numbers of past stressful life events, lower expectations of future life changes, and increasing levels of depression in the period after myocardial infarction [heart attack] presents a consistent psychosocial profile of cardiac patients with increased risk of dying. . . . This study and others show that the emotional state and relationships of patients in the period after [the heart attack] are as important as the patient's cardiovascular disease severity in determining their prognosis.

A study at Duke University in North Carolina[9] suggests that relaxation, feeling better about yourself, and managing emotional and psychological stress can profoundly reduce the risk of coronary artery disease (CAD). CAD affects 13.5 million Americans and hundreds of millions worldwide, at a price tag to the U.S. economy of at least $117 billion in lost productivity and treatment. Published in the American Medical Association's *Archives of Internal Medicine*, the five-year study with 107 patients with heart disease showed that patients who learned to manage stress reduced their risk of having another heart attack or heart problems by 74% when compared with patients receiving medication only. Reducing mental stress also proved more beneficial than getting exercise.

STOPPING EMOTIONAL DRAIN

The third theme of internal self-management is critical:

> As individuals learn to identify and plug the leaks in their own personal systems, they stop draining energy and effectiveness personally and organizationally.

You obviously have a choice in how you respond to these statistics about the relationship of emotional balance to health: react with fear that you are on the road to a life of misery, deny it, or greet the news with hope that intelligent solutions may exist. We suggest the last response. Any paradigm shift to increased peace and intelligence in the Information Age will have to include managing the emotions and bringing them in phase with the intelligence of the heart. This process builds emotional power so you can manage rapid change. People are taught in school to manage emotional outbursts, but an emotional drain of energy still goes on inside that most people do not recognize. Most people think managing emotions is just about controlling anger or the more obvious displays of emotional mismanagement. It also is about all the little hurts, disappointments, anxieties, fearful projections about the future, and so on. These more subtle emotional states drain away more vitality and intelligence capacity than people know. They are the real robbers. Once emotional energy is leaked away, deep exhaustion sets in. When we are emotionally drained, we become more vulnerable to angry outbursts and caustic behavior. The accumulated drain of emotional mismanagement is a major cause of severe anxiety and depression. A 32-year study of more than 2,000 men showed that anxiety is one of the strongest risk factors for sudden cardiac death. Men with anxiety had six times increased risk of sudden cardiac death than men who reported no symptoms of anxiety.[10]

It takes emotional buoyancy to experience a continuity of rich textures in life. When you feel buoyant, it is easier to deflect problem situations. What at times could make you angry does not seem to matter that much. Buoyancy fills you with energy. Quality of life is not just a question of lifestyle or career choice but is based on whether your emotional reserves are filled or drained. People often try to mend emotional energy drains with physical stimulation—food, exercise, drugs, sex—but still find themselves tired and worn out once the buzz has worn off. This is because the mind has continued to justify the emotional bleed-off of the unresolved situation, resulting in an ongoing inner dialogue that perpetuates more emotional drain and fatigue.

ACCUMULATE, DO NOT WASTE, YOUR ENERGY

At the Seventh International Congress on Stress in Switzerland in February 1995, the most common stress-inducing emotional drains identified were anxiety, perfectionism, guilt, resentment, perception of lack of control, and a feeling that there never is enough time or that everything takes too long.[11] All these emotional leaks can be managed as people gain access to their heart intelligence.

The energy required to sustain a "storefront"—looking good on the outside while feeling bad on the inside—is expensive. You can be mild tempered yet full of internal emotional reactions that leave you continuously below par. It takes significant energy to sustain emotional reactiveness, energy you otherwise could use for creativity, enriching your relationships, and increasing your fulfillment in all aspects of your life. A higher ratio of emotional management will bring a higher return in personal power and effectiveness.

Continuing with the first dynamic, internal self-management, we now explore a powerful tool to clear up the murky waters and move into the domain of heart intelligence—freeze frame.

NOTES

1. Richard A. Shweder, "America's Latest Export: A Stressed-Out World," *New York Times* (January 25, 1997).

2. Cited in ibid.

3. Cited in Jane E. Brody, "The Good News About Growing Old," *Atlanta Journal and Constitution* (April 14, 1996).

4. "Job Stress Affects Arteries," *British Medical Journal* 314 (1997), pp. 553–57.

5. Ibid., pp. 558–64.

6. Glen Rein, Mike Atkinson, and Rollin McCraty, "The Physiological and Psychological Effects of Compassion and Anger," *Journal of Advancement in Medicine* 8, no. 2 (1995), pp. 87–105.

7. Sue Shellenbarger, "No, You're Not Too Tough to Suffer a Bout of Burnout," *Wall Street Journal* (June 25, 1997).

8. Cited in a Reuters article, "Emotion, Stress Affect Heart Survival," *American Journal of Critical Care* 6, no. 2 (1997), pp. 116–26.

9. Brigid Schulte, "To Help Your Heart, Just Take a Chill Pill," *San Jose Mercury News* (October 20, 1997).

10. Cited in an Associated Press report, *Circulation* (May 1994). The study authors are Ichiro Kawachi, David Sparrow, Pantel Vokonas, and Scott Weiss.

11. Graham Burrows, "Stress in the Professional," in Seventh International Congress on Stress, American Institute of Stress, Montreux, Switzerland, 1995.

5

Freeze-Frame: One-Minute Stress Management

The last theme of internal self-management is this:

> Individuals can learn to increase their capacity for intelligence
> resulting in more effective decisions, greater resilience, and a
> heightened sense of well-being. This provides enormous value to
> any organization.

The research described in Chapter Three indicates that the heart-mind-body complex is inherently designed to work in energy-efficient, harmonic, synchronized ways. This is as much to maintain our energy levels when dealing with external environmental or social factors as to maximize the potential for growth. Awareness of the natural inner workings of our system, if applied with even a fraction of the energy we apply to learning external systems such as computers, technological conveniences, or any skill we throw our heart into, can have a huge payoff. The payoff starts with *paying attention.*

Freeze-frame is a powerful tool to neutralize any negative or inefficient reaction—or prevent it before it starts—by capitalizing on the built-in heart-brain communication link. Freeze-frame is a way to "pause" the scene (much like pressing the pause button on your video machine's remote control), regain neutrality, and scan for energy-saving solutions. While freeze-frame is by no means a tool just to reduce stress, regular practice of the technique greatly heightens your awareness of the noise in your system and allows you to hear a commonsense voice inside. You gain increased access to intelligence.

Freeze-frame is a fast-acting power tool for transforming stressful thoughts and emotions into clarity, allowing you to take efficient and effective action. With practice, you gain increased power to come to balance and quickly change a negative, draining response into a proactive, creative one. Here are the steps.

FREEZE-FRAME STEPS

1. Recognize the stressful feeling, and freeze-frame it. Take a time-out!
2. Make a sincere effort to shift your focus away from the racing mind or disturbed emotions to the area around your heart. Pretend you are breathing through your heart to help focus your energy in this area. Keep your focus there for ten seconds or more.
3. Recall a positive feeling or time in your life and attempt to reexperience it.
4. Now, using your intuition, common sense, and sincerity, ask your heart what would be a more efficient response to the situation, one that would minimize future stress?
5. Listen to what your heart says in answer to your question.

Step 1 requires self-awareness and the realization that learning about your internal communication network will maximize every aspect of your fulfillment. This is like scanning to see what seems out of phase, troubling, or confusing.

Step 2 sets the stage for a new approach. Focusing in the area of the heart is unfamiliar to many people but quickly becomes natural. People usually feel their most positive feelings of love, appreciation, or joy as warm sensations around their heart. Do not try to feel the heart beating or any other physiological sensation in the organ, rather focus your attention gently in that area. Try to be neutral. (Focusing first on your big toe for a few seconds, then the palm of your hand, then the center of your chest helps give you a feel for this focusing process. Once you feel comfortable focusing in the area of the heart there is no need to repeat the focus on the big toe or hand.) Breathing deeply, as though you were breathing through your heart, can help increase the sensation. The essence of step 2 is to *anchor yourself in your heart* so you are not dragged back in to the inefficient mental loops that caused you to freeze-frame in the first place.

In Step 3 you activate a positive feeling. This both neutralizes the negative emotion you had and brings increased electrical coherence to the body. This step goes beyond *visualizing* a pretty scene or having a "happy thought." The intent is to actually *feel* it. Just as the amygdala in the brain has the power to conjure up negative emotional memories that can rob clear perception, *you* can generate positive feelings which restore balance physiologically while widening perspective.

Step 4 enables you to revisit the problem from a new emotional state. At worst, you have neutralized the stress reaction and stopped a mental, emotional, and physical drain. At best, you also have gained insight that helps you solve problems or take action.

Step 5 ensures that you listen to and act on any new insights.

WHY DOES FREEZE-FRAME WORK?

By consciously shifting focus from the problem causing stress and focusing instead in the area of the heart on a positive feeling, you are withdrawing amplitude from the problem and allowing your perspective to widen. In freeze-frame, the process of shifting focus to the heart enables the power in the electrical system of the heart to work for you, resulting in new intuitive insights for dealing with the problem. Even if no new insights appear, freeze-frame can get you into neutral, buying you time for more clarity while reducing the strain on you.

> The affairs of the heart are directly connected to the brain and it's the heart's natural intelligence that must be unfolded for the brain to operate with greater efficiency.
> —JOSEPH CHILTON PEARCE, *EVOLUTION'S END*

Like Bruce, the realization that asking the heart for guidance could result in intelligent solutions came early on in my professional life. A native of North Carolina, like many of my friends, I began working at a furniture factory after a tour in the military. Conflicts erupted on the job, particularly when I felt unfairly judged. Still fairly hot-tempered, a deeper intelligence reminded me that to lose it over something trivial could cost me friends, let alone jeopardize my job. Arriving late for work one day, I was soundly humiliated by a supervisor. I was determined to tell off my supervisor, over the principle of it, but I realized this was shortsighted and foolish. Heart intelligence had saved the day—and saved my job.

Freeze-frame provides direct access to heart intelligence. As you practice, you are retraining your physiology. Your mind and body have become quite familiar with the reactive patterns—they have become habit. These are habits it clearly is in your self-interest to break. As you shift focus to your heart and freeze-frame, heart rate patterns become smoother, so the messages the heart is sending the brain facilitate the brain's activities instead of inhibit them. The more balanced emotional state freeze-frame gives you also allows for greater electrical coherence in your body, so all systems can run more effectively.

The essence of the freeze-frame process is

- Recognize
- Shift
- Activate
- Ask
- Act

Recognize the situation that needs adjusting. *Shift* your attention to the area around your heart. *Activate* a positive feeling from the past or even something fun in the future, and *ask* yourself for an energy-saving, commonsense solution that can help you come back in phase with your core values. Then, *act* on your insight. Remember, each time you act counter to your values, which spring from your heart intelligence, you are fighting yourself. It is a battle you cannot win.

In one of Doc's earlier books, *Freeze-Frame: One-Minute Stress Management*, numerous examples and applications for this tool are explained,[1] but here we simply focus on some of the most powerful.

NEUTRAL

Neutral is one of the most efficient psychological states on the planet. Neutral is a state where you are not jumping ahead too quickly nor moving too slowly. Neutral does not mean being inactive, complacent, or passive. It is a calm poise that allows new information and new possibilities to emerge before taking further action. When in neutral you actually increase your sensitivity and intuitive intelligence. Neutral is fertile ground from which new possibilities can grow.

Neutral means putting the overactive mind in check, slowing down the constant stream of thoughts and taking a deeper, unbiased look at situations big and small. Neutral saves wear and tear on our bodies. It keeps our systems working smoothly, in a flow. It is an economical approach to life. If we constantly react to every conversation, assignment, change, or random perception, we drain away valuable energy that can be needed when a definitive action needs to be taken. Again, neutral is not an unfocused, unproductive state. It is a highly intelligent, ordered awareness that observes without boxing you in. When you constantly "know what you know" without seeing things from a more neutral perspective, how can new possibilities have a chance to manifest themselves?

Neutral takes practice because the mind works at high speed and quickly forms opinions and perspectives about everything, and not always correctly. Here is a common workplace example. You hear a rumor about a management change in your organization, project negative scenarios into the future, and experience a cascade of "what ifs," devitalizing your system and compromising productivity in the process. What actually happened is that you overheard someone say that the manager of your division is going to be transferred. You did not really hear the whole conversation, just a few words. Without going to neutral you can start to think things like, "Does this mean the department is going to have to go through another reorganization? I bet Bill will get the manager's job instead of me. I just knew it. That's just not fair! If it's true and I don't get a promotion I think it's time to start looking for another job." One projection leads to another and another and before long you've painted the entire picture of a possible scenario on which you have very little information. All of that mental processing adds stress to your system and accelerates the aging process needlessly. At times like these, a dose of neutrality would go a long way. In neutral, you would put the mind projections on hold. Stay balanced and wait and see what happens. After all you really do not know the outcome of the change or, in this example, if a change really will take place.

> There has been much tragedy in my life. At least half of it actually happened.
> —MARK TWAIN

People often think they are being neutral, and to a certain extent they may be, but not in the deeper state of neutral we describe here. In continuing with the example, a coworker could ask you if you had heard anything about a possible managerial change and how you feel about it. You could say that you are doing fine, you are neutral about it. On deeper review you could be running low-grade angst inside. You believe that you have really gone to neutral because the potential change no longer is causing anguish and anxiety, but in truth you continue to subtly process the potentially unpleasant possibilities all day, devitalizing as you go. You might say you have gone to neutral on it—but not really—not to the point where you're really at peace with it. From a heart intelligent perspective, you would see there still is unfinished business to take care of, a deeper state of neutral to be actualized.

Neutrality also is not about saying things to yourself like, "Whatever. I guess it will be all right. Somehow I'll probably find a way to deal with it no matter how it goes." This kind of approach often is accompanied by feelings of resignation. You feel beaten down and have not really surrendered enthusiastically to the situation. Real neutrality contains self-security. You peacefully allow things to play out and use your available energy in more productive ways.

Getting back to a neutral state is becoming increasingly essential for enhancing personal balance and effectiveness. Research shows that if you work too long at mental tasks, your problem-solving time can decrease by up to 500 percent.[2] When you are in neutral, energy is not draining, you are not wasting gallons of energy in worry or anxiety.

THE POWER OF BECOMING NEUTRAL

Becoming neutral several times each day, even if you cannot find a positive feeling to focus on, gives you these benefits:

- It saves energy.
- It saves degenerative hormones, which do not flow through your system.
- It saves wear and tear on your nerves.
- It saves aging of your cells.
- It saves strain on your heart.

These "personal strategic moments" have enormous benefit. If not taken, the brain unplugs anyway, so we space out, lose focus, or doze off, resulting in damage to our work and relationships.

How do you get neutral? What does it feel like? Neutrality is a state of quietude inside—not total silence or the total absence of thought, but a state of greater balance than usual, a dynamic peace. As you pay attention to the thoughts and feelings that go on each day, deeper levels of neutrality can be achieved. This can seem paradoxical, but as you increase in self-management, you become more sensitized to subtle noise and incoherence in your system. What was neutral when you started can become progressively deeper awareness. From this state of neutrality, your system can recharge and new insights can unfold.

STRESS PREVENTION

Most people have numerous predictable situations that throw them off balance or cause stress—the weekly staff meeting, the daily commute, the performance appraisal, telephone calls with clients, customers or vendors. A 30-second freeze-frame prior to any of these events means you are managing yourself, saving energy, and being less of a victim.

Sit quietly at your desk, eyes open or closed, shift your focus internally to the center of your chest and breathe deeply. Recall the most positive feeling you can muster. If you are about to meet with or talk to someone with whom you have had conflict before, find something in the person to appreciate. Stay anchored in your heart and remind yourself to at least *stay neutral* if the waters get rough. (In later chapters, we describe how freeze-frame can be incorporated in all communication to ensure authenticity in what you say and depth in how you hear.)

BUTTON PUSHERS

Have you ever experienced a negative irrational reaction merely on seeing the name of the sender of an e-mail message? Do you ever think, "Oh boy, here he goes again," as soon as a certain coworker begins speaking? Do you ever jump to conclusions and start accusing your child of naughty behavior before finding out the truth? In all these examples, you could be "right" to justify the reaction—based on the emotional memory stored in the brain. However, right or not, your reaction is draining your energy, it could be clouding a more accurate perception, and it can drive a spike into the heart of an important relationship.

Staying neutral allows you to save energy *just in case* the other person was not to blame, the e-mail actually was a thank you note, or the child was innocent of the "crime" accused. Neutrality is a tremendous energy saver.

ENERGY EFFICIENCY

Focusing on internal self-management results in more efficient use of your energy on all levels—mentally, emotionally, and physically. Stop to freeze-frame, then ask yourself, "What is the most energy-efficient response in this situation?" The concept of energy efficiency became popular in the gas-guzzling 1970s, when the skyrocketing price of oil forced a rethinking of how we spend our finite energy resources. Applied to the human system, becoming more energy efficient personally can help you see a bigger picture, save energy now, and untold amounts of energy later on. Increasing personal energy efficiency is analogous to increasing profits: More spare energy is available to "invest" in fun, creative, or regenerative activities.

Each day brings multiple new opportunities to explore increasing energy efficiency. As you begin to freeze-frame several times a day, you will become more sensitized to subtle stresses in your system. You will notice more often when your actions contradict an intuitive insight. You will anticipate future problems earlier and have increased energy available to prevent problems or mitigate their damage if they already occurred. Paying attention to the energy efficiency of thoughts, reactions, and attitudes yields significant energy returns. Apply this concept to customer interactions, whether or not to hold meetings, or what type of communication is appropriate around a specific issue. Considering energy efficiency immediately shifts you into a more expansive perceptual framework, more options are seen, and wider consequences understood. Considering energy efficiency inherently involves whole-system views. If a particular course of action seems expedient to you or a key stakeholder but would dramatically alienate other key players, it clearly would not be energy efficient. The extra energy you expend to deal with the fallout could neutralize the positive benefit of the expedient decision. As you consider various scenarios this week or this year from the point of view of energy efficiency, a new balanced picture begins to emerge, often yielding surprising insights. A process for deepening these insights in problem-solving or decision-making modalities is called the *asset-deficit balance sheet*.

THE ASSET-DEFICIT BALANCE SHEET

Like freeze-frame, the asset-deficit balance sheet is a simple tool, designed to uncover new solutions to personal or business problems while reducing the drain of negative or unbalanced emotions. The concept is that, when making decisions that require deeper reflection, a careful weighing of the assets and deficits of the proposed course of action yields clarity and more energy-efficient decisions. This process, by the very act of carefully considering upsides and downsides from a neutral perspective, reduces emotional drag. Many times in our own organization, people have made proposals opposite to their original emotional impulse, once they had considered deeply all the assets and deficits. Sometimes unexpected assets came to mind that were unseen when the idea was first flown. Also common was the realization that potential deficits are easily manageable in the face of the overwhelming assets. At other times, significant deficits were revealed that would have been ignored if the first "evangelical" instinct had been followed.

Using freeze-frame to add a heart intelligence perspective is a powerful addition to this process and differentiates it considerably from the "pros and cons" decision-making approach common in business. Here is an example of how to use the process: Scan the past week and jot down all the significant positive events that occurred, both personally and professionally. Write them down on the left side of a sheet of paper under the heading *Assets*. Be thorough and feel appreciation for each item you jot down. Do not quit after two or three; keep digging and even use Freeze-Frame to uncover more assets. Now shift to the deficit side and, *from a neutral perspective*, jot down the negative personal and professional events during the same period. Note if any of the deficits occurred because you failed to listen to intuition. Also note if any deficits could be transformed—at least neutralized—through freeze-frame. Notice if the type of assets and deficits you have fall into a pattern. For example, many people say their assets are relationship based but the deficits reflect situations beyond their control. Oftentimes, people are surprised how much energy can be drained by one or two deficits, while significant assets go unnoticed. Such is the power of unmanaged emotion to distort perception and drain energy.

Continue to freeze-frame while you complete your two lists, then freeze-frame one last time to discover the essence of your week. How balanced was it? Did deficits overtake intelligence? Did activating heart intelligence—for example, using appreciation instead of impatience or staying neutral instead of judging—save energy and yield positive outcomes?

Even without using the written form of this tool, verbally evaluating ideas using this approach can ensure greater individual and organizational coherence, particularly at times when you get "bad news." Finding one or two assets in an otherwise bleak scenario can plug the emotional drain on you or a team. It can keep attitudes resilient, hopeful, yet realistic. Most important, it allows you to maximize intelligent input while minimizing strain.

BUSINESS AND WELL-BEING IMPROVEMENTS

All the clients we work with have specific business issues that need improving and are intrigued that an approach focusing on internal self management could produce measurable results. In case after case, where the freeze-frame, asset-deficit balance sheet, and other IQM tools have been taught and their practice encouraged, significant improvements occurred.

At Royal Dutch Shell in the United Kingdom, several operating companies instituted programs in the HeartMath technology after a successful initial pilot program involving middle and senior level managers. In the pilot program led by Dr. Alan Watkins and Chris Sawicki of Hunter-Kane, several significant positive changes were noted, including an overall drop in blood pressure from 126/80 to 118/78 within six weeks. Significant improvements were noted in the group with the highest level of stress. These included reductions of 65% in tension, 87% in fatigue, 65% in anger, and 44% in intentions to leave the company. A further assessment six months after HeartMath tools were introduced saw a further reduction in virtually all key parameters (see Figure 5–1).[3]

Patricia Chapman attended a HeartMath program in the fall of 1995 after a six-year bout with arrhythmia and ventricular tachycardia (an electrical malfunctioning of the heart). Her condition had involved several serious attacks, surgery, and an extended work absence. A long-time employee of one of Silicon Valley's legendary companies, she stated, "I was so used to the adrenaline rush that I did not know what it was like not to have it." After attending a weekend HeartMath seminar, Patricia's colleagues immediately noticed a difference—less stress and tension and more ease, even during a particularly hectic work period. Her arrhythmia specialists at Stanford University were also impressed and within five months after her training, they reduced her medication by 50%. "After my weekend at HeartMath, whenever that adrenaline would start to rush again, I could stop the trigger. Now I can pull myself back into balance at will." Her health improvement has now sustained for nearly three years. There have been no further episodes of ventricular tachycardia or surgery. There were no lifestyle, dietary, or exercise changes, therefore, Patricia attributes these profound improvements to the tools she learned at HeartMath.

Significant improvements in productivity and well-being also have been seen in government agencies. At a large state agency in California, improvements occurred in a pilot program involving more than 125 employees. Statistically significant reductions occurred in anger, anxiety, burnout, and physical symptoms of stress.[4]

At one of the world's largest and most powerful technology companies, similar results occurred for a high performance engineering team.[5] Tracked against a control group of engineers from the same division, the training was conducted during one of the most intense periods of growth and strain in the division.

- The test group saw a 17% reduction in fatigue compared to the control group's 1% increase.
- The test group had a 7% increase in vitality while the control group saw vitality fall 7%.

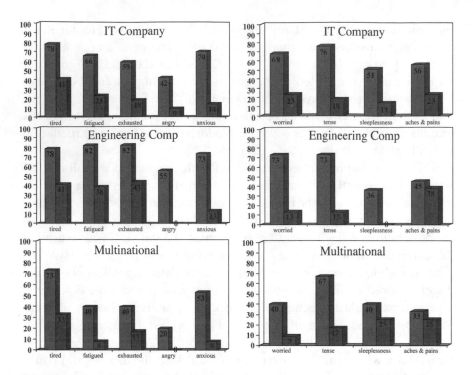

FIGURE 5–1 A summary of stress-related improvements seen in three organizations utilizing the IQM technology. Pre- and post-IQM technology values represent a six-week period. Number values represent the percentage of participants who reported the stress symptoms "often or most of the time."

- Sleeplessness improved 8% in the test group while it worsened 18% in the control group.
- Social support rose 11% in the test group while it declined by 6% in the control group.
- Anxiety fell 13% in the test group while increasing 1% in the control group.
- Rapid heartbeats declined 17% in the test group, while rising 10% in the control group.

Among the tens of thousands of people worldwide who have learned the IQM tools, one of the most common benefits people cite is having more time. Clearly, anything that could give us more time, or at least shift our perspective toward time, would give us tremendous leverage.

NOTES

1. Doc Childre, *Freeze-Frame: One-Minute Stress Management*, 2d ed. (Boulder Creek, CA: Planetary Publications, 1998).

2. Robert Cooper and Ayman Sawaf, *Executive EQ: Emotional Intelligence in Leadership and Organizations* (New York: Grosset/Putnam, 1997).

3. See the Appendix for more information.

4. The Appendix gives more details on this case study.

5. The Appendix gives more details on this case study.

6

Time, Expectations, and Other Things Difficult to Manage

We explore further one of the themes of internal self-management:

> As individuals learn to identify and plug the leaks in their own personal systems, they stop draining energy and effectiveness personally and organizationally.

One of the biggest leaks in energy for most people is their love-hate relationship with time. We experienced this firsthand while this book was being written. IHM was launched in 1991 as a not-for-profit research and education center. As we wrote this book, all the training and consulting activities were licensed to a new for-profit company, HeartMath LLC. Some reporting relationships changed, no one lost his or her job but many new jobs were added and many of our relationships were changed profoundly. Anyone who has been involved with a significant business restructuring understands the complexities involved. Add to that the legal, accounting, and tax implications of creating a new for-profit organization out of a not-for-profit one.[1] Time seemed crunched as people were challenged to do their regular jobs while spending considerable time planning and organizing the transition.

While this transition has been essential to the expansion of our work, we have not rushed it. We set milestones and goals, marshaled resources hoping to meet them, but stayed flexible in the face of business and legal realities. This change was not one we would undo, so taking our time and doing it properly—with minimal strain on the people and existing business momentum—has been essential.

We launched the institute's corporate training activities in 1993 and watched them grow at a rate of 70% per year for four years. While juggling four training and international consulting divisions, with all the strategic partners and players that implies, we remain focused on the foundation of all our work: the *inside job*.

When we contracted for this book and agreed to a completion date, we thought: "Whoa! We'll need a time shift to get all this accomplished and maintain personal balance."

What do we mean by a *time shift*? Time shifting could sound like a concept out of the movie *Back to the Future* or a similar time-warping movie. The sense we mean is far more practical yet profound. Time shifting describes an internal state so coherent that your perception of time—and your ability to shape it—changes dramatically. Every time you catch yourself before falling into a negative reaction, you have time shifted. Every time you stop long enough to find an intuitive solution instead of rushing ahead impulsively, you have time shifted. Every time you allow your intuitive intelligence to propel you out of inertia or confusion, you have time shifted. If you arrive at a solution to a difficult personal or organizational issue in five minutes instead of five hours, you have time shifted. You have jumped out of the self-limiting mental frequency that says, "Certain things just take time," into a new dimension. Time shifting means moving past standard linear time flows. Staying in the Now, more aware and sensitive to whatever is going on would be efficient use of time. We call this being *present*. Most people, however, at any given time, have a percentage of their thoughts assigned to reliving the past or projecting into the future. Not having enough time is a perception that, according to statistics, is a high-ranking source of stress yet most people do not stay as present as they could. By learning how to stay present, time is used more efficiently and stress overload is greatly reduced.

Some would say, "There is an objective reality to time; 24 hours in each day, no more, no less." Yet your perception and effectiveness in regard to time clearly changes as your perception changes. Love what you are doing and "time flies." Hate it and time stretches maddeningly. Stay stuck in an inefficient thought loop, and your effectiveness within a given time span can diminish dramatically.

Many problems people have finally do resolve but not before they have used up a lot of precious time. For example, two people have an argument at work. After the argument they replay the uncomfortable incident over and over. In an effort to feel justified, they may tell someone else about it, making their points about what they said and why. Later in the day, the mind begins to run out of gas and new thoughts like "perhaps I was a little too emotional in that exchange" or "I wish that hadn't happened. I really do like her" start to arrive. Soon, a more objective review of the argument comes on-screen and a desire to apologize or make things right starts to dominate the mental process. The next day, the apology is made and both parties feel a release. Things go back to normal and balance is regained.

In this case, what if efficiency and effectiveness had been diminished by 10, 20, or even 50% during the hours this person complained and resented? His use of time clearly was not efficient, and emotional mismanagement was the culprit. Learning to freeze-frame and neutralize the petty annoyances and disturbances saves enormous loads of energy and, in this example, could have shifted this scene in the movie of life ahead several hours. Freeze-frame helps you time shift.

How many situations face you each day where time feels like the enemy or at least a hungry competitor for your sanity and sense of balance? Snapping out of a judgmental thought process causes a time shift. Catching yourself replaying the same inner dialogue over and over—and stopping it—causes a time shift. We mean this actually. Your relationship to time fundamentally shifts when you engage heart intelligence instead of relying solely on the mind.

TIME EXPERTS

Some of the most effective people are those who are not imprisoned by incomplete perspectives of time. They are the ones who say, "Why are we rushing this decision?" Their patience usually pays off. They also are the ones who, at other times, can be quite decisive and intuitively recognize the importance of quick action because of how much time and energy could be saved by not delaying. The emotionally intelligent people recognize the objective reality of time but deeply understand how easily its grip on our perceptions can be loosened and transformed.

High performance teams seem to operate in a "parallel universe" of time and effectiveness. Southwest Airlines is a model of organizational coherence. Time efficiency is one of their bottom-line outcomes. Their on-time performance beats the competition every year. They have time shifted into a new dimension of effectiveness that their customers love and their competitors envy. When you watch many other airlines perform the same tasks, it is easy to see a marked contrast. Internal coherence—loving what they are doing and having fun doing it—is the springboard for time efficiency at Southwest.

The pressures on people today demand learning how to time shift. When faced with obviously conflicting priorities that "cannot possibly be accomplished in the time frame," what alternative is there other than mind-numbing stress? The first thing is to assume there *is* a solution that can be achieved once you get internally coherent enough to perceive it. Internal coherence is the priority and can lead to surprising time-saving convenience.

TIME CONVENIENCE

The number of conveniences that occurred for us once the decision was made to produce a finished manuscript in nine months—while maintaining a 50–60 hour workweek—have been amazing. Meetings to discuss the content and direction of the book occurred just at the "right time" on several occasions, saving us considerable energy and time. A key client, for example, postponed two sessions at a time when we needed extra writing time. Two free writing days resulted. Two divisions of another client independently decided important meetings should be held on the same day, saving several hours of travel time. We scheduled more than 60 "book days"—unbreakable appointments—and informed staff members we were unavailable those days. Life became more coherent as we did. Balancing all these priorities became a daily challenge and a game.

Then another reality set in: The rapid growth of our business made it increasingly difficult to put consistent "quality time" into writing. Many issues came up regarding our restructuring and new strategic direction that required input. To keep saying, "We are working on the book," was starting to sound hollow and even a bit irresponsible. And yet our contract with the publisher had a fixed date. The only possibility was to request a significant extension, despite concern that publication of the book would be delayed for a full season. Meanwhile, the publisher had independently realized the following season would be better anyway, so an extension was willingly granted. Time had shifted, and the shift occurred because of an internal attitude shift that acknowledged that, in the name of balance, "life" had to shift.

What are some of the key attitudes and internal perceptions underlying problems with time? How do you manage something as absolute and uncontrollable as time? The first point is to understand time itself is unmanageable. What you *can* manage is your perception of it and the events within it. Ponder deeply on this. Numerous programs exist to help us "gain mastery" over time and many systems offer practical formats and guidelines. Yet the mastery people need is over inefficient thoughts, judgments, and expectations.

EXPECTATIONS

Few things can devastate personal or professional relationships and inner peace—or cause a bigger drain on your mental and emotional balance—as much as unmet expectations. The raise we expected to get, the recognition we expected to get, the commitments we expect our colleagues to keep, the quality of work we are expected to produce—all of these unmet expectations and our reactions to them can generate a stream of disappointed thoughts and feelings. These emotions so easily can move into a torrent of frustration, resentment, and anger, all of which affect productivity at every level of life. We finally realize we have to neutralize expectations if we want to enjoy life.

The problem is *how easy reactions are to justify*. After all, you *expected* to be treated a certain way; "any rational person would have expected the same treatment," you tell yourself and anyone who will sympathize. Expectations often are based on some form of idealism. They set us up for disappointment and allow for no new possibilities to emerge. When reality does not match your mental image, the gap between your expectation and the pervading reality creates a tension that can be hard to release. If you could release or transmute the tension, you could move on quickly and adapt to the new reality. In fact, the new reality might turn out to be better than the one we expected, but if we see things through mind-sets about the way things have to be, we are cut off from new possibilities.

If your expectations have become crystallized, it takes emotional adaptability and flexibility to regain balance and security. In the absence of such powerful intelligence, the emotional residue of the expectation lingers, creating the perfect opportunity for disappointment, the primary by-product of expectation. At a more subtle level, disappointment is a convenient hiding place for judgments. You judge people, places, issues, and yourself for not meeting your expectations. You say you were not judging, you were just disappointed about the situation. But, if you looked deeper, you might find that judgment was at the root of your disappointment.

A team member you respect promises a report by 3:00. By 4:00, nothing; 4:30, still nothing; 5:30, not even a hint. At 5:45 the report finally arrives via e-mail, putting you behind schedule on your project. When the report finally arrives you say you are not mad, just disappointed that this person was not as responsible as she should be. Somewhere in this example a judgment is lurking. If you could see a transcript of the thoughts and feeling you had between 3:15 and 5:45 it would reveal a lot about how expectation led to judgment and then to disappointment. When the team member who was late tells you her child had fallen down at school and cut his hand, requiring stitches, and that she was called to the school to take the child home and just forgot to call to say the report would be late, you quickly forgive her, but the damage of expectation has already been done to your body and your mental and emotional energy reserves.

As the broken expectation lingers, a lot of energy is used to sustain the disappointment, energy no longer available for productive activities. Your mind is preoccupied, the internal dialogue races, and time once again is the enemy. Energy is drained away. Your physiology slides deeper into incoherence, making it harder still to shift perspective. Your cells actually age. It does not have to be this way.

In the process of increasing your internal self-management through heart intelligence, scan your awareness regularly for subtle as well as overt expectations of yourself and others on your team or in your family. Consider how to stay emotionally "neutral" if things do not work out as expected. Deeper management of expectations requires understanding the excitement that often spawns them and where it originates. We use salespeople as an example. Many other scenarios would tell the story equally well, but the sales process provides a convenient model.

SALES EXPECTATIONS AND "RATIOS"

We both have known many salespeople who were excellent at attracting a buyer's interest but then, in their overenthusiasm over the potential of a large sale, short-circuited the process. In the long run, they lost more sales than they made. Each time this happened, the disappointment grew, making the expectation for the next sale even harder to manage. This kind of negative feedback loop can be devastating to self-confidence. Many good salespeople have given up because of the disappointment felt from unmet expectations about a big sale.

Successful salespeople know about "ratios": Some deals close, some do not. As long as the ratio stays consistent with their goals, everything is fine. They intuitively know that overexcitement about potential sales creates the perfect breeding ground for failure. Salespeople with a balanced internal attitude understand the unpredictability of life, so such people can bounce back quickly even when the "sure thing" evaporates.

The concept of ratios is central to rapid progress in internal self-management. First you use it to balance your own expectations, then apply it to other areas. You may make rapid progress in stopping the leak of a long-standing mental habit, then feel your progress stymied when a tough situation causes you to lose your cool. You feel like you slid backward because you reacted negatively, and then you judge yourself for the slip. Slipping does not negate the genuine progress you made. What you do *next* in your internal attitude, however, sets the stage for either more progress or inertia. Losing hope, becoming despondent, or doubting yourself will leak massive quantities of energy and intelligence. *Appreciating* the increasing ratios of time you already spent in greater coherence provides a booster for sustaining them, especially when challenged. Understanding ratios helps you have sensible expectations about people, yourself, and your work instead of demanding absolute perfection and being continuously disappointed.

We have learned, from personal experience, the need to stay balanced and positive while keeping energy-draining expectations to an absolute minimum.

This attitude of allowing life and people to be their unpredictable selves, while maintaining a positive inner attitude that has security either way, can bring ever-increasing rates of success, personally and professionally. *What an irony: manage expectations and watch them be surpassed.* And if they are not, you have accumulated extra energy to move on to the next potential. Become overly crystallized and attached to a potential outcome and you often can block a more positive potential from unfolding.

Much of the noise and incoherence in organizations today results from overpromising and underdelivering. In your enthusiasm to convince a buyer of the value of your product or a colleague of the value of an idea, it is easy to set expectations at unreachable levels. Overenthusiasm based in the mind's need for stimulation is the real culprit. The greatest antidote is building more acceptance and appreciation for what is. A self-secure person knows it is much smarter to underpromise and overdeliver, but it takes inner security to hold true to that perspective.

Freeze-frame is a great tool to scan your inner radar screen for simmering expectations in yourself or those you could have created in others. As soon as you do, you will begin to get a picture of how much more energy and intelligence you could have available.

JUDGMENT

Another significant energy drain already mentioned is being judgmental. Judgment of others or yourself results from assessments made without benefit of heart intelligence. They often result from an overactive mind "sizing up" a person or situation based on limited or emotionally distorted information. Judgments have no payoff. They throw our system out of balance physiologically—in fact, you are most vulnerable to being judgmental when operating at a deficit emotionally. Being judgmental drives a wedge between yourself and the person you are judging. Judgments of oneself are particularly insidious, cloaked as they are in the robes of self-improvement. We judge ourselves because we erred, we are not improving, or we fear an unchanged pattern will doom us personally or professionally, all the while draining our emotional reserves and limiting the potential for growth. We judge others because their behavior fails to "match" our expectations, but all too often, when overstressed or overrushed, we "default" to judgment at the first sight of a certain person or before even reading the boss's e-mail. At our most immature, we feed judgments based on gender, race, profession, or academic background.

In all these cases, judgment drains and robs us of the clarity needed to build relationships or take decisive action. While it can seem stimulating, even fun, to judge, judgment actually consumes tremendous quantities of energy. Its only usefulness is as a wake-up call, letting us know we let unmanaged emotion cloud perception while accelerating our aging. Appreciating that we spotted the judgment, then quickly neutralizing the unmanaged emotion can restore balance and full intelligence.

Judgment is one of the most pervasive drains on the planet. Judgment underlies all ethnic, racial, and regional conflict. It underlies teams refusing to cooperate with others, executives overly critical of subordinates, even nations out to destroy a neighbor. Often the judgment seems justified, based on past experience. The mind constructs its memory of a past abuse, then carefully protects its viability. Judgments rarely retreat without a fight, so deeply embedded can they be in our mental, emotional, and cellular makeup.

Heart intelligence, activating positive emotional states to yield increased intuitive understanding, can pop the balloon of judgment so we regain balance. Once their fangs have been removed, judgmental attitudes can be seen as merely the inefficient product of mental-emotional imbalance. Neutralizing judgment will not rob you of the power to discriminate, assess, or evaluate. In fact, once the judgmental mind is recognized, clarity, balance, and poise all can increase.

DYNAMIC BALANCE

For businesspeople who love to work at high speed and pride themselves on being able to thrive under pressure, the notion of *balance* could seem cute but frankly rather bland and unproductive. Think of high-wire artists. Clearly these performers understand the importance of balance; in fact, for them it is a life-and-death issue. They must make hundreds of micro-adjustments to stay balanced on the wire and keep their nerves, anxiety, and visual distractions from ruining their day. Balance is key, but there is no lack of adventure, excitement, or risk. In fact, *without* balance their fun would be a one-shot thing.

Look at balance from another perspective. In the 1960s and 1970s, a great American track star, Lee Evans, set world records in the 400 meter, 500 meter, 600 meter, and 1,600 meter relay and many other distances. Many of these records were not broken until the 1980s. In his track days, Lee was known as an extremely hardworking athlete, but what set him apart was something different. Lee was not the most graceful runner, but he had learned that to go faster, the answer was not to tense up, but to relax more deeply. While running, he would tell himself to relax and find a more flowing style; he would accelerate and win nearly every race. A deeper level of balance helped him find more speed and grace.[2]

A third analogy is a high performance car. For a Ferrari to pick up speed, you need to shift gears intelligently. Each time you shift gears, the engine is able to run more efficiently so you can drive faster with less wear and tear on the engine. High performance cars like a Ferrari need constant tuning so that a dynamic balance is maintained and higher speed is possible. Without constant aligning and balancing of the engine, the wheels, proper fuel and vital fluids, the car runs poorly or, worse yet, can spin out of control. Speed still is the objective, but balance is the way to achieve it. Paying attention to the car's need for adjusting is a constant priority.

Think about how these analogies relate to your day: Are you racing to get more done, while causing increasing wear and tear, or could you create "personal strategic moments" to slow down, step back, and discover a more balanced, efficient way to get the job done—with less strain on you? What effect might that have on your sense of time, your productivity, your relationships, or the quality of all your communication?

NOTES

1. The Institute of HeartMath is a 501(c)(3) not-for-profit corporation incorporated in 1991. HeartMath LLC is the new training and consulting company, licensing the technology of the institute. HeartMath LLC is a limited liability company.
2. Lee Evans and Bruce Cryer worked together during the 1984 Olympics in Los Angeles. We had numerous conversations over several months about the disciplines and attitudes that made him a great track star, and those attitudes that kept other superb athletes mediocre.

COHERENT COMMUNICATION

1. *Achieving understanding first* is essential for effective communication. How easy it is to think we understand the views of a customer, colleague, or constituent without truly knowing.

2. *Listening nonjudgmentally* allows full intelligence and understanding to unfold. It requires careful attention to mind-sets about people and ourselves. High speed judgments of others block full understanding of their point of view.

3. *Listening for the essence* of a communication means hearing deeply the core message without being distracted by the superficial tone or quality.

4. *Authentic dialogue* brings increased clarity and reduces the noise in any system. Authenticity represents an intelligent transformation of unmanaged diatribe, antagonism, or withholding.

7

Authentic Communication

Dynamic 2, coherent communication, is the nitty-gritty of personal fulfill-ment and organizational resilience. Nearly all of us could listen better and most of us could express our own ideas and the understanding of our heart with more care, clarity, and precision. Many organizations choke on myriad communication problems—from conflict avoidance to systems confusion to sheer information overload to male-female posturing and wariness. In an era when the primary reason people leave their jobs is the inability to get along with their supervisor, improving communication rapidly is becoming a per-sonal and strategic necessity. What is missing? An obvious answer would be the heart. But, again, we do not mean just that communication needs more sentiment or emotion. Rather, compassion, mature understanding, and intu-itive sensitivity are needed to transform the communication distortions of our world.

Authentic communication implies listening and speaking with sincer-ity, security, and balance. It implies a fullness, a completeness, a directness to one's communication that arises from the core of oneself, not the storefront. As Robert Frost said, "Something we were withholding made us weak, until we found out it was ourselves." *Sincerity* is the oil that lubricates communi-cation, dissolving the metallic friction so prevalent in this information-inun-dated world. *Security* arises from a core "knowing" that everything is okay; its Latin roots mean "without fear." Balance provides the self-calibration so heart intelligence is the core frequency—the central operating system—guiding how we speak and listen.

If organizations would ever undertake to *measure* the lost productivity and stress generated because of the unexpressed concerns, fears, and antag-onism present, they would be shocked. The gap between what most people *feel* and what they *say* is huge and costly. National surveys in the United

States suggest 70% of employees are afraid to speak up at work. (In some other countries, this percentage is far higher.[1])

We are not advocating a free-for-all of truth telling for its own sake; in fact, that can be quite destructive in an emotionally immature environment. Some use authenticity, or being a "straight shooter," as a mask for unmanaged emotion and judgment. Real authenticity is not reaction; it is expression from the core—the core of compassion, understanding, and intuition. Nor is authenticity soft or tentative. The failure to be authentic and the resulting incoherence is costing more than we want to know. How do *you* feel when you fail to speak up over an insensitive decision, knowing your courage could be greeted with blackballing and isolation? What examples in your professional career have you seen where the failure to address an issue proved costly? There are some tragic examples. The problem with the O-rings in the space shuttle Challenger was known prior to launch. Failure to speak forthrightly—and for that communication to be heard—cost the lives of the entire crew. Every day in organizations around the world, people *notice* things that could be costly, but often out of fear, many of these observations go unexpressed. The personal guilt and self-blame you can experience for not speaking up can haunt you for years.

Any book on organizational theory states the obvious: Effective communication is essential for successful relationships and successful organizations. But we are suggesting something much deeper: authentic, essence level communication that catapults speaker and listener into a new dimension of clarity, resonance, and entrainment.

Robert Cooper and Ayman Sawaf's book, *Executive EQ*, narrates how a Tibetan wise man describes this heart-based authentic communication:

> You must understand . . . that this is not something only of the mind's making. It is from the heart. We call it authentic presence. It means literally, "field of power." When we live from here, from the inside, we can talk openly and honestly with each other, and say the things we deeply feel, even when it's hard to say them. We hold ourselves, and each other, accountable to our best effort in all things. We search for our calling, for the path we are born to take. Every person has this, and can face hardships and problems but not live inside them. This is a very difficult thing to do, but we can do it, we can set them aside.[2]

Underlying these fundamentals is the deep principle that to authentically communicate with others requires self-honesty and increasing levels of self-maturity. Authentic communication starts with listening to yourself, especially the sometimes challenging prompting of your heart. So many things in life can convince people to justify their reactions, throwing them back into fear or insecurity. Freeze-frame and neutrality are two tools to bring you back to balance and help you become more deeply aware of what you are feeling, the consequences of these feelings, and possible true-to-yourself solutions.

ELECTRIC COMMUNICATION

Some researchers suggest that our comprehension of a conversation is only minimally based on the words expressed. As much as 58% of our understanding is due to our interpretation (perception) of *body language*, 35% on our perception of the *tone of voice*, with only 7% based on our interpretation of the *words* themselves. Obviously, this leaves lots of room for misunderstanding and incoherence.

"What a radiant person she is!" "He has such magnetism and presence." "The room was electric as she announced the plans for next year." These and other phrases reveal a deep intuitive understanding that communication is not just auditory but also visual; *and* it is electromagnetic. Research has demonstrated that the heart produces an electromagnetic field that can be measured at least ten feet from the body using current technology. As soon as you come within ten feet of someone else, your fields interact. (Another reason why crowded subways are so hard on the nerves?) Research has established that measurable changes occur in the heart's field, depending on one's emotional state: Frustration causes "static" in the field, while appreciation or care creates increasing levels of coherence in the field (see Figure 7–1).

THE ELECTRICITY OF TOUCH

Additional research at the institute has shown that, when touching someone through a handshake or hug, a measurable transference of electrical energy between the two people takes place (see Figure 7–2). Happy, sad, loving, or insecure—it does not matter: Touching generates an electrical transference. In fact, even close proximity between two people registers an electrical effect, when people are as close as 18 inches.[3]

So, while your words communicate one message, your tone of voice another, and your body language yet another, your own heart is radiating an undeniable, hard-to-hide electrical message. Quantum theory would suggest that, although the electrical component of human communication may only transmit 10 or 12 feet, the quantum level knows no such limitations. Once again it is clear: We live in a sea of frequencies. Information is every-

ECG Frequency Spectrum

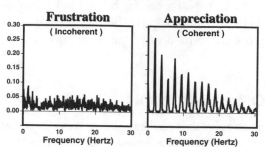

FIGURE 7-1   Feelings affect the information contained within the heart's electrical signal, which is transmitted to all the cells in your body. The graph on the left shows the "noise" created within the heart electrically when we experience a negative emotional state such as frustration. It is called an *incoherent pattern* because the signals are distorted. The graph on the right shows the coherent electrical patterns created by the heart during a positive emotional state, in this case, appreciation. Notice how the lines are clear, ordered, and harmonious.

Electricity of Touch
(Heartbeat Signal Averaged Waveforms)

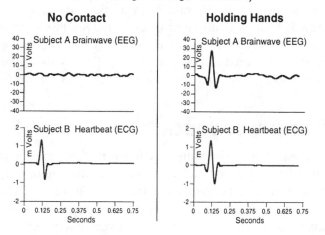

FIGURE 7-2   The electrical signal radiated by the human heart is transferred between people when they touch as shown by these two graphs. Simultaneously, two subjects were being measured: Subject A's brain waves and subject B's electrocardiogram. The graphs on the left show their respective measurements while sitting four feet apart. However, when they touch, as shown in the graphs on the right, the electrocardiogram of subject B is appearing in the brain wave pattern of subject A, showing a measurable electrical transference while the two touched.

where. We each broadcast and receive. The clarity of the reception has every-thing to do with the clarity of the receiver—you. Have you ever listened to someone a bit impatiently, tried to speed the conversation along by finishing the speaker's sentence and letting him or her know you understood, only to find out you were dead wrong and completely missed the point? Or if you cannot remember ever doing this, no doubt it has been done to you and it drove you crazy. Internal noise from unmanaged emotional stress is one of the greatest inhibitors of clear, effective, essence level communication.

DEEP LISTENING

If deeper, more authentic communication with others is the goal, how could you avoid starting with yourself—the gut feelings, the instinct, the still small voice within? How often do you ignore an intuitive sense because the mind's rationality or past experience blocks the way? Remember that intu-itive intelligence represents an underdeveloped frequency range within each person's intelligence capacity. From time to time you may get a flash of insight or glimpse of the obvious, but how random or unpredictable these intuitions can seem.

Attempting to listen to the intelligent voice of the heart requires prac tice, especially when the mind's decibel level is blaring. But it is a practice that yields payoff in every dimension of life. Mastering listening to yourself is facilitated by disciplined attempts to do so. Freeze-frame throughout your day to pick up subtle signals telling you that something is out of phase, something needs attention, "I need to deal with so and so." Pick spe-cific times in your day to scan the inner radar screen for unattended-to issues or concerns. Early monitoring during the daily commute, lunch, and other breaks are excellent times to step back, check the inner voice and respond, save, or delete. A major part of everyday stress results from failure to listen to one's own intelligent input. Can you recall any times in the past week, month, or even year when you kicked yourself for not doing some-thing or regretted saying something that in your heart you knew was not appropriate? For most people, this is fairly common. If examples are hard to come by look for it in others and freeze-frame to get more clarity yourself.

Listening to yourself as you would a child or a friend with a problem can quickly increase compassion for yourself and then for others. Most peo-ple have mastered one overused aspect of listening—the art of listening to their own self-judgment and self-blaming. They play hours of personalized "self-helpless" tapes, designed to imprison them in the familiarity of despair and unfulfillment. It requires a new, more compassionate focus to become neutral and quiet long enough to listen to a deeper intelligence beneath the emotional pain or turmoil. Of course, once you get adept at listening to yourself, authentic action is mandated from within. In the face of intelligent choices, failure to act confirms the self-defeating behaviors you are trying to transform. Acting from the heart represents a new level of self-empowerment, a new platform from which to build more internal coherence and more authentic communication.

Whether your role is to lead others or simply to lead yourself, acutely understanding what you are feeling and perceiving is the prerequisite to understanding what others think and feel. It is easy to master the "storefront" we talked about. In a society where "looking good while feeling bad" is having ever more serious consequences, it is time to let the heart's wisdom guide our actions. Start by paying closer attention to your subtle internal feelings. Attempt to verbalize them on paper or to close friends. Never stop this process if continual growth and unfolding your intelligence is a goal. Sharing one's deepest insights invariably yields unexpected clarity. Intelligence is everywhere.

BARRIERS TO EFFECTIVE COMMUNICATION

There are two types of barriers to effective, authentic communication: encoding errors and decoding errors. *Encoding* involves the meaning we ascribe to the communication we send; *decoding* is the process of making meaning out of what we hear. Encoding errors occur when we as the speaker

- Are not clear what we want to say due to excessive emotional noise.
- Do not know what we really mean.
- Use words that have meaning only to us, with no clear translation for the listener.

  Similarly, decoding errors occur when we as listeners

- Misinterpret the essence based on our perception of body language, tone, or words.
- Form judgments about the speaker.
- Listen at only the surface level.
- Make an inappropriate "match" between what the speaker is saying and some previous experience.
- Have so much internal noise that the signal is drowned out.[4]

Intuitive listening provides a technique for reducing these "errors" so greater coherence can be achieved.

INTUITIVE LISTENING

If you have taken a management development, customer service, sales training, or parenting course, you probably learned fundamentals of good listening: steady eye contact, open receptive body language, paraphrasing key points. All good storefront communication. Intuitive communication implies that a deeper level of intelligence, efficiency, and effectiveness are at play when you get past the mannequins in the window.

Good listening requires both the hardware and software, hearing and understanding. There are three distinct levels of listening:

1. The *word level* is where much miscommunication happens. How many arguments or misunderstandings are over the words said and not the real meaning? The words themselves are just the tip of the iceberg of the real communication a person is trying to make. Many times people cannot find the words to describe accurately what they want to say; others are simply not adept with words, although they might communicate their feelings in a very expressive way. What one person means by *heart*, for example, could be totally different to what someone else means. Words are cages around frequencies. They sometimes are crude attempts to capture the essence of an idea and convey it with clarity and specificity. They are necessary but not always sufficient and often the cause of confusion.

2. Beneath the words we speak is the *feeling level*, where the deeper meaning can be found. We all have listened to people who were saying one thing, but we thought they meant something quite different. Feelings are an area most people are uncomfortable discussing, and clear differences exist between men and women. Yet, this often is where relationships are made or lost. Feelings often are expressed, especially in business settings, through tone of voice and body language. Less often are they expressed authentically.

3. The deepest level of communication could be called the *essence level*. Remember a conversation with someone in which you felt so in sync, it was as though the person knew exactly what you meant or felt. This is very efficient communication that cuts through when words are inadequate or do not convey the deepest meaning. Getting to the essence saves time, facilitates understanding, and establishes a true connection.

Finding the essence means getting past the storefront to the stockroom. What is on the shelves inside, is it organized, is it carefully managed? We are using this metaphor guardedly, not so you actually will seek to understand the "inventory" in a conversation, but rather to intuitively understand the core, the real substance, underneath the surface. People lack the time to waste on just the words or hurt feelings—it is time for *essence*. There is no downside for seeking to understand the essence of an issue or another person's point of view. While it could sound time consuming, intuitive listening has as its aim a tremendous increase in mutual respect, understanding, and energy efficiency. By utilizing intuitive intelligence, you operate out of a deep part of your own essence, which is why you more easily can hear the essence of another person or message. Not only do speaker and listener *feel* better about the exchange, coherence is higher, leading to creative solutions that surpass what is possible when the air is filled with distortion and contention. In fact, this type of communication is highly energizing. When you feel heard, especially if the issue is emotionally charged, a tremendous release can occur, freeing up energy for more productive things.

Intuitive listening requires being neutral or even positive emotionally while listening to another person:

- Try to feel appreciation for the other *as a person*, so you see a fuller picture, not just a limited view created by the message being delivered or an old memory you have.
- This means allowing the person the time and space to complete thoughts without interrupting, judging, or rushing.
- It means giving your complete attention, not having your mind on other tasks because "you have so much to do."
- It involves, when necessary, repeating what you believe to be the essence of what the other person has said—to make sure the person feels heard—before responding with your perspective or opinion.
- It requires a measure of emotional maturity to not simply react defensively if the message contains feedback for you. From this foundation of maturity, a deeper relationship can be built. For customers and clients this is essential, just as it is for friends and colleagues.

When we lead intuitive listening exercises in workshops, we continuously are impressed by how deep, rich, and quick relationships can be built; and we are struck by the efficiency of intuitive communication. There is less noise and more coherence in the mind and heart of the listener, with much less time and energy spent sparring, jousting, and defending. Creative solutions arrive on the scene at high speed, through the entrained efforts of the participants. A program we did recently for a global consulting firm yielded such comments as, "I can't believe how well we got to know each other in five minutes!" "Having the other person focus on making sure I felt heard and not interrupting me actually clarified my thinking."

Each of these principles can and should be applied both to ourselves and to our communication with others. Several years ago a new member of our staff was having a challenge adapting to our unique organizational culture. An MBA with extensive consulting experience on Wall Street, he found the degree of cooperation, collaboration, and camaraderie appealing but somewhat disconcerting because of how different it was from his previous highly competitive professional experiences. At one point, he began grumbling about the dynamics within the team. We asked if he would be willing to bring up the issue openly in a team meeting. He agreed, although it took some courage on his part. During the meeting he forcefully shared his concerns, which related to a perceived gap between the senior members and the junior ones, and the intense frustration this caused him to feel. We listened nonjudgmentally, realizing we could easily have had the same perspective being in his shoes. We locked in to the essence of his words, trying not to get thrown by the emotional delivery (*neutral* came in very handy). As we listened, we appreciated his courage for speaking up and his anxiety over the gap he felt. But, before making any comments, we made sure we had understood the essence by paraphrasing it back to him, then asked if we had heard him correctly. He threw his arms up in the air and said, "Finally, someone has heard me!" The relief in his face and body was tremendous. Gone was the tension, the fear, and the insecurity that, if poorly expressed, his words could result in reprisal or isolation, a common pattern in so many corporate environments. We concluded the exchange by suggesting we talk "off-line" to make sure we understood his concerns fully.

Here is where the power of intuitive listening became so profound. While talking privately he realized that once he finally "felt heard," it became clear that most of the problem was in his perception. He thanked us for listening, and a bond of openness, security, and respect remains to this day.

Time after time, we have seen the power of intuitive intelligence transform ordinary communication. Performance reviews that neither party is looking forward to, difficult negotiations, client interactions—all these continually become more fulfilling and efficient when internal coherence is maximized, noise is reduced, and the heart provides the playing field.

A software company president from Australia offered this story:

> Today, one day after I finished the HeartMath program, I went into what I
> expected to be one of the most difficult negotiations of my life. I was nego-
> tiating the [company name] distribution agreement, which was like many
> agreements that I have negotiated in my life, except that this time I was
> negotiating with my life savings, resulting in a not insignificant increase in
> pressure. The agreement that I had received from [company name] about
> two months ago did not reflect the true spirit of the agreement that we had
> made on a handshake, and I started to feel very conflicted about this. From
> the distance of Australia, I felt that [company name] wanted to draw back
> from the agreement that we had made verbally. Actions subsequent to my
> challenging the basic conditions of the agreement were also not helpful in
> changing my opinion that they were reneging. They did not respond to
> phone calls or e-mail. Finally, and most critical, they did not send me a
> final draft of the contract as I requested. Hence, I had every reason to
> expect the worst (from a normal business point of view). Having changed
> my perceptual position with respect to [company name], these were the
> smoothest negotiations that I have ever been in. I freeze-framed often and
> poured love out of my heart for the negotiators as often as I could. They
> conceded every major point in the negotiations, about 15 in all, and only on
> one point did they not concede, which, from my point of view, was a minor
> consideration. This negotiation went like clockwork and major issues like
> term of contract, continuity, arbitration procedures, and quotas all fell the
> way that I wanted.[5]

At first glance it seems tedious to have to make sure you understand
the essence of what someone is saying. After all, don't most people talk in
slow, circuitous sentences anyway? It is much more "efficient" to cut in and
help the other person clarify his or her thoughts, isn't it? Hooked on speed,
always rushing to keep up, how easy it is to justify insensitive, ineffective
communication, veiled as it is behind the screen of judgment. The irony is
how much havoc is created by the rushed decisions and frantic thought
processes we convinced ourselves are essential to our organization or
career.

Slowing the mental chatter while neutralizing the emotional clatter
allows the high speed refined intelligence of intuition to be heard. The heart
has the power to neutralize runaway mental missiles and disarm the emotional grenades. As a side benefit of listening intuitively for the essence, a
study conducted at Johns Hopkins University showed that married people
who were able to accurately summarize the feelings of their spouse were
able to lower blood pressure.

Think of the great leaders of our time or a mentor who made a lasting impact on you. We suspect a part of your heart was awakened by the sincere spirit of that person. Most likely the person had the gift or developed the skill of deep listening, and that depth infused the words he or she spoke as well. The power and authenticity of their expression seemed to resonate from a deep passion and knowingness.

Many organizations have seen measurable benefits from applying tools of coherent communication. At a global energy company, a key strategic team had only 14% of its members feeling meetings were well organized. After six months with IQM tools, this figure had jumped to 53%. Only 43% felt they listened to each other prior to IQM training, but six months later 73% felt listening was good. And in this same team, only 57% felt free to express themselves prior to IQM. Six months after the IQM intervention, 93% felt free to express their views.

Another important dimension is the coherence of a team's communication with other parts of the organization, as well as the networks of relationships it is able to build outside its immediate sphere. Maintaining coherence within necessitates coherence without. In one study at the Harvard Business School, the way a team or unit was linked to others had a dramatic effect on its performance. In one multinational electronics company, for example, the best connected business units were able to bring products to market 30% faster than average.[6] As anyone who's ever talked on a cell phone or transmitted data through a modem knows, it's one thing to be connected, and quite another when that connection is distorted or full of noise.

ORGANIZATIONAL APPLICATIONS

The applications of coherent communication to an organization are many.

- *Meetings.* Before a meeting starts, review the key principles of intuitive listening: listening nonjudgmentally, listening for the essence, achieving understanding first, and speaking authentically. Write them on a flip chart or grease board as a reminder. Summarize key points of any discussion or presentation to make sure the whole group is in sync. Continue discussing until there is shared clarity. An intact team from Hewlett-Packard used this process to make sure the announcement of a new strategy was understood by everyone. The announcement took less than five minutes to make but more than an hour to distinguish the various interpretations from the real message expressed. Had they not taken this time, considerable uncertainty and confusion would have resulted, wasting many hours and possibly culminating in misguided decisions. Has this happened in your organization?

- *Phone conversations.* Whether dealing with a customer, vendor, or constituent, applying the principles of intuitive listening and authentic communication helps ensure a speedier, mutually beneficial outcome that can be energizing. Especially when you have no body language or other visual clues to rely on, focusing on keeping yourself emotionally neutral or positive while making sure you heard the other person is far less draining than being judgmental or making unfair or inaccurate assumptions.

- *Performance reviews.* Performance reviews are one of the most emotionally draining and commonly avoided organizational activities. Yet, they can be a rich opportunity for growth. Authentic communication in this context means putting the person's highest good as your primary objective. Make sure your appraisal allows adequate time for the person's assets to be discussed—and make sure the person hears your appreciation, sincerely. Where feedback is necessary, make sure the tone is not judgmental but is supportive and direct. Using freezeframe at the start of this process can neutralize or reduce anxiety while creating a stronger field for rapport instead of antagonism.

- *External relationships.* Evaluate the quality of communication between your team and other key divisions with the organization. Where is coherence lacking? Where is it strong? Particularly examine any areas of extended communication where people have become resigned to incoherence or antagonism. This is a high leverage point for boosting productivity. Typical examples of hardened relationships include manufacturing versus marketing, sales versus accounting, and marketing versus sales.

- *System noise.* Continue to ask where there is noise in any part of the system:
  —Sales people frustrated over level of services and support
  —Administration staff inhibited by infrastructure or process inefficiencies
  —Production people resentful over design delays or constant changes
  —Middle managers stuck in a no-man's land between senior management preoccupation with shareholder (or board) perception and rank-and-file (or membership) cynicism.

Now, from the interpersonal domain of communication, we move into the electronic domain and consider how the ideas of organizational coherence could be applied to information technology.

NOTES

1. Robert Cooper and Ayman Sawaf, *Executive EQ: Emotional Intelligence in Leadership and Organizations* (New York: Grosset/Putnam, 1997), p. 68.
2. Ibid., p xxi.
3. Rollin McCraty, Mike Atkinson, Dana Tomasino, and William Tiller, "The Electricity of Touch: Detection and Measurement of Cardiac Energy Exchange Between People," in *Proceedings of the Fifth Appalachian Conference on Neurobehavioral Dynamics: Brain and Values* (Mahwah, NJ: Lawrence Erlbaum Associates, 1998).
4. Dr. Alan Watkins, who has worked extensively with IQM tools in the United Kingdom, Europe, and Asia, contributed many of these ideas of encoding and decoding.
5. From a conversation with Gerard McMullan, president, No Fear Software Services, Sydney, Australia.
6. Cited in Sarah Cliffe, "Knowledge Management—The Well-Connected Business," *Harvard Business Review*, July-August 1998, p. 17.

8

Technology, Inner Technology, and the Measure of Human Capital

As with virtually every facet of society today, technology is in massive transition, facing significant choices for its future direction. Organizations like the Silicon Valley–based Institute for the Future carefully map the trends in information and communication technologies, while also attempting to forecast the impact of technology acceleration—economically, environmentally, socially, and personally. The picture is chaotic to be sure. With computing power now exceeding even Moore's Law of doubling of microprocessor speed every 18 months and devices becoming smaller, more compact, and more versatile, the future looks like a gadget freak's paradise. Much of this new technology will add immeasurably to our ability to learn and understand across borders and across time zones. But, at what price? Concerns about cyber-crime, children glued to computer screens, breakdown of traditional communities, a growing gap between rich and poor—connected and unconnected—are just some potential effects.[1]

Ironically, it is also a time when we are facing a truly planetary crisis—the Year 2000 computer problem. The issue, now known as Y2K, is far more than a question of mainframe computers that were inadequately programmed many years ago. Because so many technology devices are date-sensitive, it is not clear how widespread and devastating the problem may be. It is also becoming clear that it is not enough to simply have our own house in order, since making all computer systems within our organization Y2K-compliant does nothing to minimize the effect of other systems external to us that are not compliant. Life as we know it has become totally dependent on computers that function correctly, and the networks that connect them. This "cyberecology" is delicate—disruptions anywhere in the web of computers and connections could have a ripple effect throughout the entire system. So many things will be affected: banking, ATM machines, air traffic control systems, information networks, power plants, telecommunications, the embedded chips in a vast array of manufacturing and production systems. Some experts believe an economic slowdown is inevitable. Other predict a global recession; some even fear a depression.

Readers on the 20th century side of the millenium are no doubt rapidly becoming aware of the potential impact of Y2K on their business and on their personal lives. Some are preparing in rational, measured ways. Others are beginning to panic, and will make decisions out of fear and paranoia. No one really has any clear sense of how widespread the disruptions may be or how long-lasting. Readers on the other side of the millenium will look back at how we as a global community have dealt with one of the first truly global, man-made disasters. Did we prepare enough? Did we pull together in a sense of community to address the issue? Did we overreact and allow selfish interests to distort more balanced perspectives? Did the tendency to assign blame result in a frenzy of litigation? Did it give us a new perspective on how technology-dependent we, as a human species, had become? Did we look for hope in the midst of gloom? Meanwhile, the race for ever more technology speeds up.

Increasingly, communication is becoming electronic. The good news is that there are more ways to connect than ever; the bad news is that there seems to be no escape. As bandwidth (the range of available frequencies) expands to satisfy our stimulus-crazed addiction to information, so does the potential for information overload. The more information to which we gain access, the more our internal circuitry overloads, making effective processing difficult at best.

A 1997 Reuters study[2] suggests we are witnessing the "rise of a new generation of 'dataholics.'" Based on a survey of 1,000 people in the United States, United Kingdom, Ireland, Germany, Singapore, and Hong Kong, the survey cited these responses:

- More than 50% feel unable to handle all the information accumulated in their jobs.
- 61% believe information overload is present in their workplace, with 80% predicting the situation will worsen.

- 47% take material home or work longer hours to keep up with the amount of information accumulated.
- 55% are concerned children will become information junkies, with 36% "extremely worried" their children were overexposed to information.
- Nearly half of all parents said their children prefer PCs to peers.

Two researchers have determined that as much as 85% of the population feels uncomfortable with technology.[3] The 15% who are comfortable still fall prey to frustration, intimidation, or distress. Even the techno-literati feel the pressure. The number of messages and other demands on our attention—whether phone calls, e-mail, TV ads, Internet "junk mail" (affectionately called *spam*), or other kinds of messages—number in the tens of thousands daily. As we were working on this book, a call came in from a client, a senior executive of a global technology corporation, who was lamenting the incredible drain on his energy required to deal with the 200–250 daily e-mail messages he receives. Most get deleted without being read. And yet the senders thought they had "communicated."

E-mail can rapidly aggravate organizational incoherence. React negatively, even mistakenly, to a new policy or any situation, and you can instantly broadcast your displeasure to dozens of people. Here is a simple story. In a large financial services firm, an irate employee gave hostile feedback via e-mail to a coworker and sent copies to 15 other people, including the boss of the coworker's boss. The team director then had to sort out the issue, while responding to two higher levels of management and calming down the coworker who had been publicly and unfairly humiliated, electronically. Similarly, customer complaints electronically can snake their way very high into an organization, involving many people emotionally in the drama. In both examples, e-mail is not the villain; it is neutral. But e-mail has become a convenient vehicle in the transmission of incoherence and emotional mismanagement.

The information overload phenomenon increasingly is global. Another survey done by Reuters,[4] conducted with management personnel in the United Kingdom, United States, Australia, Hong Kong, and Singapore, revealed a tremendous amount of mental anguish and physical illness resulting from "information fatigue."

- 1 in 4 of the 1,300 managers surveyed admitted to suffering ill health as a result of the volume of information they must handle.
- 48% agreed that the Internet will play a primary role in further aggravating the problem over the next few years.

- Two thirds of managers reported that tension with work colleagues and loss of job satisfaction arise because of stress associated with information overload.
- 43% of senior managers suffered from ill health as a direct consequence of stress associated with information overload.
- 62% testified that their personal relationships suffered as a result of information overload.
- 44% believed the cost of collecting information exceeds its value to business.

The angst, strain, and paralysis of Year 2000 related crises are easy to imagine, further aggravating this bleak picture. Readers in the next millennium will know how we did. How much of this craze for information—and the personal and organizational inefficiency it spawns—arises out of insecurity and fear—fear we will be left behind, fear someone else will do the deal or get to the market faster, insecurity that if we are not constantly "connected" our value and worth will be questioned and ultimately cast aside?

It is fascinating to step back and realize how quickly information technology became central to our lives. Can you remember when you did not own a VCR, nobody sent faxes, nobody used e-mail, personal computers were a novelty (even in business), pagers did not exist, and phones in cars were for presidents and prime ministers? This pastoral scene is 1980! Fast forward to the present and we, in the developed countries, clearly live in an entirely different world. Today, many of us—more all the time—work and live in technology-intensive environments. Our homes increasingly reflect the technology frenzy in organizations. And, by all accounts, the intensity and speed of change will only increase. There is no end in sight for this trend to slow down or shift direction.[5] Only when the negative consequences cost us dearly are we likely to challenge the basic assumption that an ever-increasing volume of raw information is inherently good. (One can die of too much of *anything*, including water.)

In a very short time—15 years or so—computers and information technology rapidly became the primary physical asset of corporations and central to their operations. Today, close to half of all capital expenditures made by companies are on computers, networks, and software, the largest single category of expenditure.[6] Almost every employee of public and private sector organizations must be able to operate at least one but usually several kinds of information technology device: computers, laptops, modems, fax machines, e-mail, pagers, cellular phones, and other similar equipment.

A HEART INTELLIGENT RESPONSE TO INFORMATION TECHNOLOGY

With information technology rapidly pervading our work and home environments, we can expect change only to continue and to accelerate. How do we cope with all this? Pull the plug on technology and go back to simpler living? Unplugging is not practical nor possible for organizations, though we clearly have a choice at home. Furthermore, our *perceptions* of technology and the kinds of demands and changes on our lives that come with it are key to whether technology's value exceeds its price.

The first step is to recognize the essential paradox of technology. "Technology does not place us into an idyllic garden of paradise but rather into an unsettling garden of paradox," asserts David Glen Mick of the University of Wisconsin in Madison.[7] "The essence of a paradox is that it cannot be resolved. It creates an emotional conflict within a person that can be a source of considerable stress, and the need to cope with that stress affects how the person behaves as a consumer." Mick and fellow researcher Susan Fournier of the Harvard Business School have identified eight paradoxes that characterize the relationship between consumers and technology:

- The way in which technology insures greater *control* or exacerbates *chaos*.
- Whether technology promises *freedom* or creates new *enslavement*.
- The need for the latest *new* technology versus the fear of becoming *obsolete*.
- The way technology boosts our *intelligence* while at times humiliating us into a feeling of *stupidity*.
- The promise of increased *efficiency* versus the reality of extra new chores creating *inefficiency*.
- The premise technology will *fulfill needs*, while in fact creating *new needs*.
- The value of technology in increasing *assimilation* and connection between people, versus its tendency to create isolation by *diminishing* face-to-face contact.

The information age requires a new type of intelligence for people to sort through, filter, and effectively process all the data and choices now available. Whether you are a consumer of technology or a product developer, learning to develop "heart intelligence" gives you increased insight to assess the essential value of information—or a new product—from a wider perspective. Without heart intelligence—when operating solely from an overtaxed mind—people quickly are overwhelmed and respond to only the loudest and most persistent information or "default" to old, familiar processes. An intelligent assessment of new information is difficult at best. In the extreme, you may defensively shut down and not really assimilate much information at all. As the knowledge base is built and you achieve competence in reducing your internal noise, you can use intuition to search the internal knowledge base at lightning speed, bypassing a more linear search process. The internal knowledge base, coupled with intuition, allows one to leap beyond known possibilities to find unique new solutions when necessary. *This represents tremendous leverage for anyone in organizations today.*

So if technology has radically increased the bandwidth of possible information transfer—more ways in which to connect, more conduits for knowledge flow, and more opportunities to be overwhelmed—what if technology was actively being used to enhance the quality of that information?

> It was Arno Penzias, the 1978 Nobel laureate in physics, who first theorized that computing had met communicating to form connectivity and that, in effect, everything eventually will be connected. Computing, in short, was never about data crunching. Data crunching was the means; connectivity was the end, which is why the data-pigs and cyber-pioneers will never inherit the Earth. Nor was the communications revolution about the machines and services that spawned it. Fax machines, modems, interactive TV, and Internet providers were all the means; connectivity was the end. Computing and communicating did more than intersect; they fused. And when they fused, connectivity was born. But connectivity finally is not the end, either. Connectivity is a state of existence, nothing more. The true end is what happens when things are in connection, what happens when connectivity itself fuses with information.[8]

To which we add this: Connectivity is great if the signals are clear and the content has enduring value. But, how much noise is present in the connection, the noise of incoherence on the part of the sender or receiver? What is the enduring value of the messages being sent? How do we improve the inner quality of the *people* operating the technology?

Torrey Byles is a business economist and writer on electronic and digital commerce. His view is that:

> If we can effectively manage our perceptions, we can not only deal with the demands of the new technological world, we can go further and truly take advantage of the incredible possibilities that technology brings to us. The key to managing perceptions is first balancing our emotional and bodily states. Combining heart with information technology is the next step—a quantum

leap—in the roll-out of technology in our work and home lives. It's the only way I can see to keep it all in balance. I believe that the only way to fully realize the potentials of information technology will be, ironically, to go more deeply to the heart. We will go outside the technology dimension, we will rise to a higher dimension, in order to place technology into balance with the needs of the person and of the planet. I have found that HeartMath tools allow you to utilize coherent heart intelligence first, then in a joint venture with the mind, find perceptions that are in positive, enthusiastic moods, not moods of anxiety and despair.[9]

ENHANCING HUMAN PRODUCTIVITY WITH HEART AND INFORMATION TECHNOLOGY

Byles points out that computers, like any other tool, above all are intended to enhance human productivity. For example, call-center and customer support departments use computers to quickly bring up the account file of a customer who calls in. The call-center representatives are far more productive in dealing with the specific issues, requests, and other pertinent information concerning the customer than if they had no ready access to the customer files, which the computer provides. The result, we all hope, is a customer who remains loyal to the company and satisfied with his or her interaction with it. But what about the internal attitude of the representative? Does the customer feel understood or respected during the interaction or just efficiently handled so another call can be taken? Technological efficiency can enhance, but never replace, the warmth of human respect and sincere listening.

Ask anyone in virtually any organization today; he or she will tell you that using information technology is stressful—you cannot get the devices to do what you want them to do and they are always breaking, crashing, or acting independent of reasonable human behavior.

Another example is the researcher in a governmental health agency. She uses computers for many purposes including searching databases of research papers or other information, building simulations and models of natural processes, and conducting statistical analyses of laboratory experiments. In both of these examples, computers make a big difference in allowing workers to achieve the desired outcomes. Without computers in these examples, either drastically more workers would be required to achieve the same results or else the same results just could not be accomplished in the same period of time and for the same cost to the organization. Unfortunately, computer systems can be poorly designed and implemented into workplaces, so that they counteract productive human work. In these cases, computers only frustrate, overwhelm, or otherwise block the efficient flow of work.

Byles goes on to suggest that the heart—and personal emotional balance—plays a critical role in getting the most productivity out of information systems.

> In the design and deployment of computers, balanced emotions on the part of the designers will result in effective computer systems for the end-users. In the day-to-day use of computers by end-users at work, balanced emotions will allow workers to use the systems in the manner in which they are intended, and to avoid being frustrated and overwhelmed by them. In other words, by combining emotionally balanced people with the powers of information technology, companies can achieve breakthroughs in performance.[10]

THE HEART AND HUMAN CAPITAL

To what extent computers have truly added to human productivity is a significant debate among economists and business leaders currently. At a client lunch where the flood tide of e-mail overload was being lamented, one high-tech company executive sincerely asked whether we felt technology had enough positive benefits to outweigh its obvious stress-producing downside. In an age where the mass consciousness seems to assume more technology is inherently better, many say that no well-grounded measurements unequivocally show that computers have enhanced workers' output. Others say that, because computers wholly change the nature of output (in terms of quality of product, ability to customize product to individual customer preferences, speed of production, worker skill requirements, and other factors), the impact of computers is almost impossible to measure in an "apples-to-apples" fashion. Nevertheless, most economists and others in the financial community agree that computers and information technology are features of a new understanding of human economic growth: intellectual capital and the knowledge economy.

In this new understanding, the content of people's intellect (their imagination, knowledge, creative ideas, skill sets, assessments, designs, ability to make requests and promises, future expectations, etc.) is the source of all wealth. Material products are only by-products of the intellect. Material, tangible things come into existence only after people have conceived of them, worked to attain them, and used specific practical ways of attaining them. The intangible and intellectual precedes—and is inherently more valuable than—the tangible and material. (Clearly our view is that intellect is only one aspect of human and organizational intelligence. But how refreshing that something as intangible as intellect actually is being measured in organizations.)

Leif Edvinsson, the world's first vice president of intellectual capital at Sweden's Skandia, and Michael S. Malone, a noted business writer, sum up this point well in their book, *Intellectual Capital*:

> All individual capabilities, the knowledge, skill, and experience of the companies' employees and managers, is included under the term human capital. But it must be more than simply the sum of these measures; rather, it also must capture the dynamics of an intelligent organization in a changing competitive environment. For example: Are employees and managers constantly upgrading their skills and adding new ones? Are these new skills and competencies recognized by the company and incorporated into its operations? And are these new skills, as well as the experiences of company veterans, being shared throughout the organization? Or, alternatively, is the company still drawing on a body of aging and increasingly obsolete skills, ignoring (even punishing) new competencies gained by employees, and locking up knowledge as a way of cornering power and influence with the organization?[11]

Given that we are beginning to see how important—and measurably valuable—the intellect is, what does this tell us about the emotional and intuitive sides of being human? What would happen if we could coherently orchestrate a balance of all human factors, changeable and dynamic though they are? The fruits of the intellect's powers are conditioned by the emotional state of the person. An angry or depressed scientist is a scientist whose intellectual capital is low. A joyous, enthusiastic plumber is a plumber who brings tremendous intellectual capital (creativity, knowledge, skills, etc.) to making a wonderful human habitat. At the same time that some businesses have discovered "intellectual capital," we are discovering "human capital." Good human capital—in other words, intellectual and emotional balance—is a prerequisite for a person to gain access to his or her intellectual capital.

Byles makes a further point worth pondering. Humans have invented many incredible tools over the millennia. (Anthropologists say that tool making is a fundamental human trait.) The species has now advanced to the point where we recognize that our tools are not only physical but nonphysical as well. We are now working to systematically create and exploit nonphysical tools—in software programs, education and training, and knowledge that is recorded in various electronic media. The information age with its information tools (namely, computers) is the dawning of an age where a common and widespread practice in human society is to use intangible tools at work. Computers are somewhat of a bridge tool: part physical and part nonphysical. They connect the physical world with the intellectual world, the world of ideas and intellect.[12] Emotional management practices are another set of intangible tools. Where information technology has been viewed as the tool of the intellect, the intellect is a far more powerful tool when fueled by managed emotions. Heart intelligence is the operating system.

The Institute of HeartMath has created an instrument that measures key aspects of human capital and pinpoints where stress is inhibiting its full leverage. The Personal and Organizational Quality Assessment (POQA) measures 19 separate constructs, tracking health and business performance indicators. The organizational constructs measured by the POQA are social support, goal clarity, mental clarity, job satisfaction, productivity, and communication effectiveness. The personal constructs measured are global negative affect (mood), sadness, depression, anger, distress, fatigue, positive affect (mood), peacefulness, and vitality. The stress symptoms measured are sleeplessness, anxiety, body aches, indigestion, and rapid heartbeats.

The POQA is used to compare the health and human capital of an organization against a database of world-class organizations and measure changes resulting from the application of the IQM technology. (The case studies data cited in the Appendix were generated through the POQA, with the exception of the biomedical data, which was generated through standard medical monitoring.) As this information is fed back to participants and management, clear steps can be taken to reduce the noise, resulting in higher value human capital.

USING INTUITIVE INTELLIGENCE TO ENHANCE INFORMATION SHARING

Clearly, the coherent sharing of information is a key to success in the future—and a primary way to reduce stress. As technology continues to expand the bandwidth of communication, people still must oversee the quality. Inner quality management emphasizes helping individuals understand how to boost their own inner quality—to improve the internal communication within themselves—then take that to their team (or family), their department (or social circle), their organization (or community), and the like.

We found that this sharing of information is easy to sermonize about but harder to actualize when business operates at ever-increasing speeds. For people to stop long enough to remember the importance of sharing (when they have "a million other things to do"), they need specific tools for the process of stepping back. The ability to pull back and recognize frustration, irritation, anger, or anxiety is the first important step toward finding an effective energy-saving solution, to move from chaos to coherence.

FREEZE-FRAME AND INNER TECHNOLOGY

Freeze-frame is a powerful tool to instantly widen the bandwidth of available intelligence: more information with which to make decisions and more care to add to oneself and the situation one is in. In terms of the communication process itself, this creates what we call *value-added information*, with the potential for much greater impact and broader application. When true care is at the core of the desire to share, the quality of all subsequent activities shifts into another domain of power and effectiveness.

Another way to look at this is that it is one thing to recognize the importance of a broadcast, another to spend the time ensuring that the receiver is properly tuned and distortion free. Most organizations are fairly good at the former but completely ignore the latter. Real sharing of information requires understanding the subtleties and nuances of information transfer between *people*. Then it becomes the transfer of *living information.*

As soon as humans are involved, we need to remember that we are dealing with nonlinear systems who *feel* as well as *think*. The human being, physiologically and psychologically, is a living example of chaos theory in action. Skill in human understanding provides the resonant field to allow seamless, static-free information transfer. Put simply, when you remember to be compassionate and caring in your communication, it is much easier for the listener to hear the message. This is a skill that requires practice to develop and the positive, public reinforcement of its merits. For example, *stopping to deeply consider the range of responses* to a piece of e-mail you are about to broadcast can save considerable stress and increase productivity. Considering the most appropriate means of communication—even multiple modes—ensures a higher level of receptivity to and sustainability of the message. "But I sent you e-mail about this!" is no excuse for insufficient communication.

A CREATIVE VISION OF THE FUTURE OF INFORMATION TECHNOLOGY

Information technology today is very primitive compared to what it will be in the future. In 20 years, we will look back at today's computers, wireless communication devices, the Internet, and so forth and think that these are very simple tools, some perhaps even misguided. Byles believes "information technologies will be designed around principles of emotional management and other core human characteristics."[13] Arguably there is no other alternative. What do we do in the meantime?

Practical examples of stress-reducing ways of handling technology overload include the following. Take a moment to freeze-frame *before* reading and responding to e-mail. Ask yourself, what is the highest priority information here and what is the most efficient way to respond? Stay "neutral" to keep your reactions in check as you pore through otherwise non-essential information. Remaining emotionally neutral means stress will not subtly accumulate on the back of judgmental thoughts, concerns, or frustrations. Be strategic as to when and how you respond. Remember that if you are operating in a reactive mode, you will not respond with full intelligence or care.

At HeartMath LLC, we implemented a simple method that has saved considerable time in e-mail reading and setting priorities. Since some e-mail messages need be only a simple phrase, such as "Be there at 3 for the meeting" or "Report needed by 4:30," we established a protocol that any message that could be summarized in a few words would start with a * symbol. This * symbol in the subject lets the reader know the entire message is contained in the subject line, therefore no need to open the e-mail since there is nothing else there to read. For example, our administrator sends us a reminder phrased like this: *Itinerary in your in box!

We simply read this subject line in the list of e-mails, then delete. You would be delighted how much time this simple process can save, especially when you consider the number of employees, the number of hours spent on e-mail, the number of days at work. While this does not solve the whole problem of overuse of e-mail in many organizations, it does encourage an attitude of efficient, concise communication that is sensitive to the needs and workload of the receiver.

We heard of at least one multibillion-dollar organization giving permission to overworked employees not to respond to e-mail for 24–48 hours, to encourage greater balance in the face of e-overload. The policy achieved mixed results since the culture continues to covertly reward overwork and employees' work habits are slow to change. The attitudinal level is where the real work must occur.

As mentioned in the previous chapter, organizations need to *discuss* how communication is working, in what ways people are feeling overwhelmed, where they feel underinformed, so the mind and heart together can design effective ways to communicate that are efficient for all concerned.

Intuitive intelligence increases as you continually step off the treadmill and ponder a more effective response. One of the most precious commodities for all of us is time, and we could all do a lot better job of respecting each other's and our own.

Voice mail is yet another ubiquitous form of communication radically changing the nature of how we communicate. (When was the last time you called a significant size organization and heard a busy signal? We heard one recently and, for a moment, didn't know what to do.) Responding to the number of voice mail messages and the frequently strained or angry tone is a significant source of anguish and dread, sapping coherence in virtually all organizations. What if your computer system could monitor the incoherence generated during and after listening to voice mail and could track the impaired decision making, the health consequences, and the loss of productivity? You probably would be shocked at the data. Taking a moment to freeze-frame and find "neutral" before and during voice mail can keep your system more in balance, as well as help you hear beneath the angry or impatient tone to the underlying essence of the message. Intuitive listening can ensure you are hearing the essence of the message and responding from that depth. The alternative is ever-increasing levels of incoherence, personally and professionally.

Technology can be a vehicle for positive experience beyond intellectual stimulation in many other ways, too. Screen savers could remind you to value important elements of your life. Digitized images on your computer monitor could help you recall a feeling of peace and rejuvenation. While some organizations frown on personalized use of computers, ever-worsening productivity and deepening malaise eventually will reveal that computers and information systems must become vehicles for the positive reinforcement of behaviors that boost the organizational climate.

One of the most popular follow-up tools we ever devised is a simple Internet group subscribed to by past IQM program attendees. Each week more than 1,000 people around the world receive a two to three paragraph e-mail message about the application of one of the tools they have learned. We continually hear that these simple e-mail messages quickly are read and absorbed, so sure are the readers that this will be a totally positive, useful, and caring message. (Perhaps the only one they receive all week!) Nothing else to do, no response required, no reports to fill out. Just a brief interlude to remind them what is important, to regain coherence, to move past mechanical habits and get the mind and heart in sync. We have helped client organizations set up similar discussion groups to keep organizational coherence themes alive amid the din of work.

What if computers and other information devices in the future were able to monitor your physical or emotional state and remind you how to shift perception? What if they could display on the screen your out-of-sync heart rhythms, then at the touch of a button, you could rebalance them and refresh your entire system for the next few hours? (We are developing PC-based technology to do just this, in conjunction with the freeze-frame technique, to help users boost internal efficiency and productivity while interacting with video-game type animation. As they freeze-frame and balance the heart rhythms, their internal coherence will affect the images on the screen.) What if designer music, played through your CD-ROM drive, were regularly used to boost productivity, clarity of thought, and achieve new creative breakthroughs? What if hardware and software engineers in the future continually explored how to make these tools servants of our growth as people, not just vehicles for more information?

In the words of Singapore's prime minister, Goh Chok Tong, "We should focus on building capabilities, resilience, and heartware for the future."[14] The caring and efficient integration of tools for internal self-management and coherent communication underpin the next dynamic: organizational climate.

NOTES

1. The Institute for the Future is a not-for-profit research organization. Robert Johansen, its president, also is the author of *Global Work: Bridging Distance, Culture and Time*, with Mary O'Hara-Devereaux (San Francisco, Jossey-Bass, 1994), and (with Rob Swigart) *Upsizing the Individual in the Downsized Organization* (Reading, MA: Addison-Wesley, 1996). Contact the firm at 2744 Sand Hill Road, Menlo Park, California, 94025-7020, phone at 415-854-6322.

2. "Study Reveals Growing Danger of Information Addiction," *Reuters* (December 10, 1997).

3. Conversation with *Technostress* authors Michelle M. Weid and Larry D. Rosen, October 25, 1997.

4. "Information Fatigue Syndrome," *Reuters* (October 25, 1997).

5. Many measurements of technology improvement, such as the all important price-performance ratio of silicon densities/microprocessors and data transmission characteristics of light, show that many core information technologies are in the early stages of commercial exploitation and that several generations are to come before we start running up against physical limits. The implication is that, while we may be awed—and stressed out!—by computers and the Internet today, we ain't seen nothing yet.

6. From conversations with Torrey Byles, an economic analyst and consultant specializing in Internet commerce and the digital economy, August to December

1997. Torrey can be reached at Granada Research, P.O. Box 2601, El Granada, California, 94018, phone at 650-726-3002.

7. Cited in David Champion, "Marketing: Technology's Garden of Paradox," *Harvard Business Review* (July-August 1998), p. 12.

8. Jim Taylor and Watts Wacker, with Howard Means, *The 500-Year Delta: What Happens After What Comes Next* (New York: HarperCollins, 1997), p. 115.

9. From a conversation with Torrey Byles.

10. Ibid.

11. Leif Edvinsson and Michael S. Malone, *Intellectual Capital: Realizing Your Company's True Value by Finding Its Hidden Brainpower* (New York: HarperCollins, 1997), p. 34.

12. From a conversation with Byles.

13. Ibid.

14. Prime Minister Goh Chok Tong's vision for Singapore 21, as reported in *The Straits Times* (June 7, 1997). Singapore 21 is a high-level government initiative for helping the country maintain its excellence into the 21st century, while ensuring increasing levels of balance for the people.

BOOSTING THE ORGANIZATIONAL CLIMATE

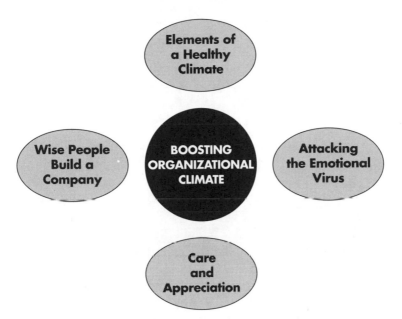

1. A healthy organizational climate is now proven to boost productivity. These elements include *supportive management, contribution, self-expression, recognition, clarity,* and *challenge.*

2. An *emotional virus* is attacking many organizations today. It is the result of emotional mismanagement and shortsighted management practices. And a corollary of this is *organizational learning thrives when the organizational "immune system" is strong and vibrant.*

3. Human qualities such as *adaptability, flexibility, care,* and *appreciation* underlie sustainable organizational climates.

4. Understanding the distinction between *knowledge* and *wisdom* is essential to organizational leadership. Building wise companies through developing wise people is the next organizational frontier.

9

Organizational Climate and the Emotional Virus

Most of us intuitively understand that the climate of one's workplace has an impact on how people feel and on how they perform. Dynamic 3, boosting organizational climate, will explore several dimensions of this intuitive belief, including a review of studies linking climate and productivity. More important, we explore solutions as well as ways to measure this ephemeral notion called *climate*.

In using the term *climate*, we refer to the collective atmosphere of a workplace: the attitudes, perceptions, and dynamics that affect how people perform on a daily basis. Climate, like the weather, is not static and unchanging. Nevertheless, as with any locale, certain climate patterns are unique to each organization. More important, unlike the weather, we all are involved in creating our organizational climate on a daily basis. Initially, we explore the first theme of this dynamic:

A healthy organizational climate is proven to boost productivity. The elements of this include supportive management, contribution, self-expression, recognition, clarity, and challenge.

For almost a century researchers have explored the causes of work-related injuries, a major cost to any organization and one of the earliest measures of organizational incoherence. At first, it was believed certain employees were more "accident prone" than others, but studies failed to support this contention as a definitive personality trait. Research then shifted to uncovering the personality traits that differentiated workers who were hurt from those who avoided injury. Looking into the psychology of safety became

111

essential as organizations such as OSHA and the National Safety Board in the United States determined that 90% of all accidents are caused by unsafe acts, while only 10% are caused by unsafe working conditions.[1]

The vast majority of workers today are employed in nonmanufacturing jobs, where workplace safety concerns focus more around issues such as ergonomics, workload, and mental and emotional processes, as opposed to the heavy labor of our forefathers. Yet workers' compensation claims are soaring in many nonmanufacturing sectors of the economy. And health, safety, and environmental issues are growing in importance, especially in industries such as technology, petroleum, and aviation, where disregard for these issues can be catastrophic.

According to Dr. Phil Smith, an organizational psychologist working in the United Kingdom and Hong Kong, a review of 61 studies of job burnout concludes that

> of the three facets of burnout—*emotional exhaustion*, *depersonalization* and *diminished personal accomplishment*—emotional exhaustion is most sensitive to factors which negatively influence workplace climate, and is the strongest predictor of attachment to the organization. Interestingly, job stressors such as role stress, workload and role conflict have a disproportionate impact on emotional exhaustion, not equaled by the relief provided by resources such as social support, job enhancement and reward structure. This implies that attempts to compensate for the effects of stressful work environments by the provision of additional resources may not be successful.[2]

Dr. Smith goes on to suggest that, "While a good emotional climate is not by itself sufficient to ensure success, a bad climate is certain to prevent it."

THE BROWN AND LEIGH STUDY

Underlying the inner quality management model is the understanding that your effectiveness in anything you attempt—career, marriage, relationships, fun—is based on activating the most intelligent perceptions of yourself, your environment, and those with whom you interact. Most of us would agree with this principle. Research showing a direct, measurable link between one's perception of the climate of one's workplace and one's own performance has been lacking, however. A ground-breaking study by Steven P. Brown and Thomas V. Leigh, published in 1996 in the *Journal of Applied Psychology*, sought to investigate the process by which workplace climate is related to employee involvement, effort, and performance.[3] A refreshing aspect of the study was that the researchers chose 178 salespeople in three different companies as the test subjects. Sales results were monitored and correlated with the study's predictions, providing a bottom-line context for the study outcomes.

Based on numerous previous studies, Brown, a professor at the Cox School of Business at Southern Methodist University, and Leigh, a professor at the Terry College of Business at the University of Georgia, designed their study to examine six dimensions of a workplace's psychological climate (see Figure 9–1):[4]

- *Supportive management.* The extent to which people feel supported by their immediate manager.
- *Clarity.* The degree of clarity about what is expected of an individual.
- *Contribution.* The feeling that one's contribution is worthwhile.
- *Recognition.* The feeling that one's contribution is recognized and appreciated.
- *Self-expression.* Feeling free to question the way things are done.
- *Challenge.* The feeling that one's work is challenging.

Each of these was considered to be an indicator of how psychologically safe and meaningful the employee/salesperson perceived the organizational environment to be, and the dimensions build on the work of the past century in linking job satisfaction and specific organizational outcomes.

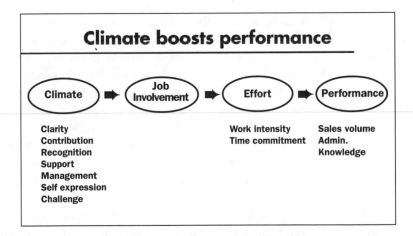

FIGURE 9–1   Brown and Leigh study of organizational climate. Source: Reprinted with permission from Steven P. Brown and Thomas V. Leigh, "A New Look at Psychological Climate and Its Relationship to Job Involvement, Effort and Performance," *Journal of Applied Psychology* 81, no. 4 (1996), pp. 358–68.

The 178 salespeople, one group of which represented a paper goods manufacturer and the others represent office products companies, were surveyed on these six aspects of their managers' attitudes and the workplace climate. The salespeople in turn were measured by their managers on three dimensions of work performance: achieving sales objectives, extent of technical knowledge, and administrative performance.

The study results were significant and supported the researchers' predictions. An organizational climate perceived by employees as psychologically safe and meaningful positively affects productivity. This occurs when

- Management is perceived as supportive.
- Work roles are well-defined.
- Employees feel free to express and be themselves.
- Employees feel that they are making a meaningful contribution.
- Employees are appropriately recognized for their contribution.
- Employees perceive their work as challenging.

Then, employees are more involved in their job and exert greater effort.[5] This leads to measurable improvement in sales, administrative performance, and product knowledge. (Described later is a way to measure and productively address these discussions of climate.)

IGNORING THE CLIMATE

The health consequences of ignoring the workplace climate was researched in a long-term study of British civil servants. The study indicated that employees with little control over their working environment face a significantly higher risk of heart disease than those with authority to influence their job conditions. "Our research suggests that illness in the workplace is to some extent a management issue," says Michael G. Marmot, director of the International Centre for Health and Society at University College in London and lead author of the report.[6] "The way work is organized appears to make an important contribution" to the link between socioeconomic status and heart-attack risk, he adds. The study, which tracked nearly 7,400 men and women in London civil-service jobs for an average of more than five years, found that those in low-grade positions with little control over their responsibilities were at a 50% higher risk of developing symptoms of coronary heart disease than those in higher level jobs. Since 1992, the United Kingdom has made companies liable for employee stress. Numerous lawsuits brought by employees against employers who created stressful environments have been won. Similar legislation in the United States so far has been blocked. In the highly litigious American culture, one can imagine the economic and social chaos that would be wrought by such legal actions. Liability issues aside, organizations the world over must deal on a daily basis with the consequences of unhealthy climates.

TRACKING AND TAMING THE EMOTIONAL VIRUS

This leads us to the second principle of Dynamic 3:

> An "emotional virus" is attacking many organizations today. It is the net effect of emotional mismanagement and shortsighted management practices. And its corollary is this: organizational learning thrives when the organizational "immune system" is strong and vibrant.

We have begun hearing some change agents in organizations call themselves *organizational viruses*, hoping to infect the organization with their view of needed transformation. Their intent, like a computer hacker's, is to get in and out fast, before the organizational immune system kicks in to throw out the invader. This analogy is intriguing and quite appropriate but we would like to *invert it*.

An organization is much like an organism. It requires a wide variety of nutrients and resources to be healthy; it can get sick in response to external stressors or internal imbalance and, unless it learns to heal itself, eventually becomes sick and dies.

Typically, today, when an organization recognizes something's not right, the solutions are to focus on cost cutting, process reengineering, product improvements, or improving customer service. While these well-intentioned initiatives are usually necessary, they are not sufficient. They focus on the *symptoms*, not the *cause*. In many organizations, this classic Band-Aid approach actually creates more frustration, anger, and anxiety, while the organization, or organism, becomes even sicker. Once people are drained emotionally, the creative energy needed to develop new innovations is sapped. Additional energy is then expended in inefficient ways that put added strain on the people, and the downward spiral accelerates. Acrimony, mistrust, antagonism, and blame are just a few of the emotional reactions that take up residence in the workplace. Finger pointing becomes the preferred exercise program, and left unchecked, the very creative source for the organization is drained.

The 1994 CSC (Computer Sciences Corporation) Index "State of Reengineering Report" revealed these statistics undermining many organizational climates:

- 50% of the companies studied reported that the most difficult part of reengineering is dealing with fear and anxiety in their organizations.
- 73% of the companies said that they were using reengineering to eliminate, on average, 21% of the jobs.
- Of 99 completed reengineering initiatives, 67% were judged as producing mediocre, marginal, or failed results.

Consider this analogy. An executive goes for his annual physical. Nothing seems to be wrong healthwise, just a routine check-up. Of course, he had been feeling a little tired lately, but who wouldn't be with all the international travel, round the clock pressure, and "never enough help." The doctor reviews the lab reports, checks the vital signs, then rechecks. His face turns serious. The executive expects the worst. "Your blood pressure is at the edge of stage two hypertension, cholesterol is nearly off the chart, and you have the beginning stages of arrhythmia. I'm putting you on a program of increased exercise, no-fat diet, and no more stress!" To the executive, his life has just been turned upside down. A radical rethinking of his entire lifestyle has been necessitated by the doctor's shocking discovery. No second opinion is going to lower that blood pressure or cholesterol. And how is he going to have no stress?

Compare this to the business that is humming along successfully, taking its market by storm, feeling indomitable. Its new technology is the buzz of Wall Street and a cover story in *Fortune* is in the works. A few systems seem to be straining every so often, but this is considered just growing pains. However, a series of late product releases and the departure of two key executives have people edgy. Before long stock analysts worry the share price is overvalued, and the company cannot meet the demand for its technology, so management brings in a consultant team that says the company needs to reengineer. But the situation quickly turns critical. After two consecutive quarters of losses, the Board of Directors steps in and orders a downsizing. Now everyone feels like they have just been hit by the flu, but there is no Alka-Seltzer for this sickness.

In an era of corporate chaos, we are now seeing a new phenomenon: the emotional virus. The virus hits its victim organizations unexpectedly, seemingly without symptoms, until suddenly the organism is quite sick and may be in need of radical surgery. The roots of the sickness are emotional. The virus grows and thrives on emotional imbalance, insensitivity, and overreaction in the organization. It is the antithesis of organizational coherence. The greater is the incoherence, the more nutrients the virus has to feed on.

WHAT IS THE VIRUS?

Doc first coined the term *emotional virus* while he was consulting with a CEO who had attended an IQM program in California. The executive was concerned about the internal backbiting among several of his management teams, which was clearly affecting not only morale but also productivity in a key division. The emotional virus was described this way: It is the net effect of emotional mismanagement within an organization. As with *other* viruses, the emotional virus is highly infectious. People think it is okay to complain, whine, and sarcastically laugh—about the imbalanced coworker, the stressed out boss who ignores voice mail or e-mail, the department that just cannot get its act together—not realizing they have caught the emotional virus bug.

Each casual complaint and unconscious judgment is like coughing in a coworker's face, thus spreading the germs of negative emotions and creating a caustic, unfulfilling environment. Once an outbreak of the emotional virus has been detected, the workplace should be quarantined until proper medicine arrives, but that is not the way business works—yet.

In evaluating long-term growth, companies that spend time and money on eliminating the emotional virus will see a big return on their investment. Ignoring it and staying on the track of believing "that is just the way it is" is a dangerous move on the chessboard of future business. People are changing and the worker of tomorrow will have a different set of standards for evaluating job satisfaction. This already is happening. The workforce already is demanding more harmonious working relationships. Salary, although still important, is not as high on the list as it used to be. Workers often are "cashing out," taking less pay and moving into jobs more in line with their core values. Working in an environment where people do not stab each other in the back, where management and employees can have a more open dialogue, and where the employee feels connected to and proud of the company and its products are among the career core values people are adopting. The emotional virus eats away at these organizational qualities and many people are seeking a place to work where they do not have to witness watercooler and break room character assassinations. It isn't that people can't take it. Millions do daily. Times are changing, however. As Doc told the CEO, "In the name of smart business, increased productivity, less employee turnover and lower health care cost, I believe the emotional virus eventually will have to be dealt with."

The workplace is not the only location where an emotional virus is on the attack. Many employees leave home or community environments full of viral activity. Without tools for effective self-management, people become drained emotionally because of the increasing pressures in society, family life, and their workplace. They are unable to recoup the lost energy, and the people around them soon become affected or infected. Like any virus, it spreads quickly if the organizational immune system already is weak.

The only way we have seen to eliminate the emotional virus or stop it before it gets out of control is to educate individuals who make up an organization on how to manage their thoughts and emotions. It has to come from the individual change of perspective within the people who make up an organization. It is usually essential to start right at the top with the senior management but it can start in a team of line workers and be highly effective. Just as the emotional virus spreads from person to person so does the antidote. As people in the organization, especially the most visible and influential ones, begin to actualize change within themselves, others soon will follow suit or move on to another environment that resonates with their attitudes. Start by fostering an atmosphere of appreciation. Do not allow judgments to go on without pointing them out. Put more care into communication and use heart intelligence to make decisions, big and small, especially when the decision affects others. There is more but these suggestions, if applied with sincerity and consistency, at least will save you from becoming infected and go a long way toward helping your coworkers and your organization.

WHO IS TO BLAME?

Executives or other highly visible employees often take the blame for being the carriers of the virus that has hit the company. Witness the unpleasant public departures of CEOs at Apple three times within five years, a company once noted for its innovative vision and people-oriented culture. Or the blindness of American automakers to their companies' sickness while the Japanese gained dominance and market share. Many business magazines write gloating postmortems of once-hot executives, helping their demise become public. No company is immune from the emotional virus or its ravages. Yet, rarely do analysts look at the emotional coherence of the organization, so easy is it to blame missed product deadlines, bad decisions, or other external factors that have a deeper cause.

It could be tempting to see the emotional virus as an isolated phenomenon. "It won't happen here." Reconsider some of the global statistics cited earlier. The sudden collapse of several Asian economies in 1997 has forced a major reexamination of business potentials in that part of the world while affecting global commerce. What role has emotional mismanagement—greed, unhealthy competition, and the like—played in that drama? Similarly, could many of the stress-related health care and productivity-related costs of doing business today in Europe and North America be based, at least in part, on underlying emotional mismanagement and organizational structures that ensure a fertile environment for continued viral growth? Is the procrastination in many organizations around Year 2000 issues an outcome of emotional overload on the part of these managers? We anticipate the situation will worsen as increasing globalization creates conditions perfect to mutate new strains of the emotional virus. As with populations that were isolated for centuries then devastated by disease brought by their conquerors, few have built the emotional resilience required to manage unprecedented change and uncertainty. In an age of connectivity, no one is isolated anymore.

HOW TO STRENGTHEN THE ORGANIZATIONAL IMMUNE SYSTEM

Recent research in human physiology has revealed key aspects of immune system health with remarkable parallels in organizational behavior—the organization as an organism. In the human body, feelings like anger, frustration, and irritation weaken the immune system and drain vitality, leaving you more susceptible to colds, flu, and more serious illnesses. A recent Institute of HeartMath research study,[7] published in the *Journal for Advancement of Medicine*, shows that even a five-minute episode of recalling an angry experience can suppress a key component of the immune system for as much as six hours. This research is showing the converse is also true: Attitudes like appreciation, care, and compassion significantly boost the immune system, and give you more resilience and strength to withstand sickness (see Figure 9–2). With these positive feelings operating in your system, even if you do get sick, you recover more quickly and recoup lost energy. The more your system is balanced, the more intuitive insight you are capable of—intuition that can anticipate problems before they turn ugly.

Organizations are strikingly similar. Work environments characterized by excess stress, contention, and anxiety breed insecurity and unproductivity and inhibit creativity. People do not want to come to work in these

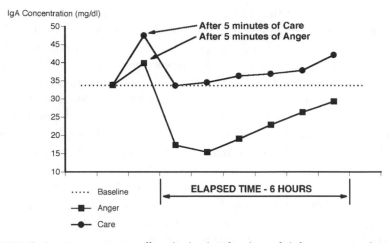

FIGURE 9–2   Emotions can affect the body's first line of defense against bacteria, viruses, or pathogens. In this study, IgA (secretory immunoglobulin A), a key immune system antibody, was found to be suppressed for nearly six hours after a five-minute period of recalled anger. On the other hand, a five-minute period of feeling sincere care caused a significant short-term rise in IgA, and a gradual increase over a six-hour period.

rigid, inflexible environments. The negative attitudes compound the pressure on an already strained organization. The last place most people look for answers is within; the first thing many will do is find someone or something to blame, reinforcing the organizational rigidity.

The same attitudes proven to boost a person's immune system are the ones known to create a harmonious, productive and creative workplace. Where people are valued, appreciated and cared for, they produce more, have greater loyalty to their employer, and have higher levels of creativity (see Figure 9–3). Attitudes like appreciation, care, and compassion are not just sweet; they are powerful medicine for the virus.

HOW TO SPOT THE EMOTIONAL VIRUS

The challenge in tracking and curing the emotional virus again is one of perception. Like the fish growing up in the Hudson River, assuming the polluted water was "real" water, many of the symptoms of the emotional virus are so prevalent, there seems no alternative, or they seem invisible, so maladapted are we to their effects. Common symptoms include:

- Caustic humor
- Constant stream of complaints

Attrition Data

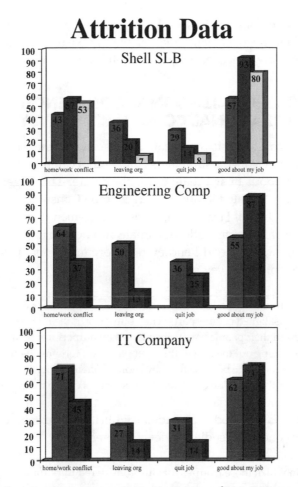

FIGURE 9-3 Attrition improvements. A summary of improving employee attitudes in three organizations utilizing the IQM technology. Data reflects responses to questions on home and work conflict, desire to leave the organization, desire to quit the job, and feeling good about the job. Data was collected over six months, showing a significant improvement in all measures. For each category, three bars represent predata, postdata (six weeks), and post-postdata (six months).

- Defeatism
- Resentment
- Us vs. them mentality
- Suspicion
- Frequent communication breakdowns
- Ongoing fatigue or an overrushed pace of work
- Anxiety, fear, intolerance, resignation, antagonism, despair

All these symptoms can be seen, heard, and felt in lunchrooms, around the coffee machine, by the copier, in mail rooms and boardrooms, and around the dinner table. Early detection and prevention is the best insurance policy.

ASSESSING ORGANIZATIONAL COHERENCE: THE ORGANIZATIONAL COHERENCE SURVEY

Building on the considerable organizational research of the past 100 years, the institute has developed a survey instrument that carefully assesses how employees feel about their organizational climate. The Organizational Coherence Survey,[8] created jointly by Edgecumbe Consulting Group Ltd. (UK) and the Institute of HeartMath, gives management focused information on the state of the organizational climate and how to improve it. Edgecumbe's chairman, Dr. David Pendleton, an organizational psychologist and codeveloper of the survey, says,

> There is an increasing body of evidence that coherent organizations do better than their misaligned counterparts. They outperform the market and bring out the best in their people. We believe that they outperform their competitors *because* they bring out the best in their people. They certainly gain clear and predictable advantage because they are more efficiently coordinated. In the public sector, they provide consistently superior service to their constituents.[9]

The survey is designed to provide insights into the extent to which an organization is coherent. Pendleton views coherence as

> the state in which those features that are considered important by the stakeholders are performed to a high standard in the organization. It is the consistency between expectations and reality that goes beyond mere "alignment," a buzzword of the '80s and '90s. Aligned organizations may consistently implement norms that do harm to their people. Coherent organizations are aligned around norms that bring out the best in people at work.[10]

Organizations usually do not become incoherent by deliberate actions. They usually are not sabotaged into an incoherent state, nor do most managers act maliciously. They are undermined by subtle factors that are easily ignored or missed in the high speed world inhabited by most organizations. The survey is designed to act as an early detection mechanism and identify how appropriate actions may be taken. A unique aspect of the survey's design is that questions are asked two ways: "How do you feel about the issue?" *and* "How important is it to you to feel good about it?" The distinction between *importance* and *current feelings* shows the gap between expectations and reality and the sources of organizational noise and incoherence. *The emotional virus lives and thrives in the gap between expectations and perceived reality.*

CONTENT

The survey investigates how the respondents are feeling in general. It seeks to determine the extent to which they enjoy their work, feel motivated, feel (un)stressed, feel valued, feel proud to be a member of their organization, and feel committed to it. It also asks how they feel when they have finished a typical day. These outcomes represent their responses to how they are treated at work, and how they feel about their experiences there.

The six topics explored in the Organizational Coherence Survey (see Figure 9–4) are as follows:

1. *Taking care of business.* The extent to which each key group of employees takes care of the interests of its customers, staff members, and shareholders.

	Feel bad about item's current performance	Feel good about item's current performance
High importance	**Fix** Important items that are not currently performing well	**Celebrate** Important items that are performing well
Low importance	**Ignore** Since these items are relatively unimportant, they do not currently require attention despite not currently performing well	**Question** There may be some redundant effort here, so can the resources taken by these items be reallocated?

Importance (vertical axis) — *Current Performance* ⟶ (horizontal axis)

FIGURE 9–4 Organizational coherence survey. All items within each of the six topics are plotted in a scattergram format, yielding information on priority and importance. Depending on where in the graph each item falls, it can be characterized as *fix, celebrate, ignore,* or *question.*

2. *A sense of well-being at work*. How people feel in their workplace.
3. *Relationships at work*. How people feel about their relationships with key individuals and groups.
4. *Managing people*. The style of management that brings out the best in the employees surveyed and sustains their efforts in the longer term.
5. *Managing the organization*. How people feel about the balance between their work effort and the rewards they receive.
6. *The working climate*. How people feel working for their particular manager (this topic investigates the six dimensions explored in the Brown and Leigh study).

Once the information is clear on how the organization perceives itself and its management practices and behaviors, clear priorities can be established and action plans built for continuous improvement. Many organizations do annual or biannual employee satisfaction surveys. Because most such surveys ask only how employees *feel*, while neglecting to ask the *importance*, the information is far less focused and meaningful.

One client is a rapidly growing company within a large health care organization. Rapid growth meant new systems and processes were required that had been unnecessary when the company was small and entrepreneurial. Rapid growth also meant lots of hiring, so the unique West Coast culture of innovation and friendliness began to be diluted. The strain in the company was showing up in declining employee satisfaction scores. In 1995, an outsider was named VP of marketing while the popular previous VP assumed a larger role. The new VP was greeted with mistrust and suspicion, and satisfaction scores in marketing plummeted. Hoping to turn around the decline in her organization and uncover the emotional virus, the VP asked us to provide the Organizational Coherence Survey to pinpoint the areas of incoherence and find the virus. Several parallels with their own employee satisfaction survey were found, allowing for targeted discussions and solutions. Six months later, satisfaction survey scores had doubled or tripled, even though it had been a period of significant turbulence in the department. Along the way, the company saw revenues increase to record levels and market share increase, while the top priority in marketing and customer service had become "organizational climate."

The survey was not administered in isolation. Marketing and customer services staff members were trained in IQM tools, the tools became integrated in staff meetings and performance reviews, and a coaching series was initiated for managers. The Organizational Coherence Survey is designed for continuous feedback. After an initial survey of the entire organization or division, representative samples are frequently tested—say, every three months—so the information is kept current and feedback to employees can happen quickly.

The assumption, too, is that employees must be given tools to manage their perceptions and emotional reactions so they become active creators of a healthier climate, not just victims of management whims. Analyzing organizational incoherence—while giving employees practical tools for managing and leveraging their emotional and intellectual processes—represents a powerful parallel approach to regaining organizational vitality. Next, we explore tools and attitudes to enhance organizational climate, from the inside out.

NOTES

1. Jon Gice, "The Relationship Between Job Satisfaction and Workers' Compensation Claims," *CPCU Journal* 48, no. 3 (September 1995), pp. 178–84.

2. Phil Smith, "Emotional Climate Is More Than Just a Feeling," *The Edge Newsletter*, Edgecumbe Consulting Group (August 1997). The Edgecumbe Consulting Group can be reached at Edgecumbe Hall, Richmond Hill, Clifton, Bristol BS8 1AT, United Kingdom, phone at 0117-973-8899.

3. Steven P. Brown and Thomas V. Leigh, "A New Look at Psychological Climate and Its Relationship to Job Involvement, Effort and Performance," *Journal of Applied Psychology* 81, no. 4 (1996), pp. 358–68.

4. Ibid., p. 361.

5. Ibid.

6. Reported in article by Ron Winslow, "Underused Skills Raise Risks of Developing Heart Disease," *The Wall Street Journal* (July 25, 1997).

7. Glen Rein, Mike Atkinson, and Rollin McCraty, "The Physiological and Psychological Effects of Compassion and Anger," *Journal of Advancement in Medicine* 8, no. 2 (1995), pp. 87–105.

8. Contact HeartMath LLC for complete information.

9. David Pendleton, *Organizational Coherence Survey Manual*, Institute of HeartMath, 14700 West Park Avenue, Boulder Creek, CA, 95006, phone at 408-338-8500.

10. Ibid.

10

Core Values: The Foundation of Sustainability

With the demise of the myth of job security, the accelerating pace of change, and the increasing ambiguity and complexity of our world, people who depend on external structures to provide continuity and stability run the very real risk of having their moorings ripped away. The only truly reliable source of stability is a strong inner core and the willingness to change and adapt everything except that core.   —JAMES C. COLLINS AND JERRY PORRAS[1]

Unswerving at the core—remaining true to one's heart—is the prerequisite to building resilience and flexibility mentally, emotionally, and physically. The model of coherence states that coherence at the heart of a system, personal or organizational, is the foundation for rapid shifts in effectiveness, growth, and motivation. Our research into human efficiency, performance and fulfillment has yielded this conclusion, the third principle of Dynamic 3:

> Human qualities such as adaptability, flexibility, care, and appreciation underlie sustainable organizational cultures.

CORE VALUES AS A FOUNDATION

As we and others have delved deeply into the common principles and best practices of visionary companies, that search has yielded a common conclusion. At the heart of all successful organizations—and indeed successful people—is a set of firmly held core values for which the organization feels passion. These values, more than profits or the thrill of competition, are the source of the organization's creative energy. Business leaders and their organizations need to make sure that as business strategies change, adapt, and morph into new activities uniquely suited to the time and the locale, core values and purpose remain stable and protected.

It is no different in our personal lives. When we are fulfilled, it is because of coherence between the values of our hearts and the actions we carry out in our professional and family lives. While our relationships will vary depending on the depth of trust, love, and commitment, the core—the heart—out of which we act does not change. In fact, the more consistently we act from our core values, the more the intelligence of these values unfolds, increasing our ability to adapt intelligently to the world around us.

Indeed core values are powerful because they are the embodiment of intelligent operating principles for our lives or our organizations. *Values as intelligence* may be a new twist on this fundamental principle, and yet each of us could see how the values we hold most dear represent a highly intelligent use of our energy. Intelligent not in the context merely of being intellectually astute, but rather energy efficient. Our perceptions are clearer, decisions more balanced, communication more caring and well-reasoned. Core values do not lead to mushy actions or sentimentality; they are the battery chargers for wisdom. We are *smarter* when in phase with our core values. As internal coherence increases by becoming more consistently in phase with the heart's core values, leaps in perception, creativity, and adaptability are possible. That's intelligence!

ADAPTABILITY REVISITED

Why would adaptability be an essential characteristic? According to research conducted by the authors of *The Service-Profit Chain*,[2] the clear differentiator between high and low performing firms, all with strong cultures, was the ability of each firm to *adapt* to changing environments, whether legal, technological, social, or competitive. The authors discovered that the single most important indicator of adaptability was the *adherence by management to a clear set of core values stressing the importance of delivering results to various constituencies, especially customers and employees,* as part of an effort to deliver profits to owners. They concluded:

1. Strong cultures don't win as consistently as adaptable ones,
2. Adaptability is a "state of the management mind" resulting from a set of core values that include an emphasis on the importance of change, and
3. Organizations that vigorously practice these core values and install devices for maintaining adaptability not only greatly improve their

chances of sustaining high performance over time, they increase their chances of achieving successful transitions from one leader to another.[3]

The true meaning of adaptability implies healthy adjustments to external factors, as opposed to the maladaptation process discussed earlier in the rigidifying way most people react to stressors. True adaptability is the ability to assess from the mind *and* the heart—to analyze and feel—then shift attitude and action. How we respond to a crisis or unexpected occurrence underpins true adaptability.

THE ROLE OF SIGNIFICANCE

Your response to each event of your day is based largely on the *significance* you ascribe to it. Consider significance from an emotional perspective. How significant something becomes is directly proportional to the amount of emotional energy you assign it. When you feel secure and confident, unpleasant events have much less significance than when you are emotionally imbalanced. You see things in perspective. But when operating at a deficit, the tone of voice, the inflection or the implied message in a conversation can easily become magnified in your perception. Then, your internal video machine replays the "story" repeatedly while you work yourself up into greater emotional turmoil. All of this because of the *significance* you placed on the event.

Certain people overinvest in making things significant. They make a big deal out of nearly everything. From a balanced, heart-driven perspective people can see more easily how much of their own vital, precious energy needs to be given to each daily event. If everything is significant it becomes difficult to not eventually feel drained and victimized by emotions. People who do well long term and can handle pressure are often the ones who naturally are more even keeled. They do not make things overly significant. This does not make them better or worse than others, but it is a gift that saves energy and sustains personal productivity. All of us can learn to take the significance out of things. The concept and practice of "taking out the significance" is powerful. It seems so simple and it is, but when applied as a tool or technique the amount of your unnecessary, inefficient energy expenditures will decrease significantly.

There is a fine line between an attitude of irresponsibility or simply brushing things off as opposed to intelligently withdrawing some of the significance out of life's tricky events. This kind of discrimination is a by-product of heart intelligence. It is intuitive intelligence in action to know how much of your emotional energy to give to something. Some things are more important than we at first perceive, while other things are not as important as we make them out to be. Overdramatizing and adding significance to anything amplifies it, just like throwing a log on a fire causes the fire to burn brighter and hotter. Use heart discrimination to decide what kind of fires you want to build.

Taking out the significance is an important skill for developing adaptability. It saves energy that can be used to adapt when needed. Adaptability is an energetic flexing of our inner muscles, that requires extra energy. It builds reserves in the system that manifest themselves as more genuine care. As you learn to take the significance out of things that you know will not serve your best interests, you will see a natural increase in your ability to care.

It is much easier for people to adapt to change when the environment supports them, as the Brown and Leigh study implies. However, if your organizational climate clearly is filled with an emotional virus, it is still in your *interest* to adapt as fully as possible, even if that adaptation process involves an intelligent exit from the unhealthy environment. (Being a "doormat" for abuse or incoherence is not the intelligent insight of truly caring perspectives.) This is as true at the individual level as at the team or organizational level when faced with unhealthy competition, unethical practices, or attitudes that contradict your deeply held core values. Adaptability in this context, especially, requires centering ever more deeply in your core values and, from that position of strength and wisdom, determining the most energy-efficient, coherent response possible.

Organizational life today is full of such bombardment that true adaptability rests on your ability to heartfully adapt to all the mini-crises and disturbances, using heart intelligence as an inner guidance system. This can be as simple as stopping long enough to ask yourself, "What is the best way to adapt to this situation, for the good of all involved?" Your heart, if asked, can supply surprising wisdom. When you learn to adapt first then become internally coherent, you can discover more coherent solutions.

Learning to take the significance out of situations that really are minor blips on the screen saves energy for those issues of real significance—the core values and viability of you and your organization. With unnecessary significance kept to a minimum, the energy to adapt, flex, and innovate is maximized.

CARE

A basic human instinct is to care. In our work, we have seen that care is central to personal or organizational effectiveness, when balanced with efficiency:

Efficiency + Care = Effectiveness

Consider this simple equation both personally and organizationally. Biomedical research cited in the last chapter suggests that feeling sincere care for something or someone actually boosts immune system function, as measured by the antibody IgA. A study by Harvard psychologist David McClellan and C. Kirshnit in 1988[4] showed that inducing the feeling of care could boost levels of IgA, the body's first line of defense against pathogenic invaders such as viruses or bacteria. Clearly, care is a good investment of energy. You receive a payoff for you when you care, beyond just being nice. Care is rejuvenating for both the giver and receiver. It acts like a lubricant on mental, emotional, and physical levels, increasing adaptability mentally, emotionally, and physically.

Here we present one of the prime personal and organizational challenges in this age of transition: Care is its own reward, as poets and philosophers have said for centuries. Whether or not the other person sees your actions as caring, by adapting to stress through the heart, you have saved untold amounts of energy, potentially saved a decision that could have proven costly to the organization, and stopped an emotional and physiological drain in your own system.

REVIVING THE CORPORATE HEART

The research cited in the last chapter revealed organizational benefits of caring. Consider how you and your organization could apply care to the six dimensions of climate:

- Recognition
- Clarity
- Contribution
- Supportive management
- Self-expression
- Challenge

Even asking the questions would be an act of caring, but be prepared to follow through sincerely on the responses or the efforts will backfire, being viewed cynically as yet another example of management paying lip service to employee perceptions and concerns, with no intention of acting on them.

A practical application for caring in the workplace is to ask your managers to have their people assess their own assets and deficits on each of the six dimensions of climate, then discuss with them key patterns in the feedback and how to best address them. Do the same yourself with those who report to you or, if you do not manage others, with your closest colleagues. Discuss in your next staff meeting how your department or division, as well as the organization as a whole, stacks up on each dimension. By evaluating deficits and assets you can understand what areas require attention, while appreciating those areas deserving appreciation and celebration. This activity can lead to a sense of excitement and pride as you recognize what is good in the climate you created. Sincere appreciation builds a solid foundation for future growth.

SINCERE CARE

Underlying the application of care in your workplace is sincerity. Without sincerity caring acts ring hollow. Sincere care is required to achieve a true service attitude with people. When care is mechanical or insincere, it causes resistance and reaction in others, undermining adaptability. Coworkers, family, clients, and superiors can tell the difference between *required courtesy* and *sincere care*. Put simply, it is much easier to adapt to unpleasant or unexpected circumstances when we feel our workplace or social environment is caring. Care is the glue that keeps relationships together once the novelty has worn off. This is as true in organizational life as in the personal domain.

Tom Peters said:

> Store shelves groan under the weight of new products, but few have heart. Service offerings are about as lifeless. Most hotels, for example, spent the last decade buffing their customer service. The mechanics are better. Bravo. But the heart is usually absent: the sincere sense of "Welcome to my home" as opposed to "I've gotta remember to act like I care."[5]

The Mandarin Oriental Hotel in San Francisco is different. An award-winning hotel in the heart of San Francisco's financial district, it has consistently provided exceptional value and service to its guests since opening in the late 1980s. And yet like any other high performing organization, management recognized its staff members were being held to ever-higher standards while facing greater personal pressures as societal stress increased. IQM tools were instituted at all levels of the hotel staff to help ensure a high level of balance of personal and professional effectiveness. At the Mandarin, there is an understanding that care for oneself and for colleagues goes hand in hand with exceptional care for customers.

"Caregivers"—whether social workers, health care professionals, or counselors—are at their best when providing the kind of support that makes it easier for the patient to adapt to and recover from the illness, injury, or personal setback. The caregivers themselves, however, must learn when the care is enhancing their own and others' adaptability and when it is detracting. A 1990 study[6] on caregiving among nurses observed that caring did not lead to burnout but it was the lack of caring or overcaring that did. The study reported that "caring itself allows nurses to access a very important source of energy and renewal." When nurses became overly emotionally identified with the plight of their patients, their care turned to burnout. Whether your job involves caring for patients, caring for customers, or requires extra care in times of high stress and pressure, keeping your care balanced and rejuvenating requires vigilance and close attention. This is one of the greatest challenges in an age of chaos and complexity. When care depletes, it becomes *overcare*.

THE DRAIN OF OVERCARE

Overcaring is caring that crossed the line into anxiety and worry, ceased to be nurturing for the giver and receiver, and is close to the top of the list of personal and organizational energy drains. Overcaring begins as caring, but because of unmanaged emotions such as unrealistic expectations, emotional attachment, or mental preoccupation, the caring becomes tainted and diminished in its effectiveness. In the extreme, overcaring is debilitating for all concerned, driving a wedge between you and the object of your overcaring. Clear examples of overcaring would be these:

- The micro-manager who must have a hand in every detail of his division, causing stress and inefficiency in those he supervises, and confining himself to a self-created environment of obsessive mental activity, cut off from the nourishing power of the heart.
- The parent who hovers over a sick child, creating an environment not of caring support but of overbearing intrusion.

Overcaring is tricky because, in our achievement-oriented society, the only alternative to overcaring seems to be uncaring or apathy. The truth is that overcaring is so emotionally and physically draining, chronic overcaring eventually leads to *not caring*. But there is a healthy, balanced alternative. The challenge is to identify overcaring early on and utilize heart intelligence to determine a more balanced and caring response. A simple question can help distinguish caring from its kissing cousin overcaring: "Is my care *stress producing* or *stress reducing*?" If it is overcaring, you will sense stress in your system; if balanced caring, you will experience more contentment and peace.

IDENTIFYING OVERCARE

Overcare is defined not by the specific behavior or action but by the underlying attitude. This often is experienced as ongoing anxiety and concern, which may briefly subside in moments of appreciation but continues to drain energy and occupy attention like a hammerlock. While there are no pat rules for what actions are overcaring and what are caring, here are some examples. Working overtime to complete a project could be an act of true caring, so long as the internal attitude was not fueled by worry and fear. How much more energized do you feel by any project when you are positively motivated to complete it instead of fearing the consequences of its lack of completion? When worry or fear is the fuel, you still may complete the project in the allotted time—maybe even faster—but at a significant cost to your health and balance on all levels. Similarly, failing to address a difficult employee issue could be the result of overcaring about how the employee might react. The caring action would be to ask the heart for a clear perspective on the situation and how to most effectively resolve the situation for the good of all concerned. The effects of these stressful, overcaring behaviors do not just go "poof!" and disappear. They live on in our bodies as diminished vitality and the emotional memories of the overcaring events that replay themselves.

In our work at HeartMath with organizational clients, we continually ask ourselves if the "something extra" we think we should do for the client truly adds value or is it just going to add stress to us and provide nothing beneficial to the client. Keeping overcaring in check is a tremendous energy saver, with the added benefit that the effect of care on clients, customers, and staff members is increased significantly. In our staff meetings we ask each other what areas of overcare we have around workload, deadlines, or performance, then get help to diminish the load or explore new perspectives on the reality of the pressures. Stopping overcare in its tracks frees up tremendous energy that allows you, or your team, to jump to a whole new level of efficiency and effectiveness that translates into improved business results.

How easy it is to spend hours watching an internal movie of possible horrific future scenarios, all the result of overcaring. If they fail to manifest themselves, we still have aged our bodies in the hours or days or weeks we spent overcaring. Clearly, not an efficient investment of energy! But, once again, the alternative to overcaring should not be *not caring* but rather *bal-*

anced caring. It is incumbent on us as leaders, managers, or parents to take seriously potential threats to the health and safety of our organization or our loved ones. Overcaring can be the wake-up call that a new perspective and action are necessary to deal with a potential stressor. However, once overcaring is recognized, we would do well to adapt our attitude, neutralize our stress reaction, then proceed with whatever balanced caring would be appropriate.

From a business and personal perspective, overcaring blocks effectiveness. It is *noise* that distorts clear communication, whether you are the receiver or the transmitter. It limits our ability to satisfy internal or external customers or be as productive and fulfilled as we can be. The good news is that all overcaring starts out as caring, but unmanaged emotions dilute the caring and keep us stuck in perspectives that tend to perpetuate the overcaring. The challenge is to bring the caring back into balance. Overcaring creates the breeding ground for actions and attitudes that will self-fulfill the underlying overcaring. Overcaring breeds more overcaring. Unchecked, overcaring can lead to reactions and attitudes that allow the emotional virus to thrive.

What examples of overcare in yourself or others can you think of? Take a moment and list a few key examples of overcare in your life. Then, recognize the current effect on you, the other person, your energy level, effectiveness, health, and so on. One of the most powerful tools for neutralizing overcaring is freeze-frame. Most overcaring is just "one attitude adjustment away" from a caring, balanced attitude and action, but without stopping and consulting the heart, the answers easily can evade your awareness. Use freeze-frame to ask yourself how to bring the overcaring back into balance and uncover intelligent alternatives.

Certain segments of an organization are especially vulnerable to overcaring, such as customer service and sales. Because these positions normally deal directly with the public or consumers, those working in them live in a precarious world of loyalty to two masters. Caring for both, it is often hard to discern the appropriate action—look after the needs of the customer or look after the company? The pat answer would be that, in taking care of the customer, the company will be taken care of. In a general sense, this is true, but when an irrational or out-of-control customer is in your face, such a perspective lacks credibility and practicality. In the real world, people get upset, expectations are not met, insecurity is high, and things are said or done that do not reflect the deeper core values of that person. Recognizing, neutralizing, then moving past the overcaring can bring balanced solutions or, at least, minimize the drain.

Overcare is a powerful inhibitor of personal and organizational effectiveness, cloaked as it is in the robes of care and concern. In many organizational cultures, we are rewarded for overcaring. "How dare you leave the office at 5:00 to be with your family, don't you care?" "Why aren't you worried about the production delay, don't you care?" "Why aren't you anxious about the client presentation, don't you realize the significance of this account?" In our extremist, stimulus-addicted culture, there appears no alternative to chronic, debilitating overcaring, other than total apathy or self-centeredness. Yet research on the effects of chronic anxiety or worry on health, let alone the emotional drain on the organization of constantly being on edge, should suggest overcaring already is costing us dearly. Organizations require an alternative, and there is one.

If you manage people, you would do well to examine areas of overcaring in your management style. Overcaring disempowers others. Overcaring in leaders robs them of the magnetism necessary to inspire confidence and hope. Overcaring is caring made incoherent. When people resist change, overcaring accumulates. As you adapt intelligently to change, that is caring. Care regenerates; overcare depletes. When overcaring is recognized in a team or in yourself, specific steps can be taken to regain balanced care.

SELF-CARE REVISITED

A powerful element in the reduction of overcaring and achievement of organizational adaptability is *self-care*. In many cultures, self-care is almost taboo, because the fear is that any focus on self-care will lead to self-obsession and attitudes that undermine the collective well-being. The Asian focus on collective culture makes it challenging to justify the importance of self-care. American culture by contrast could seem to be self-indulgent and self-caring to the extreme. And yet, in a stimulus-addicted society, *balanced* self-care is nearly nonexistent. For many people, self-care goes no deeper than self-medicating with drugs, alcohol, or a once-a-year vacation that is often stressful, a strain to prepare for, and over far too quickly. The notion of self-care can conjure up images of mandatory exercise, less junk food and high-cholesterol meals, restricting or eliminating ingestion of substances such as alcohol or tobacco—in short, self-care seems to be self-*denial*. What we are suggesting is something much more core to each person—the balanced care of oneself. People take for granted that children need care to grow and mature, that plants need regular attention and care to thrive, that pets need care to be the happy playmates we want them to be. Are you any different?

Deep self-care would mean regular reflection on your core values, assessing where your life lacks coherence and balance, evaluating how much and in what way you want to attend to physical health—in short, caring for all the dimensions of your life.

By focusing self-care in the mental and emotional domains and achieving balance there through the activation of heart intelligence, significant jumps in effectiveness can occur. An organization where self-care is a valued quality is far more coherent than one that denies its importance. Imagine a car refusing the offer of a fresh tank of gas!

THE HEART LOCK-IN

A powerful tool for increasing internal coherence through self-care is the heart lock-in. In this tool, the objective is to practice staying focused in the heart "frequencies" of care and appreciation. It is called a *lock-in* because you attempt to lock in to the heart feeling domain, like a jet fighter pilot directs radar to lock onto a target or a great athlete stays locked in to "the zone," keeping mental and emotional distractions to a minimum so performance is optimized. *Heart Zones*[7] is music specially designed to facilitate heart lock-ins. This four-song concept (composed and performed by Doc Childre) takes you through a "cardiovascular workout" for your mind and emotions, leaving you feeling refreshed and energized. The first song is like a warm-up, helping you relax and release tension. The second song picks up the pace and stirs things up. The third song is very dynamic and helps activate a "go for it" feeling in yourself. The fourth song is the cool-down, bringing a feeling of completion. The overall intention is to calm and reenergize. As with a freeze-frame, you attempt to keep your focus in the area of the heart, but if thoughts or concerns arise, you note them, then return to a focus in the heart. Many organizations today incorporate this simple 5–15 minute centering tool in meetings or planning sessions. The rationale? By increasing internal coherence, you increase team coherence.

Over the past 25 years, we explored many tools for adaptability, increased intelligence, and self-care. We have found the heart lock-in technique to be an extremely powerful tool, providing a daily boost and surprising clarity. With consistent use, levels of physical, mental, and emotional resilience increase dramatically. As a state of internal balance more frequently is reached, it becomes much easier to quickly adapt to unexpected change. The heart lock-in was designed to help people build a strong muscle for internal self-management, making it much easier to find a neutral or positive perspective when they freeze-frame. An entire organization using this tool enhances its adaptability, creativity, and climate.

We had a recent example of the benefits of frequent heart lock-ins in Kuala Lumpur. While testing the presentation technology at the Top Performers Leadership Center, we realized the power converter had been broken in transit. When an alternate converter was finally found, we plugged in all the equipment and watched as a key biomedical device began to smoke, while brown oil leaked from the switch. Our hosts became quite concerned, and all our attention went to how best to adapt. We stayed calm, scanned for alternatives in the event the unit was damaged beyond repair, knowing the nearest repair shop was 10,000 miles away. By staying in balance, our hosts also kept their concerns to a minimum. By the time the unit was successfully repaired by a highly ingenious man named Siva, we had kept stress from grabbing our vitality. Heart lock-in techniques helped us sustain health, clarity, and focus.

In the past two chapters, we discussed the role of climate in organizational performance, the primacy of core values to organizational longevity, and essential qualities such as adaptability, care, self-care, and appreciation. In the background during this discussion lurked the fourth principle of Dynamic 3:

> Understanding the distinction between knowledge and wisdom is essential to organizational sustainability. Building wise companies through developing wise people is the next organizational frontier.

It no longer is enough to be smart—all the technological tools in the world add meaning and value only if they enhance our core values, the deepest part of our heart. Acquiring knowledge is no guarantee of practical, useful application. Wisdom implies a mature integration of appropriate knowledge, a seasoned ability to filter the inessential from the essential. Self-management and internal coherence are central to the emergence of wisdom personally and organizationally. A healthy, adaptive climate makes the journey all the easier. Wisdom also will emerge as information overload—knowledge addiction—pervades more corners of our lives. For some, pain or tragedy will force the issue. For others, deeper promptings from the heart will urge a shift in perception, an insistence on living in integrity with our hearts, of putting care for self and others as a prerequisite to survival and fulfillment in the next millennium. The markets, the constituents, the members will expect this from us. They want it, too.

NOTES

1. James C. Collins and Jerry Porras, *Built to Last: Successful Habits of Visionary Companies* (New York: HarperBusiness, 1994), p. xx.

2. James L. Heskett, W. Earl Sasser, Jr., and Leonard A. Schlesinger, *The Service-Profit Chain: How Leading Companies Link Profit and Growth to Loyalty, Satisfaction, and Value* (New York: The Free Press, 1997).

3. Ibid., p. 249.

4. D. C. McClelland and C. Kirshnit, "The Effects of Motivational Arousal Through Films on Salivary Immunoglobulin A," *Psychological Health* 2 (1988), pp. 31–52.

5. Tom Peters, "You Gotta Have Heart," *Canadian Airlines Magazine* (February 1994).

6. Carol Montgomery, "The Care-Giving Relationship: Paradoxical and Transcendent Aspects," *Journal of Transpersonal Psychology* 23, no. 2 (1991).

7. An album of music designed to enhance mental and emotional balance. Doc Lew Childre, *Heart Zones*, Planetary Publications, 1994.

11

Male-Female Balance

In the journey toward building coherent organizations, one of the most prominent obstacles is the dynamic between men and women in the workplace. While many issues of diversity, such as multiculturalism, same-sex partners, and age discrimination can have a negative impact on organizational coherence, the absence of Dynamics 1 and 2, internal self-management and coherent communication, is particularly apparent in the level of incoherence around male-female issues. By one estimate, at least $10 billion is spent each year by American corporations wanting, or forced by legal actions, to teach greater sensitivity and understanding in the increasingly diverse and multicultural workplace.[1]

How much noise exists in your organization today because of male-female issues? How many male managers are given poor ratings by the women who work for them due to gender insensitivity? Do any female managers try to be "male" and appear insensitive or overly aggressive? How many men are confused about what is appropriate in an environment, especially in the United States, where the slightest gesture toward a member of the opposite sex can be construed as grounds for a sexual harassment lawsuit? And how many women feel so burned by mistreatment by male senior managers, they are afraid to be themselves and reveal their sincere desire for greater personal balance or afraid to point out the organization's imbalance for fear of being written off as soft or overly sentimental? These are just a few of the current themes blurring organizational clarity.

THE BIOLOGY OF GENDER

The confusion may begin with biology. There are fundamental biological differences between men and women, which existed long before society taught us what gender roles are supposed to be. In fact, contrasting brain structures of men and women account for significant differences in perception, language and skills, and the aging process itself. At birth through six weeks old, hormones in the brain have very different characteristics. As children grow up, clear divergences in behavior tend to emerge. Hormonally, the male and female brains process things differently as well. However, environmental influences play a big part in the development of male-female characteristics as we grow up. As discussed earlier, while DNA provides the basic patterns and blueprint of brain development, responses to the environment as we grow up determine the neural circuitry.

MALE AND FEMALE BRAINS

The corpus callosum, a key portion of the brain associated with intuitive capacity, is larger in women so the two sides of the brain have more connectors. Women naturally are "wired" to see a larger global perspective than men and have a deeper understanding of what is or what could be, because more interaction is happening between the two sides during the thought process. Dr. Karl Pribram, discoverer of the limbic system in the brain and developer of the "holographic brain theory," has stated that the female brain develops from the front to the back, while the male brain develops from the back to the front.[2]

Consider these neurological differences between men and women:

- Studies show that, when faced with the same problem to solve, men will tend to use one localized portion of one side of their brain, while women will use a much more diffused range of tissues on both sides of the brain due to the structural differences in the brains of men and women.
- Women's diffused way of gathering and processing information may be why men tend to believe that women lack focus in problem solving or may be why creative thinkers were considered scatterbrained. This ability to "think outside the box," if properly nurtured, can be a tremendous asset in jobs requiring the ability to consider different points of view (like managing, selling, or negotiating) or requiring creativity (e.g., strategic planning, product planning).
- The difference in functional brain organization in men and women is believed to be responsible for women's ability to consider multiple paths and multiple solutions. As women solve problems, their brains process a variety of sensory, memory, and other data before they draw any conclusions; and then they may draw multiple conclusions. Their

male counterparts solve problems more linearly, using only one side of their brains, and tend to draw a single conclusion.[3]

LANGUAGE DIFFERENCES BETWEEN MEN AND WOMEN

Differences between men and women are as basic as how we process language. Women naturally process languages in both of the brain hemispheres, where men tend to process language only in the left brain.[4] Men can learn to process language in the right brain and women can learn to be more linear and assertive in their communication. It is a matter of seeing where you are out of balance and what qualities you would like to develop.

Success in organizational life often is dependent on how well you communicate and sell ideas, both verbally and in writing. Employees who represent their ideas most effectively often get the best projects, the most funding, the most visibility. They have more opportunity to impress others with their competence and their skills and to gain key assignments that will help them get ahead. Quite often, the only exposure many employees have to top management is in briefings, where communication skills are really put to the test. Having a natural tendency toward strong verbal and written communication skills clearly is a key advantage.

EMOTIONS AND GENDER

Emotions and the heart have been equated for centuries. Sir William Harvey, who was the first to demonstrate the function of the heart and how blood circulates in the body, noted in 1628 that, "every affliction of the mind that is attended to, either with pain or pleasure, hope or fear, is the cause of an agitation whose influence extends to the heart." Emotions flow through the body at a subtle electrical level, much faster than information flows along nerve pathways. Research is showing that when we *qualify* our perceptions and feelings from the heart, the mind guides a different energy flow than if we perceive and react from the mind alone. Emotions qualified or directed only through the mind often act like water that floods the landscape, whereas heart-directed emotions use that same water to quench your thirst and give substance to life. Increasing your internal coherence enables you to call the shots on the water distribution; incoherence results in being a victim of the random flows of the emotional spills.

Women are often viewed by men as being overly emotional and sentimental, which colors their decision-making ability. When balanced with the activation of heart intelligence, women's sensitivities enhance intuitive clarity and decision making. The "feeling world" of a person is critical to intelligent decision making. Without feeling, the mind's reasoning and thinking ability are not enough, a classic case of *necessary* but not *sufficient*. The balanced integration of feeling and reason brings the highest intelligence, wisdom, clarity, and fulfillment.

HORMONAL ZONES

The human system has three primary hormonal zones. The lower body produces steroid hormones (which deal with responses to stress), produces DHEA, and also the sex hormones estrogen, progesterone, and testosterone. The upper body produces brain hormones, such as noradrenaline, serotonin, and dopamine. Many of these brain hormones affect feelings, perception, and attitude. For example, the pituitary gland releases oxytocin and vasopressin, which relate to emotional bonding. Oxytocin has a longer lasting effect than most hormones. Oxytocin is released when you fall in love. That is why your first love is often so hard to get over. In mammals that secrete high levels of oxytocin at first mating, the emotional bonding created is for life. Mammals with low levels of oxytocin have levels of high promiscuity.

Upper and lower body hormones affect the entire body. Cortisol is released from the adrenal glands in the lower body. It is called a *stress* hormone because it rises when we feel stress, especially emotional stress such as anger, irritation, frustration, or anxiety. Chronically high cortisol levels are known to age and destroy brain cells. The amount of cortisol produced is regulated by the sympathetic nervous system and hypothalamus, both of which are activated by stress. An astounding 30% of women and men say they experience "high stress" nearly every day. Under stress, your glands churn out adrenaline and cortisol, which cause a rise in blood pressure, a speeding up of breathing and heart rate, and a release of sugar and fats in the body. Under chronic stress, hypertension (high blood pressure) can set in. It is now estimated that one in four women and men aged 18 and older have hypertension, the leading risk factor for heart disease and stroke[5]— and over half of those with hypertension are overweight.

The third primary hormonal zone, the heart, lies right in the middle— between the upper and lower zones. The heart also produces two hormones, BNP (brain natriuretic peptide) and ANP (atrial natriuretic peptide). ANP, often referred to as the *balancing hormone* by scientists, has receptors in both the upper and lower body. It affects the brain's pituitary gland and the kidneys. The heart helps to balance the upper and lower hormonal zones. The parasympathetic and sympathetic branches of the nervous system, which travel from the upper to the lower body, also are balanced by the heart. Differences in how each gender processes "heart hormones" are not known. However, for all people, positive emotion significantly reduces the sympathetic signals from the brain and increases the parasympathetic signals, which protect the heart and body, lower blood pressure, and increase immune system activity. Could the reason why core values exert such a powerful force in people and successful organizations be their very balancing effect on cells and the heart itself? Heart intelligence unfolds as people consistently focus on the heart and its highly complex and integrated functions.

EMOTIONAL INTELLIGENCE IN WOMEN AND MEN

When it comes to emotional intelligence, both genders appear to have it in relatively equal measure, but according to a new study, there are several notable differences between men and women. While women seem to have significantly stronger interpersonal skills, men appear to have a stronger sense of self. A study measured the emotional intelligence of 1,500 men and 3,200 women in the United States and Canada using the BarOn Emotional Quotient Inventory test. According to study author Dr. Steven Stein, "Our results suggest that women are more aware of their feelings and those of others and are more socially responsible, whereas men seem to have stronger self-regard and cope better with stress."

When having to determine an emotion in someone else, the woman's brain is less active than a man's brain. Men have to work harder to determine an emotion on a woman's face, what a woman is feeling, and how to read her response. As a result, many men have a hard time reading women's emotions. This could explain why men easily get frustrated trying to understand women's emotions and one of the reasons communicating between the sexes is difficult.

One reason many women have been extraordinarily successful in sales is that their innate ability to read people and respond to their needs has won them many clients. Client care surveys have shown over and over that many clients believe women listen to their requirements better than men and are more conscientious about responding to them. These clients had an overall feeling that they were more than just an account number to these sales reps and that their business truly mattered and was appreciated.[6]

COMMUNICATION STYLES

Men's and women's communication styles obviously are different, can cause much confusion, and can be misunderstood in a male-dominated workplace. Since in top level positions most of the senior executives are men, it is important to keep in mind some of the confusing signals that can happen during communication:

- Some women try as hard as they can to be prepared for a presentation or a meeting but feel inadequate on the inside. If your heart intelligence is registering an incoherent emotion, like fear, anxiety, or insecurity, that electromagnetic signal is being radiated, even though your words and outward appearance may be calm, cool, and collected. This may help explain why women often are ignored in putting out ideas and the man who reiterates it often gets the credit.
- Both men and women can be indirect communicators in different ways. Men often are indirect around the topic of feelings or emotions. Women often can be indirect around giving orders to subordinates. Men tend to be direct when asking others to do something and might consider a woman's indirectness to be weakness or indecisiveness. Communicating by listening intuitively and using freeze-frame before speaking is one of the best ways to add flexibility and strength to your communicating style. This helps you gather intuitive intelligence on how to communicate appropriately with the other person.
- Women might spend a great deal of time considering their words, the consequences, and impact on others. Many women tend to inject "please" and "thank you" into their business language more often than men so they do not offend. It also is common for women to try to make people feel comfortable, but this trait can be viewed as a reluctance to take charge. Again, utilizing the most powerful part of your human physiology to determine how much to inject these phrases and how you interact will be key to how you connect with others without contradicting your real core values.

MALE-FEMALE DIFFERENCES: A GLOBAL PERSPECTIVE

Deeper societal issues around male-female dynamics can affect organizational coherence. Women's rights have advanced in many nations, yet for most of the globe, women still are second-class citizens. Underdeveloped countries look to the West for leadership, yet the breakdown of the modern

American family and the challenges American women face today are not necessarily the future that developing countries envision or want to embrace. How women in the United States address these issues will determine whether or not they will be a positive role model for the rest of the world.

We recently met with the five highest-ranking women executives of a large multinational corporation. They explained that, in their organization, the role of women had deteriorated in the last few years because of the trend toward political correctness. Twenty or 30 years ago, men were openly hostile toward women trying to climb up the organization. Now, in the view of these successful women, these same male executives know that such public comments are taboo, but the women feel the ostracism just the same. Only now it is more covert. These women longed for "the old days" when the hostility was at least clear and expressed.

Many women feel advancement is encouraged until the point that the men in control decide to put a cap on it. Meanwhile, many men complain that women seem to want it both ways: They want to be taken care of, nurtured, and pampered *and* have all the corporate perks and control as well. This is seen by many men as a double message that is confusing and often threatening to the male ego. Sexual harassment, physical aggression, rape, and abuse are all on the rise. The 1990s have become a period of tremendous frustration and rage between the sexes. "Crude, rude, anger, let it all hang out," have become social release valves. However, release is not relief. The ongoing trend of many women and women's groups has been to blame men, parents, government, society, or anyone for these problems. But blame is disempowering and increases feelings of victimization. From a biological point of view, it keeps you locked in a self-created world of hormonal and electrical imbalance. There is a high price to be paid for blame, on the part of men or women.

WHAT WOMEN CAN DO

Women's intuition is not just an old wives' tale, it is intelligent inner power, which increases in clarity and reliability as you access it consistently. In general, women often seem to have an easier time gaining access to intuition, allowing them to see the bigger picture sooner. That is not to say that men are not intuitive or that women always catch new perspectives quicker. Intuition can be developed in everyone. Women may have an advantage in that their nurturing side seems to make them more sensitive in certain areas.

Individual intuitive development increases personal sensitivity, authenticity, and understanding, which in turn increases magnetic effectiveness, particularly in a male-dominated environment. Authentic power and effectiveness come from developing coherence in your whole system, especially the power and intelligence of your heart. The negative backlash associated with power comes when the power emanates from a strong ego drive without the heart directing the intention. In other words, it might be more productive to find another way to get past the glass ceiling than smashing through it. If you break through by force you still have to deal with all that falling glass.

To power up the whole system involves learning to bring the heart and mind into a creative joint venture. Heart intelligence supplies balanced strength and allows more of one's individual spirit—the passionate actualization of one's core values—to come "on-line" regarding male-female issues, work issues, family issues, health issues, or social issues. Heart power is the conduit for real spirit and intelligence to manifest themselves in any area of life.

Women could do well by better using their natural intuition and sensitivity in relating to men in the workplace and navigating the organizational environment. This is not to imply a passive approach to gender equality issues in the workplace but rather an intelligent one that embodies balance and poise while moving forward with purposeful intent. A balanced woman's strength and intelligence are formidable and should be honored and respected. Too often women lose respect from men when they try to compete through aggression. It can be frustrating for women when they feel inequality, and things do need to change in regard to the role of women in society. Women, however, should be careful not to let that frustration cut off some of the natural abilities that give them their strength, easier access to intuition and a more caring and sensitive nature.

Practicing the IQM tools will develop coherent heart intelligence and free the spirit in the complete woman and man. Balance is the key. Women can become respected high achievers without losing their womanly qualities. Both genders are trying to be achievers but often fall short because of trying to activate the spirit from the mind alone without the heart. This activates unbalanced ego drive, without the needed sensitivity and mutual respect. While women dislike the insensitive male ego drive, they have to be careful not to copy that method in their efforts to achieve equality. Equality without "quality" equals fatigue and stress. This is no real achievement. What is the achievement if you lose balance, fulfillment, and health? Then you are just living to *survive*, not really *living*.

Go for it from a perspective of mature balance. Things are changing, and the role of women in business actually is in a state of high-speed positive transformation. It may not seem like it at times but have patience. Consult with your heart if you have gender-based issues at work and use your intuitive intelligence to help guide and direct your actions in these matters. Equality will happen quicker when you use your heart to attain it, and you will maintain your peace in the process.

HEART BALANCE

Balance is the missing social keynote as we approach the millennium and beyond. Workplaces clearly have been out of balance; perspectives about ourselves, the opposite gender, and other cultures have been narrow, rigid, and self-limiting. Unmanaged mental and emotional reactions have built concrete-hard mind-sets that turn in to what we call *mind stances*. The fullness of male and female intelligence will come on-line when stances relax. When women take a mind stance—having a fixed goal in mind and fighting hard to achieve it—they repeat the male domination approach that has battered men and women alike. "Been there, done that."

A HEART STAND

To avoid repeating the same energy-draining fights of the past 30 years and accomplish something lasting, the coherent self-empowered woman will learn to bypass reactive, energy-draining stances. She will recognize it is more intelligent and effective to do so. Taking a heart stand facilitates a whole new level of power and renewal by being the vehicle for actualizing core values, free of mental and emotional reactiveness that add more noise to a noisy system. Conscious heart intention is the first step, derived from the intuitive link and balance between mind and heart, increasing the power of both. A coherent heart stand may not change policies, male attitudes, or laws immediately nor change society overnight, but men will take a new, respectful "stop, look, listen" approach. It is hard to argue with coherent intelligence.

We found that the balanced approach to male-female issues is achieved through intuitive intelligence. As two men, we do not believe women are trying to *take over*, just asking men to *move over* and let both drive and point the way together. We are dedicated to the manifestation of equalization, while respecting the different strengths of both genders. In our experience, the vast majority of women want to be players not conquerors and have an equal part in the scheme of things. This need not be a threat to the male ego. It will take both women and men to create an intelligent, coherent whole. Women's nurturing sensitivities mean they tend to use power and intelligence to try to make a difference in the lives of other people and the world. Men tend to be more absorbed in structures and plans. However, men are not merely power-hungry slugs. Men are learning to build coherence and balance just as women are. The challenge for men is finding a new maturity while releasing a dinosaur of convenience—the male-dominated society. The mark of wise players is the capacity to use the strengths of both male and female potentials for the betterment of the whole, through balance. Globalization and the Internet are just examples of this inexorable trend for balance. That is the new paradigm from which new solutions will be born.

INNER MALE-FEMALE BALANCE

Just as an electrical circuit is powered by both male and female polarities, so is the human system. When these internal polarities are balanced, we gain self-empowerment, which takes nothing away from being a man or a woman but empowers us as individuals.

- Typical qualities considered to be "male": Aggression, power, strength, courage.
- Typical qualities considered to be "female": Nurturing, care, sensitivity, receptivity.

The heart has both male and female qualities. The "soft heart" is receptive, nurturing, and feminine in polarity. The "strong heart" is courageous, assertive, and masculine in polarity. A balance of both is needed for coherent power in a woman, a man, or an organization. Entrainment is the state when the internal male and female polarities come together in synchronization.

As you balance the inner masculine and feminine polarities, your electromagnetism—and therefore your effectiveness—increases. Some women feel the need to become more aggressive to be respected by men, especially in the workplace. Often they do not know how to balance assertiveness with the nurturing side of themselves. The underlying dynamic of the feminist movement was an effort on the part of women to bring the male side of their nature into balance with their female side. The smaller but highly publicized men's movement was primarily a quest by men to develop the nurturing side of themselves and to be free to *feel*. The intent of both movements was increased empowerment. However, without individual balance, power is short-circuited and stress, anger, rage, and blame toward the opposite sex is often the result. If a new women's effort attempts the old approach to female-male issues, it will only perpetuate anger, separatism, and nonconstructive competition. A balanced, compassionate approach will lead to balance, respect, and creative possibilities for the whole. Bringing female-male problems out in the open is a beginning. Often, men do not really know the depths of intimidation and inner anguish that certain comments and gestures put women through. Many men, themselves the victims of emotional abuse at some point in their lives, want balance, too.

As we have seen in numerous client interventions, when women and men practice IQM tools, it balances their mental-emotional equilibrium. As you practice living intelligently from your heart both at work and at home, you will see how to shift and balance your energies and find appropriate responses in the moment. When male-female issues arise, shift your focus from justified emotional reactions to the intuitive intelligence in the heart. Focus on your heart and let your intuition guide you on how to effectively and intelligently deal with any issue.

DIMINISHING MALE-FEMALE COMPETITIVENESS

Ego drive can be a serious problem when it is not balanced and managed through intuition. Intuition from the heart creates a balancing energy so that ego drive can be intelligently directed and sustained without resulting in fatigue and burnout. This balancing process is the new trick to be learned for regeneration and fulfillment. Otherwise, ego drive thrives on stimulation and burns energy within your system faster than your capacity to self-nourish and renew. People associate the stimulation of ego drive with happiness and success. Yet, constant stimulation without the *balance of heart nourishment* yields a high ratio of burnout. This leaves people wondering "What happened?" when they thought they were on a roll. The energy burned needing to outdo each other, especially in the name of gender superiority, has no real payoff, but plenty of penalties.

Unmanaged ego drive creates a similar scenario to the stimulation of drug addiction, except it is a slower process. Many men and women have a stimulation addiction that they justify by achievement or survival needs, resulting in a seemingly fun trail to exhaustion. The pursuit of fulfillment through unrealized ambition actually is the *source* of many problems in male or female attempts to achieve happiness and completion. Discovering the power and nourishment potential of heart intelligence is key to simultaneously having ego stimulation and balance within the human system. This brings both inner peace and outer prosperity.

The extremism of the competitive or achievement orientation in many organizations causes people to use their ego drive to helplessly venture from their own balance, resulting in mental and emotional drain. Men have been doing this for years, creating the male-dominant society. Nations have done this, too, contributing to the imbalance between rich and poor in the world. In the name of progress and equality, many women also have increased their ambition. The resulting mental and emotional drain has a trickle down effect on the physical body, increasing the potential for various ailments. The result often is cardboard living, having to maintain a store-front momentum without experiencing the deeper textures in life.

NEXT STEPS

Why is it like this? Why are men threatened? Where do we go from here? It is not the glass ceiling, equal work for equal pay, sexual harassment, or other issues that aggravate equality, as much as men being stuck in the loop of viewing internal power through the lens of external exploitation. It is a non-pay-off investment, though in the short term, it seems high leverage to many men. Through activating the intelligent power of their core values, women casually can generate intelligent magnetics to attract fairness (equality). This new power creates an energy field that magnetizes a new respect and fair interchange in male-female interactions and policy making. We believe this approach to equality will be much faster than issue bashing. Let us be clear—policies and issues need to be dealt with on the front line, but they will find resolution much more quickly if powered from heart intelligence. Organizations, to build coherence, must become aware of the imbalances within. At the same time, men and women in organizations have a deep, life-long responsibility to seek and maintain balance in themselves.

The challenges of male-female balance as we enter the millennium can be summarized as follows:

- Personally, we each have an opportunity—and a responsibility—to generate greater male-female balance in ourselves (which is the foundation of greater respect for others). This means enhancing qualities that are dormant or sleepy, while toning down overdone traits that drain vitality and cause alienation in others.
- Personally, we can apply the principles of coherent communication so male-female (and multicultural) differences are understood and

respected. It is time to reach a new level of maturity in how we treat people different from ourselves. We would expect no less from others.

- Organizations have a responsibility to uncover areas of incoherence related to male-female issues, work-life balance, and particularly understanding the actual perceptions operating in the workplace.
- Balance will be the operating principle guiding new organizational attitudes and actions that reduce unhealthy competition, exclusion, and unfairness.

Many organizations will not yet see the importance of such issues or they may assume "we have no problem here." However, deeper reflection could reveal that even high-performing, world-class teams face challenges that can be subtle yet profound. Stability today can be shockingly threatened tomorrow. The potential for leaps in creativity, collaboration, and effectiveness that even moderate improvements in male-female coherence could provide clearly are worth the effort.

NOTES

1. Seth Lubove, "Damned If You Do, Damned If You Don't," *Forbes* (December 15, 1997).
2. Karl H. Pribram and Deborah Rozman, "Early Childhood Development and Learning: What New Research on the Heart and Brain Tells Us About Our Youngest Children," presented at the White House Conference on Early Childhood Development and Learning, San Francisco, 1997.
3. Janet C. Wylie, *Chances and Choices: How Women Can Succeed in Today's Knowledge-Based Businesses* (Vienna, VA: EBW Press, 1996).
4. Cited in the Reuters article, "Language Regions of Brain Are Larger in Women," from a study by Jenny Harasty, *Archives of Neurology* 54 (1997), pp. 171–76.
5. "Common Sense About Feeling Tense," *Heart at Work Program*, American Heart Association, 1995.
6. Wylie, *Chances and Choices*.

STRATEGIC PROCESSES AND RENEWAL

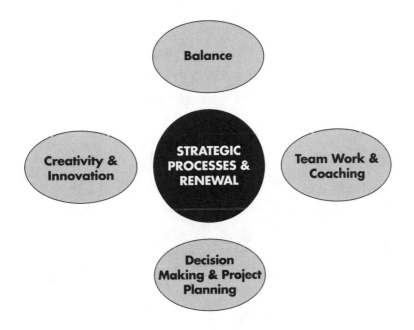

1. *Balance* is the keynote for self-renewing organizations.

2. Key management skills will be seen as strategic imperatives:
   - Building effective *teams* can be achieved based on the model of entrained systems.
   - *Coaching* guarantees ongoing renewal and growth of the coherent organization.

3. *Complex decision making and project planning* require "big picture" thinking.

4. *Creativity and innovation* arise out of coherent people and coherent processes.

12

Managing a Coherent Organization

The IQM technology builds renewal at the individual, team, and organizational levels. Excellent organizations behave like self-renewing systems, finding continual nourishment, internally and externally. They are alert to subtle or profound changes in the environment inside or outside the organization that can be intelligently adapted to. This is the strategic imperative for success in an age of unprecedented acceleration.

Typically the term *strategy* is used to describe the clear vision and comprehensive plans that are designed to accomplish specific organizational or personal objectives. The problem today is the rapid obsolescence of most strategic thinking. Excessive strategizing based solely on analytical thinking or competitive analyses is contradictory to the very principles of innovation and flexibility required today. So many corporations today link strategy only to short-term profitability, to the great detriment of the organization's viability. As a mind-set, this approach puts planning ahead of all the stakeholders—customers, employees, vendors, and the community. In the future, strategy will be seen as simply one factor—albeit an essential one—ensuring viability, with individual and organizational coherence as the foundation. We believe the *critical strategic imperatives* for success in the 21st century are building adaptability, coherence, and heart into all levels of the organization.

The first theme in Dynamic 4 is this:

Balance is the keynote for self-renewing organizations.

A balance of all four dynamics of IQM—internal self-management, coherent communication, boosting organizational climate, and strategic renewal—can ensure that the organization is resilient, nimble, and always innovating.

155

Balance in this context does not imply that the organization is static or still, but rather intelligently and dynamically aware of itself and its environment, fine-tuning itself when it gets thrown off course. Renewal at the organizational level can go as deep as individuals themselves are encouraged and rewarded for renewing themselves.

THE SERVICE-PROFIT CHAIN

This first theme in Dynamic 4 is expressed through some striking organizational research. How do high-performing organizations consistently renew themselves? Patterns of organizational renewal were described in 1994 when James Heskett, W. Earl Strasser, Jr., and Leonard A. Schlesinger at the Harvard University Graduate School of Business Administration reported ground-breaking research around an idea called the *service-profit chain*.[1] The service-profit chain (see Figure 12–1) was developed from analyses of successful service organizations such as Southwest Airlines, Wal-Mart, Intuit Corporation, Taco Bell, and MCI. It establishes clear relationships between profitability, customer loyalty, and employee satisfaction, loyalty, and productivity. The links in the chain are as follows:

- *Profit and growth* are stimulated primarily by customer loyalty.
- *Loyalty* is a direct result of customer satisfaction.

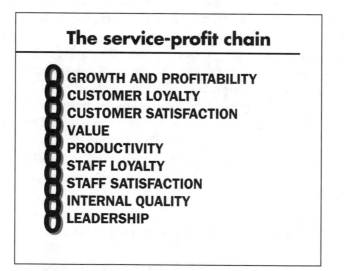

The service-profit chain

- GROWTH AND PROFITABILITY
- CUSTOMER LOYALTY
- CUSTOMER SATISFACTION
- VALUE
- PRODUCTIVITY
- STAFF LOYALTY
- STAFF SATISFACTION
- INTERNAL QUALITY
- LEADERSHIP

FIGURE 12–1   The service-profit chain. Source: Reprinted with permission from Simon and Schuster, New York, 1997.

- *Satisfaction* is influenced largely by the value of services provided to customers.
- *Value* is created by satisfied, loyal, and productive employees.
- *Productivity* is largely the result of employee satisfaction.
- *Employee satisfaction*, in turn, results from high-quality support services and policies—the internal quality of an organization—that enable employees to deliver results to customers.
- *Internal quality* results from *leadership*, which understands that frontline workers and customers need to be the center of management concern.

The IQM model of organizational coherence maps well to this research. The absence or presence of internal self-management, coherent communication, a healthy organizational climate, and strategic renewal can be seen in every link in the chain. The service-profit chain focuses management thinking on two very important ideas:

1. Do what is necessary to detect the needs and ensure the satisfaction and loyalty of targeted customers.
2. Achieve this, in most cases, by giving employees the latitude and support necessary to deliver high value to desired customers.

In short, create coherence and balance within the organization around each link in the chain.

In looking deeper at the service-profit chain model, some interesting observations come to the surface. Heskett and his coauthors note that the accomplishments of the organizations they cite did not happen by chance. Nor did they happen completely by excellent planning and design either.

> They resulted from extraordinary leadership by a small group of exceptional people who understood implicitly the relationships embodied in the service profit chain, who put them to work to create organizations capable of detecting and adapting to changing customer needs, and who have seen to it that cultures have been created in their organizations that will sustain them during future ups and downs.[2]

The focus at Southwest Airlines, an airline we actually have fun flying on, is this: high value for customers needing frequent transportation over relatively short distances at a cost comparable to the cost of driving their own car. For these customers, Southwest means high quality, reflected in frequent departures and on-time arrivals. High quality also means first-name recognition by loyal employees who have worked the ticket counters long enough to be able to recognize hundreds of frequent flyers by name.[3] It is arguably a highly coherent organization, clear and focused on its people and those they serve.

As any jazz musician knows, it takes flexibility and adaptability for improvisation to create beauty. This clearly has become the hallmark of Southwest Airlines' organizational culture. In an article in *Leader to Leader*, a brilliant magazine published by the Peter F. Drucker Foundation, Herb Kelleher, Southwest's maverick founder and CEO, says this about people in the organization:

> What's the secret to building a great organization? How do you sustain consistent growth, profits and service in an industry that can literally change overnight? And how do you build a culture of commitment and performance when the notion of loyalty—on the part of customers, employees, and employers—seems like a quaint anachronism? I can answer basically in two words: *be yourself.*[4]

How effective do you feel this approach would be if there was no fairly high level of balance and coherence *within the individuals* serving the customers? It is impossible to *mandate* this kind of attitude. If the organizational culture did not help the individual feel good about his or her job, resources, autonomy, sense of family, and sense of balance, how effective would the efforts really be? If the culture is supportive, then it still is up to the individual *whether or not to be himself or herself.*

In high-performing organizations, management recognizes the value of collaboration. Antagonism and unhealthy competition are the antitheses of the qualities needed by nimble adaptive organizations in the future. What management skills are primary in the development of such adaptive, authentic, dynamic workplaces?

MANAGEMENT SKILL

The second theme in Dynamic 4 describes key management skills as these:

- Building effective teams can be achieved based on the model of entrained systems.
- Coaching guarantees ongoing renewal and growth of the coherent organization.

Managers today have unprecedented levels of responsibility. Not only must they master ever-changing technology, be aware of workplace policies and laws, and study market conditions, they also must attend to the needs of their people. They are asked to be supportive, to appreciate, to provide clear direction without micro-managing, to delegate authority for the empowerment of others—all this while balancing their own home and work priorities. It can be daunting, to say the least. As a manager's responsibilities grow, self-management becomes increasingly important. So does improving communication and neutralizing incoherence. Diversity in the workplace also requires attending to the climate managers create. The load can be overwhelming, yet the potential for personal and professional development possible through the development of heart intelligence, along with a focus on developing teams and coaching skills, can springboard any manager into the next level of efficiency and effectiveness.

A study at Cornell University's Johnson Graduate School of Management[5] found that compassion and building teamwork will be two of the most important characteristics business leaders will need for success a decade from now. The study involved interviews with executives at Fortune 1000 companies. By contrast recent MBA graduates in the same study ranked results orientation much higher and disagreed with their more seasoned counterparts about the importance of social issues. "The results may indicate that experience cultivates a broader definition of corporate responsibility. It would be interesting to survey the MBA students 20 years from now and see if their positions have changed."

We learned earlier that entrainment is a natural state of synchronization seen throughout the biological world—flocks of birds, schools of fish, the pacemaker cells in our own heart, all working in a synchronized way, are just a few examples. Without knowing the term, we all experienced entrainment in our social or professional lives or at least we have admired it from a distance. The principle here is that complex systems such as teams require coherent individual parts to attain new levels of coherence as a whole. As the individual components, team members, become more self-managed and communication distortion is reduced, the system entrains. Once entrained, a jump to a new level of effectiveness is possible. Without entrainment in your system, energy is wasted. Without coherence between your core values and actions, there is a lag in your system and the energy of spirit is blocked from fully manifesting itself.

The same is true organizationally. Teams lacking entrainment often have conflict, withhold critical information, and are separated from a common vision. Lip service is useless, while the outcomes of such teams are unmistakable. It is essential to get at the root of what inhibits teams, what unspoken dynamics jam frequencies for potential coherence, what resentments keep the whole system from clicking in to its next level of power and effectiveness. Perfection is not the goal; consistent improvement in balance is.

> Love is the force that ignites the spirit and binds teams together.
> —PHIL JACKSON, *SACRED HOOPS*

When teams lack entrainment, there is a gap between what the head sees and what the heart wants. Without heart intelligence engaged, the head often will see the myriad of tasks and details and easily feel overwhelmed. Teams stuck in the mind lack the compassionate qualities that foster sharing and easing of each other's workloads. They see only the burden, the deadlines, the pressure. No coherent vision can penetrate the density of the collective malaise, unless the noise increases to the point a crack in the facade appears. All too often these days the openings occur because of pain or tragedy—sickness or death of a teammate, colleague, or even an employee in another division. The wake-up call can be stunning in its effects.

Before becoming a client, one of the world's largest and most successful global organizations saw three suicides among its executive ranks in one year. One of the executives stabbed himself in the heart, he was in such emotional pain. Another multinational recognized it needed to deal forthrightly with the stress-coherence issue after two suicides, one on the shop floor, rocked its employees. "Going postal" has become a cynical cliché to describe the behavior of any disgruntled employee.

We have measured the effectiveness of teams pre- and post-IQM training in many organizations. At a global energy company, over a six-month period, the percentage of the team reporting worry "often or most of the time" dropped from 47% to 7%, anxiety dropped from 33% to 7%, and anger dropped from 20% to 13%. This same team saw significant physical benefits. Rapid heartbeats dropped from 47% to 26%, tension reduced from 40% to 7%, aches and pains dropped from 27% to 7%, and sleeplessness fell from 33% reporting sleep problems often or most of the time to only 7% reporting sleeplessness six months later.

At a global electronics firm, a critical design team saw anxiety drop from 70% to 14%, anger drop from 42% to 9%, and fatigue drop from 66% to 23%. At the same time, sleeplessness fell from 51% to 14%, tension dropped from 76% to 16%, and aches and pains reduced from 56% to 23%.

Were these engineers simply becoming more docile and passive? Hardly. While the team was becoming less stressed and more coherent, creativity went from 68% to 82%, efficiency soared from 48% to 80%, and 83% of the team reported producing good results, up from only 38% two months earlier.

At another powerful high-tech company, results were less dramatic until compared to data from a control group. In this intervention, two teams of design engineers were selected from the same division of the firm. One team received a one-day IQM course with three short follow-up sessions over the next three months. The other team acted as the control, with no extra intervention provided to the control group. During the three-month period, the IQM group saw an 8% improvement in sleeplessness, while the control group saw sleeplessness rise by 18%. The IQM group saw a 17% reduction in rapid heartbeats, while the control group saw a 10% increase in rapid heartbeats. At the same time, the IQM team set aggressive new goals to avoid falling behind the rest of the division, and exceeded all their goals. Greater productivity, less stress. The manager of the control group, seeing his team's performance falling behind the IQM group, immediately asked to have his team go through training.

ENERGIZING TEAMS

IQM tools can be integrated into team structures and processes to stop the negative spiral of team dynamics and begin building entrainment in numerous ways:

- Freeze-frame is an excellent tool to increase coherence at the start of team meetings. Freeze-frame can also be used throughout meetings to refocus, clarify direction after breaks, or deepen creative input.
- Asset-deficit sheets can be used to evaluate proposals or recommendations or for the meeting process itself. These also are excellent self-evaluation tools, helping people maturely assess their progress, celebrate their success, and learn from obstacles.
- The intuitive listening skill can be the foundation of dramatically more efficient meetings. Posting the steps and reminding participants that using intuitive listening will be one of the "ground rules" is very effective.
- Intuitive listening is powerful in any size meeting to ensure coherence around new policies or decisions. The process of carefully checking that participants have heard the core message and that they will transmit it without an inappropriate "spin" saves tremendous energy.
- Within a team, an open discussion of individual or organizational overcaring often can identify problem areas before they become viruses affecting organizational health.
- Appreciation is key to meetings having momentum and buoyancy, events participants look forward to instead of dreading.

APPRECIATION

Of all the building blocks that underlie effective teams, appreciation is one of its cornerstones. Appreciation, as said earlier, implies an increase in value. Anything that is appreciated increases in value. This is as true for relationships and the creativity and skills of a team as it is for tangible assets such as real estate, stock, or the family car. (Tangible goods in most cases depreciate after purchase, of course, but the rate of depreciation is significantly altered if care is applied to the upkeep of the asset.) Many teams regularly examine the gaps in their performance to continuously improve. This deficit-focused approach clearly can boost performance but at what human cost? An individual who never feels good enough, whose performance is never quite to the highest standard, probably lives in a world of nonstop anxiety. Such people second-guess themselves regularly, so their performance is marked by stops and starts, rushing and hesitating. There is no flow to their work; anxiety blocks the pathways to greater coherence. Biologically, we know such anxiety equates to noise in the heart-brain communication system, impairing performance and obstructing optimal health. While old-school management theories still insist that encouraging anxiety in employees keeps them "hungry," appreciation is a far more efficient modality and one that enhances every link in the service-profit chain.

For appreciation to have value organizationally, it must be *sincere.* Employee of the month awards and special parking places are well-intentioned efforts to appreciate the individual, but in many cases inbred cynicism in the workplace neutralizes the positive effect of such efforts. Many overburdened managers are taught to show appreciation to employees to boost morale. In one case we recently about heard about from the U.S. Air Force, a training officer complained of insincerity on the part of her supervisor. "Super job!" was the consistent reply on every memo or report she delivered to her boss. Tiring of this lack of authenticity, she questioned coworkers who reported to the same supervisor, only to discover everyone's reports always were greeted with "Super job!" The lack of sincerity had bred an emotional virus the supervisor was too aloof to detect. Yet the intent had been to show appreciation.

> When pure sincerity forms within, it is outwardly realized in other people's hearts.   —LAO TZU, 6TH CENTURY B.C.

If lack of sincerity runs counter to all efforts in appreciation, *sincerity multiplies its effectiveness.* Sincere appreciation reduces static in an individual or team and gives a power boost to all subsequent efforts. Recall a time when you were sincerely appreciated by a supervisor, coworker, or customer (if this is difficult to remember, your organizational culture may be in need of heart). The appreciation you received was energizing, motivating, and confirming. It still brings a *feeling* of accomplishment if residual doubts or fatigue linger after a project is completed. It boosts confidence and frees the spirit to do more of what was already worthy of appreciating. Some old-school managers still believe appreciation makes people complacent or egotistical, yet if done from the heart the opposite occurs. Teams that sincerely appreciate each other's efforts, skills, and diversity are far stronger than those constantly competing for the spotlight. Many teams would say they value and appreciate each other, yet in our experience, sitting down to go over the assets of each team member can create an entrainment few other activities could. Highly touted experiential team-building activities, even though they can create shared memories and fun, rarely build the kind of rapport as does the consistent expression of sincere appreciation. Time after time, we have seen teams move from mediocre to exceptional when appreciation becomes an operating principle.

BIG PICTURE AND LITTLE PICTURE

Appreciation is a powerful tool to shift perspective. Finding something to appreciate during a difficult situation quickly moves the perspective to the *big picture* from the *little picture*. On hearing of a mistake by someone you supervise, you have a choice—immediately criticize the individual for a lack of critical thinking and overdramatize the potential effect or appreciate what other strains may have been affecting the performance and still give the necessary feedback. Seeing the bigger picture involves understanding the life of this individual, the stress he or she is under, the long-term viability of the organization, how well you are feeling at this moment, as well as the problem that needs addressing. Stuck in the "little picture" you see only the problem, often magnified beyond reason. Appreciation is a tool to keep your perspectives refreshed and balanced.

OVERACHIEVING?

The concept of the overachiever is an intriguing one when considering effective teamwork. Whether in sports or business, teams we call overachievers invariably are performing "above their level." How do they do this? Our view is that the overachievers are so in sync, so unself-conscious, so entrained and balanced, that they achieve a whole new standard of performance. Appreciation of each other is a hallmark of overachieving teams.

Sometimes, external "lucky" events are the catalyst, or it could be a powerful leader whose magnetic expression of unifying core values inspires the team members to move past self-limiting beliefs or mind-sets. Once the old mind-sets are put to rest, the team is primed for a jump into a surprising level of effectiveness, creativity, and potency. Calling such teams *overachievers* is inaccurate. These individuals and teams actually have reached a state of optimized potential, made possible by the achievement of coherence. What if traditional views of human potential are consistently distorted, looking as we are through the filters of incoherence?

Underachievers are the opposite. High on talent, rich in intelligent capacity and potential, they fail to meet expectations because of some underlying incoherence or imbalance in them or the environment. Often emotional mismanagement is spoiling the talent and isolating them from teammates. Sometimes, an inordinate ego-centrism is so off-putting to fellow team members, the static and distortion becomes deafening, undermining coherent effectiveness. Such individuals or teams drop well below the plateau of their potential, creating a new subpar standard of disappointment and negative self-worth.

SERVICE STRAIGHT FROM THE HEART

The cabin crew of a 747 must be a model of synchronized activity. In the competitive world of long-haul international flights, the care and efficiency given to passengers while onboard the plane has a powerful influence on a passenger's future decision on a carrier. Hong Kong–based Cathay Pacific Airways has long been considered one of the premier airlines flying in and out of Asia, winning numerous awards in the process. Seeking to differentiate itself from other high-quality carriers, a new marketing campaign was launched in 1995, Service Straight from the Heart. As with all marketing campaigns promising unique, memorable service, the challenge then became to deliver on the promise. Peter Buecking, then general manager for in-flight services, recognized that providing unique customized service to passengers was key to differentiating Cathay from its competitors. But he also recognized that the capability of the individuals within the cabin crew to consistently provide exceptional service was related directly to their ability to reduce stress and keep work-life priorities in balance. The strategy was to initially introduce the IQM technology to the ground staff for in-flight services, so the flight crews would see a model of extra caring and efficient service at the home base. Through the leadership of David Ling, training director, nearly 300 staff members have gone through the program and increases in team entrainment, efficiency, and effectiveness have been significant. In 1998, the airline received the Air Transport World Passenger Service Award, the Oscar of the airline industry.

COACHING

Great managers are those who, in spite of their obvious individual talent, intelligence, and creativity, choose to spread their innate skill and grace, helping others become far better in their *presence*. Such people are magnetic and inspiring because they have chosen to *radiate* their gifts, instead of internalize them. We delight in the expansive presence they create. Their very heart-based coherence, absent as it is of any meanness of spirit, enhances the talents, the capabilities, and the very processes around them.

And yet, in an age of such rapid transition and acceleration of intelligence, the temptations to waver from that coherence are everywhere. How demoralizing it is, how stung we feel in our gut, when a hero falls or a human frailty finally is exposed. We long to believe there is, somewhere or in someone, a coherence that can rise out of the chaos and the confusion. It brings hope when we see it in another.

Which brings us back to ourselves. Hope, fulfillment, and inspiration can be ignited externally for us, but we must stoke the fire daily. We must recognize the personal inefficiencies, the unconscious drains in our thoughts, the external and self-judgments. We must be responsible for ourselves and then make the necessary adjustments so we can explore and unfold our own heart intelligence and, in relationship with others, continue to refine the capacities that are our gifts.

Margaret Wheatley, a brilliant author and organizational theorist, has similar views on how to create coherent leadership for coherent organizations:

> We will need to stop describing tasks and instead facilitate *process*. We will need to become savvy about how to build relationships, how to nurture growing, evolving things. All of us will need better skills in listening, communicating, and facilitating groups, because these are the talents that build strong relationships. It is well known that the era of the rugged individual has been replaced by the era of the team player. But this is only the beginning. The quantum world has demolished the concept of the unconnected individual. . . . Those who relate through coercion, or from a disregard for the other person, create negative energy. Those who are open to others and

who see others in their fullness create positive energy. Love in organizations, then, is the most potent source of power we have available.[6]

Most managers, by the sheer volume of their life and professional experience, have much to share that can make any organization far more efficient. Time spent coaching people in the behaviors, attitudes, and skills known to produce results is time extremely well spent. Understanding the value of this time can be difficult when time itself is at such a premium.

One organization that has operationalized coaching is Thorlo, a premium manufacturer of sock products, activity-specific socks for every occasion—walking, hiking, trekking, running, tennis, basketball, you name it. Their patented designs and innovative use of textiles have created a fanatically loyal customer following (us too!). Their sock products are simply so comfortable, you quickly become spoiled by how good your feet feel. These are high-priced products, but most customers feel the value easily exceeds the price. Theirs also is a fascinating corporate culture. Located in the heart of North Carolina's textile region near Charlotte, the 350-employee company has built a culture where coaching is practiced actively at all levels of the organization. Thorlo chairman Jim Throneburg[7] recognized that, to create an enduring company in which core values infused everything, constant coaching would be required. An early adopter of team processes, Throneburg was quick to see that the team could flounder without a coaching mechanism to ensure appropriate knowledge and wisdom transfer. His was not a mild commitment: Four hours each week—10% of the employees' paid time—are spent in team formation, building coherence around every aspect of the Thorlo culture. Each of Thorlo's 40-plus teams has rotating coach facilitators who are "coached" in performing their role clearly but without excessive domination.

Several aspects of Thorlo's culture are striking and support the observations of the other authors cited here. A strong, unwavering set of core values is at the heart of the Thorlo culture. People, employees and customers, clearly matter. Helping employees gain flexibility and adaptability is also key. Thorlo U., an internal curriculum for personal and professional development, has been developed, unusual in a company of less than 500 employees. IQM tools are provided to employees to enhance their sense of work-life balance. For all its progressive policies and people-friendly climate, this company is not without significant challenges: Key product patents expire in the next few years, making it all the more essential for the organizational culture to have heightened innovation, creativity, and resilience. While the Thorlo model represents a highly structured commitment to a coaching model, the principle of mentoring and guiding employees into greater coherence is a hallmark of all great organizations.

MILITARY COHERENCE

The military arguably is a model of operational coherence. Even though in the United States, the end of the Cold War and shrinking defense budgets have created a crisis of confidence in the ranks—and many of the same issues of downsizing faced in the private sector—significant lessons on leadership can be learned. Patrick L. Townsend and Joan E. Gebhardt, writing in the journal *Leader to Leader*, point out the coherence throughout the military on its three leadership priorities: "The first is to accomplish the mission; the second, to take care of personnel; and the third, to create new leaders." There must be coherence around each of these interdependent priorities.[8] Incoherence and lack of focus around any one dramatically weakens the others and the chance of the mission's success. Townsend and Gebhardt then ask some tough questions of their corporate colleagues:

> Can the same be said about a civilian organization? Does everyone share not only the commitment to the mission but the commitment to their colleagues? Ask most civilians about their second priority at work and the response is likely to concern personal career enhancement. Military people are not angels; they are as concerned with their careers as anyone else. They know, however, that advancement is a by-product of success in meeting leadership priorities, not a goal in itself.

Increasingly managers and executives are realizing the very talents that catapulted them to the senior levels of their organization may not be the ones that keep them there. Also true is that each new level requires a broader, more global view. We usually do not "know what we do not know" until we get there. Most organizations are operating in uncharted territory, and the challenge to continually renew oneself is becoming ever more critical. The IQM tools, processes, and survey instruments can help organizations keep a vigilant and caring eye on the organizational health.

But, who is doing the same for the senior executives themselves? Often isolated and removed from the day to day operations, no longer doing some of the "roll up your sleeves" jobs that make business fun, executives find that their perspectives and attitudes can grow stale and cut off. Increasingly coaches are being brought in for these executives for the kind of private mentoring around professional growth and strategies necessary for renewed vitality. Whether coaching teams in a factory or coaching an executive whose performance has been found wanting, coaching is yet another opportunity for the activation and transfer of heart intelligence, a caring and bottom-line approach for organizational renewal.

Clearly, effectiveness in teams will be a prerequisite in the future. Getting hearts and minds in sync will be expected. With the world marching inexorably toward collaboration and cooperation, a practical tool for synthesizing the complexity of the mind with the clarity of the heart is Mind- and HeartMapping.

HEARTMAPPING®

Another key theme of Dynamic 4 is this:

> Complex decision making and project planning require "big picture" thinking.

MindMapping was developed in the 1960s by educators hoping to synchronize both hemispheres of the brain into a coherent whole, leading to breakthroughs in creativity and innovation. MindMapping is a highly creative approach to complex planning and decision making. To this well-researched technique, we integrated heart intelligence. Once a traditional MindMap is developed, participants freeze-frame, reflect on their core values, and ask themselves how to integrate these values and how they want to feel during the project they are mapping. A second map is created, which usually reveals information totally absent from the MindMap, which by intention is more tactical and pragmatic. The combination of the two maps, mind and heart, creates a compelling coherent vision of how to proceed. It provides a practical tool for individuals or teams to get a broader, more global view of key issues so that the perspectives generated are strategically sound, not just tactically driven.

MindMaps normally generate ideas as to *what* the group or individual needs to do. The ideas tend to be very action oriented, theoretical, and already known. This is good, so that an individual or group producing the MindMap clearly sees all the known items as well as links between issues and potential redundancies. In some cases, the ideas generated tend to be either already done, successfully or unsuccessfully, or too theoretical to actually drive any concrete changes. Experience suggests that concentrating solely on the ideas generated in a MindMap usually does not produce the significant improvements desired nor does it keep a focus on the human dynamics and balance of the team. This is why creating a HeartMap adds much more depth to the process.

The HeartMap normally generates a completely different set of ideas to the MindMap, as seen in the example that follows. The ideas tend to be much more to do with *how* the group needs to change—the feeling or climate a team is seeking to achieve—rather than simply what the group needs to do. The ideas tend to be more people based, pragmatic, and qualitative and less theoretical. If the group is to make the significant improvements it desires, it needs to address the human qualities generated by the HeartMap to enable the good theoretical ideas generated by the MindMap to become a sustainable reality.

If the task being mapped is particularly large or complex, key branches of the maps often require their own maps. In a group HeartMapping session, this is accomplished by a subgroup taking on the task of HeartMapping that branch. The final crucial phase of HeartMapping is creating an action plan from the two maps. This involves stepping back again from the maps to consider the timing, resources, and personnel needed as well as to assign specific timelines. While the entire HeartMapping process resembles other planning processes, the emphasis on coherent communication and the utilization of heart intelligence yields much richer information than most traditional planning methods.

HEARTMAPPING IMPROVED TEAMWORK

Dr. Alan Watkins and Chris Sawicki led a European team for a global electronics firm utilizing the Mind- and HeartMapping tool to enhance their teamwork skills. Ideas generated by the whole group during the MindMap exercise included

1. Have effective leadership.
2. Establish common goals, identifying targets, timetables, and sense of urgency.
3. Ensure correct composition and diversity of team members.
4. Assign specific responsibilities to team members.
5. Pay attention to building teams.
6. Identify resources available to teams.
7. Run meetings better, with attention to schedule and venue.
8. Improve communication.
9. Identify key information for sharing.
10. Establish rewards and incentives for all team members.

11. Identify win-win solutions.
12. Be competent, have clarity.
13. Trust team members.
14. Deliver results.
15. Celebrate success and have fun.

Ideas generated by the whole group in a HeartMap (after a four-minute freeze-frame) were

1. Promote friendship and camaraderie.
2. Place higher importance on appreciation and understanding.
3. Help each other, interindividual coaching.
4. Promote a sense of togetherness.
5. Learn and evolve together.
6. Promote harmony.
7. Reward openness.
8. Pay attention to "team chemistry."
9. Celebrate more often and put greater value on a "positive atmosphere."
10. Identify and work from the "team's spirit and soul."

In this example, there are similarities in the ideas generated on each map, but there is a qualitative difference. The MindMap is more tactical and theoretical; the HeartMap more collaborative and people driven. The combination of the two creates a powerful vision for improved teamwork. Six months later, significant business improvements in the team were being sustained.

A project team at National Semiconductor used this process powerfully as part of a cross-functional team offsite seminar using IQM tools. Participants came from National and five other vendor companies working with them on a major global project. The technical complexity of the project was amplified by the fact that local standards in several countries had to be integrated into the plan. The cross-functional team was spread out on three continents, so meeting times were also a major challenge. During the seminar, subgroups HeartMapped key areas of the project, then reported back to the whole team for feedback. (All team members had learned freeze-frame, intuitive listening, and the concepts of appreciation and overcaring prior to the start of the HeartMapping session.) In a five hour session, more than 30 pages of action plans were developed from the Mind- and HeartMaps, a process the team said normally would have taken several months to complete. As important as these tangible outcomes was the fun and efficiency of the process. Several months later, the team still was marveling at how much more effectively, and with so much less stress, this team had been able to perform. The message once again is this: Create individual and team coherence first and highly efficient results will follow (see Figure 12–2).

HEARTMAPPING APPLICATIONS

The HeartMapping tool has a variety of powerful applications because it is fun, surprisingly efficient, and reinforces the need to step back out of the high speed routine to get a bigger picture. In a group setting especially, it is essential that the process be *nonjudgmental* and founded on the principles of coherent communication. This means encouraging and mapping out *all* potential ideas, not just those voiced most strongly. It means not debating any ideas at first because you are building coherence within the team doing the HeartMapping. Hearing all perspectives is critical to creating the most comprehensive and effective outcome while uncovering creative ideas that otherwise could have been missed. Also essential is that the facilitator not edit or show any bias toward any particular theme but merely guide and draw out all possible ideas.

In our organization, HeartMapping is used regularly by teams during product brainstorming sessions. All possible ideas, customer needs, market issues, pricing considerations, and so forth are mapped out in creating an initial picture of the parameters of the product. It is best not to be linear and sequential at this stage, so you do not stay locked in traditional ways of thinking about the idea.

It is also an excellent tool for client development or enhancing customer satisfaction as well as to assess the status of a project. Using Heart-Mapping for setting personal priorities is particularly powerful. To set priorities for the month (or any other defined time period), start by building a MindMap of all potential and urgent tasks to accomplish during the month. Be as thorough as possible, especially including those easy-to-avoid items you are dreading or that are particularly tricky and complex. Freeze-frame throughout the creation of the MindMap to ask yourself what other items have not been mapped out. Then, once you feel the map is complete, freeze-frame and ask your heart what are the key priorities, the highest leverage activities that absolutely must get done. Build a HeartMap from the answers to your questions. Keep freeze-framing to remember this is the time to ensure that *balance* is at the core of your activities. This is not the time to rush back into the details and become paralyzed by the sheer volume of work you could be doing. Then create an

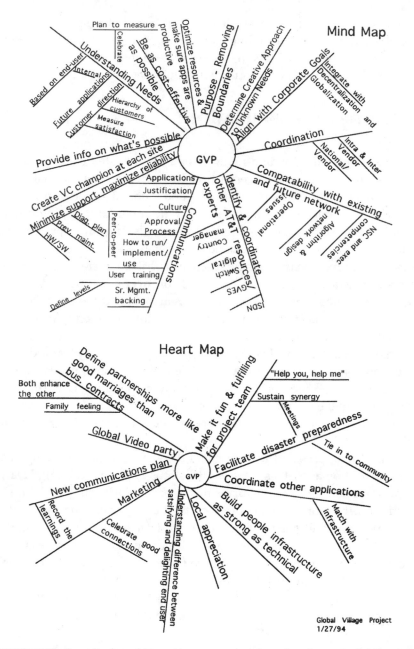

FIGURE 12–2 Mind- and HeartMaps were generated at the start of the session to give an overview of the entire project. Out of these maps, subgroups developed more detailed maps and plans (opposite), resulting in numerous plans for the successful implementation of the project. Source: Reprinted by permission from the Institute of HeartMath.

INNER QUALITY MANAGEMENT®					

Heart Map Action Plan™

PROJECT TITLE:	Global Video Project
OBJECTIVES:	Sites Operational by 1995:
	Delight (not just satisfy) the end user

TARGET DATE	HRS	TASKS—ACTIONS	WHO	DONE
Mar. 1		Understand needs	Stuart,Mike Judith	
Mar. 1		Id & Coord. other AT&T Resources	Mike, Gabe Bruce P.	
ongoing		Optimize resources- build people infrastructure		All
		as strong as tech.		
Mar. 10		Compat. w/ existing & future network	Mike, Gabe, Stuart, Gene, Judith, Kathy	
Mar 1.		Coordination - define partnerships like a good	All	
		marriage, not just business, contacts-family feeling		
Mar. 15		New communications plan- create	NSC Team	
Various		VC champion at each site	NSC Team	
Ongoing		Local Appreciation	NSC Team	
Mar 15		Coordinate other applications	Mike,Kathy E. Stuart,Judith	
Always		Make it fun & fulfilling for project team-global video	All	
TBA		Party- Celebrate good connections w/ ea. other	Mike,Bruce P. Stuart, Judith	
Ongoing		End User DELIGHT	All	
	COMPLETION DATE:			

◆INSTITUTE OF HEARTMATH • P.O. Box 1463 • Boulder Creek, CA 95006 • Tel. 408-338-8700 • fax 408-338-9861

FIGURE 12–2 *continued*

action plan from both maps, letting the core values revealed in your Heart-Map drive the plan.

HeartMapping represents yet another way to activate your full intelligence, instead of relying solely on a linear, analytical approach or responding only to the loudest needs. It opens up new creative potentials where noise once predominated.

NOTES

1. James L. Heskett, W. Earl Sasser, Jr., and Leonard A. Schlesinger, *The Service-Profit Chain: How Leading Companies Link Profit and Growth to Loyalty, Satisfaction, and Value* (New York: The Free Press, 1997).

2. Ibid., p. 237.

3. Ibid., p. 238.

4. Herb Kelleher, "A Culture of Commitment," *Leader to Leader*, no. 4 (Spring 1997), p. 20.

5. "Executive Survey: 'Compassion' Is Important for Future Business Leaders," *Cornell Chronicle* 28, no. 10 (October 24, 1996). Cornell University Johnson Graduate School of Management. www.gsm.cornell.edu/Newideas/leadershipsurvey2.html.

6. Margaret J. Wheatley, *Leadership and the New Science: Learning about Organization from an Orderly Universe* (San Francisco: Berrett-Koehler, 1992), pp. 38–39.

7. Jim Throneburg, chairman of Thorlo, has attended several HeartMath programs at our facility in California. We also provided training and consulting services to the company at its facilities in North Carolina.

8. Patrick L. Townsend and Joan E. Gebhardt, "The Three Priorities of Leadership," *Leader to Leader*, no. 4 (Spring 1997), p. 13.

13

Creating a Quantum Future

The inner quality management model suggests that four integrated dynamics underlie excellence, now and in the future. We presented many facts and well-researched studies to serve as a wake-up call that the issues of stress, human performance, and organizational climate need to become critical business strategies, not just brown-bag lunch topics dreamed up by a well-intentioned HR department. While the four dynamics represent a coherent package that any organization can apply, we are not so naive as to think life is always as neat and well-ordered. In fact, the very unpredictability and acceleration felt in organizations today propelled us to create the IQM methodology.

There is a science to business effectiveness, and there must be heart for that science to have meaning. The science presented has been built not on dogma and rigid principles but on coherence and the liquid intelligence of flexibility and adaptability. The four dynamics of IQM are not rules to follow so much as frequencies to make real and uniquely integrated to your culture. The perception of each reader will determine to a great extent how these ideas and tools come alive in the organization.

CREATING THE FUTURE

The power of perception has been an underlying theme of this entire book. During our lifetime, as for many generations before us, human perceptions of what is intelligent and what is power, and indeed what is time and the nature of our fulfillment, have undergone radical shifts. As information has exploded, the scholars among us have sought to build bridges and see connections between otherwise disparate fields of study. Laws of chaos theory and quantum physics are discussed in business schools, biomedical information influences our hiring practices and employee training, psychological studies inform our workplace designs.

It also is safe to say "we ain't seen nothing yet." Every generation looks at its breakthroughs as startling when compared to the past, and arguably the speed of transformation today is greater than at any time in human history. It is tempting to believe the latest breakthrough insight is the final answer. Yet, we would be wise to remember that for every insight, another far more powerful set of understandings await our intelligent exploration. For centuries people were absolutely convinced—and their observation confirmed—that the earth was flat. Later observation convinced them the earth was the center of the universe, with the sun rotating around it. Now expanded lenses of perception at both ends of the spectrum—from the Hubble telescope revealing never before seen worlds to the theoretical viewing of quantum particles—stretch the limits of what we can observe. We suggest here that the lens of heart intelligence presents the next frontier of how we see and interact with life.

New intelligence is available now that can bring into coherence much of the chaos and confusion of the past. Each age of human history has been marked by profound increases in human intelligence, but the flaws and distortion in human interaction have kept the impact of much of this intelligence limited. As a planet we have progressed in technology and in personal convenience, in information availability, in transportation, and in a myriad of other ways. Our standard of living has improved in many parts of the world, but fundamental social relations remain mired in immaturity and antagonism.

Viewed through the lens of history, nothing we know now could be seen as final, as the last word, or even as a resting point for knowledge. An irony here is that, in the search for meaning, the answers often get quirkier and more basic. Quantum scientists develop names for particles like quarks and mesons; astronomers theorize the existence of MACHOs—massive compact holo objects—that emit no light. The computer world and indeed most organizational cultures are filled with cheerful acronyms and new words or old words with new meanings. There is a bemusement in much of the discovery going on today; a sense that the real answers we have been looking for are at once simpler and even more ironic than we would have imagined.

A Hindu myth has it that the gods were trying to decide where to hide the secret of life. One god suggested, "Let's hide it in the mountains." But another god said, "No, they'll look there." So one of the gods said, "Let's hide it in the sky," but this suggestion again was met with "No, they'll look there." At which point the wisest among them said, "Let's hide it in the heart; they'll never look there."

Human beings show an impetus for self-organizing, from the formation of our identity to the way we manipulate our environment—how we make our beds, brush our teeth, file our papers, develop strategic or vacation plans. We attempt to manage the present with the future in mind. Left to the mechanicality of habituated mind-sets and emotional programs from our past, we usually do an adequate job. But, what are we not seeing, what subtle signals of our intelligence are we too busy to listen to?

Creativity and innovation are central facets of all human activity. Darwin saw spontaneous genetic mutations that provided adaptability and competitive advantages and, therefore, survivability. It has been noticed that these mutations happened in discontinuous jumps, not a steady progression of minute changes. To a bird, growing one extra feather made little difference to flying ability; growing many would make a significant difference. In the world of physics, electrons shift orbital states in discontinuous jumps, absorbing or emitting energy in quanta as they do so.

The shifts in organizations can be just as sudden. We believe coherence is the underlying principle that will guide quantum leaps in future effectiveness. Out of "nowhere," a new organization will become prominent. The sustainable organizations will be those founded on unshakable core values providing the operating system for coherence. As these organizations hit each new level of coherence, innovations will occur out of the self-renewing creativity. When faced with adversity, instead of overreacting emotionally to the challenge, they will organize themselves through intelligent coherence to deal with the local conditions. This is real innovation. The consistent ability to innovate will emerge from the underlying flexibility and coherence in every aspect of the health of the organization and the individual.

In the past we could antagonize a person or a system into innovating, just as we could use fear as a motivator and point to its success. But, with the new intelligence, these old methods will be seen as wholly inefficient, energy-draining strategies. Nature does not seek chaos; it intelligently organizes to ensure its survival in spite of the chaos. Coherence brings energy efficiency to a chaotic world.

Innovation is the spurt, the discontinuous jump of intelligence, applied in a new way. Innovation is not pat or static; there is no *best* way that is universal. Local solutions that work are critical, just as, on the individual level, being "present" means having full intelligence available to deal with each unique situation.

QUANTUM MANAGEMENT

Being in the moment—alert, awake, and neutral—will become a management imperative. Living in the past or worrying about the future wastes energy and resources. No organization can long survive living with time warped by history or distorted by future anxiety.

Popular culture leads us to believe that *quantum* means large. In fact, quantum means an elemental building block, too small to be actually measured. Small, even infinitesimally small, however, does not mean insignificant. In fact, the paradox may be that the smaller you look, the more powerful is the potential effect. Clearly, size is not everything: Massive stars explode into supernova or end up as black holes. Massive companies, bureaucracies, and empires have been forced to get smaller or crumble. AT&T, Soviet central industrial planning, and the British Empire are just a few celebrated examples.

Quantum management implies using full intelligence to deal effectively with each elemental building block—this moment. Organizations will be challenged to find local solutions—*now*—that work in an era of increasing complexity, chaos, and stress. The challenge will be to achieve the coherence and internal quiet necessary to perceive the deeper order embedded in what appears to be chaos. Unmanaged emotion is expert at turning discomfort into misery. Finding that deeper order is a key to adaptability and survivability. Leadership of any organization must be involved in the detection, management, and direction of change with adaptation strategies taught at the individual level. Key strategies will be uncovered by unfolding the intelligence and self-organizing potential of people in the organization. The four dynamics of IQM can provide an evolving, flexible road map for intelligently meeting the challenges of adapting to a new future.

Self-security will be a hallmark of the leaders and exceptional organizations of the future. Self-security in an individual or a system brings a high ratio of coherence. Leaders or organizations with self-security can push power and authority downstream and develop centers of innovation and excellence at all levels of the organization.

Sweden's Skandia, a global financial and insurance services firm and a key innovator in the drive to value and measure human capital, has established futures centers to explore new technologies central to its future. But, more important, as its operations, product offerings, and workforce become ever more diverse and complex, it has created a "heart office" to ensure that the company's core values are effectively transmitted. Self-organization will happen at the local level, but Skandia ensures that it will unfold in coherence with the intelligence of the core.[1]

Quantum management involves guiding the evolution of people and systems in response to change, creating "genetic" adaptations in discontinuous jumps in the blueprint of how the organization sees itself and how it transmutes itself to offer new capabilities. Quantum management will ensure that the "small and insignificant" will not be ignored; it will be clear when the problem is that we are moving too fast in a mental or emotional mode and failing to understand the significance of an event and not that the individual or issue is too small to warrant our attention. This requires paying *attention*— attention that is balanced, coherent, and aligned with our core values. Quantum jumps will happen then, allowing an organization to keep and grow its niche in the economic environment while maintaining meaning. Quantum management requires the coherent guidance of human and system capability into self-regenerating, upwardly spiraling patterns, unfolding in the individual new layers of embedded DNA potential, while unfolding new layers of market potential, human potential, and innovation potential. Pulling out of the gravity and density in ourselves and our organizations will be key.

CREATING YOUR PLAN

Your opportunity now is to maximize the investment you made in reading this book and create your own plan to apply the tools and insights gained. Where are you headed? What questions have been stirring about your personal balance, your career, the viability of the organization you work in? A glossary follows, with definitions of the key concepts and tools in this book, but we briefly summarize the tools here.

- Internal self-management
  - —Freeze-frame
  - —Asset-deficit balance sheet
  - —Neutral
  - —Managing time and expectations
- Coherent communication
  - —Intuitive listening
  - —Authentic dialogue
- Boosting the organizational climate
  - —Distinguishing caring from overcaring
  - —Self-care
  - —Organizational coherence survey
  - —Tracking the emotional virus
  - —Heart lock-in
- Strategic processes and renewal
  - —HeartMapping
  - —Asset-deficit balance sheet

—Coaching
—Teamwork

Consider now your basic routine on a daily, weekly, and monthly basis. How much of your day is spent on the phone, in meetings, planning, traveling, responding to voice mail and e-mail? Of all the concepts and tools outlined here, which seem easiest to integrate into your schedule? Which seem challenging, yet the pay-off probably would be worth it? Create a MindMap of all the possible ways you can integrate and apply the tools, referring to the preceding list. Then create a HeartMap of the highest lever-age activities, the ones most in sync with your values. Include in these maps the need to meet with any individuals to resolve conflict and build more coherent communication. Remember, especially, to focus on developing greater balance and coherence in *you*. The next to last step is to build an action plan of those tools you can commit to doing. The final step is doing.

PRESENCE

A by-product of the IQM process is the building of *presence*. Presence is a rare quality in a world of 20-second sound bites, nonstop stimulation, and gnawing anxiety. What underlies presence? Clearly, it is not intellectual prowess or Mensa would rule the world. More than once we all have been bored to tears by the intellectual aloofness of someone disconnected from everyday reality, adrift in a conceptual universe of his or her own creation. In the world of the performing arts, many have great *talent*, but few have real presence. Could presence be heart-generated coherence in the world of personal magnetics? People with presence have an ineffable quality about them; they are "present," meaning surprisingly attentive and undistracted. A fullness, a centeredness, a wholeness radiates from them. We enjoy being "in their presence." Presence can be built and is the natural radiance of heart security.

Many things can rob people and organizations of presence:

- Unresolved conflicts.
- Living apart from the heart's core values.
- Unmanaged mental processes that spin out of control.
- Judgment of oneself and others.

Presence undoubtedly is more tangible than we know and probably one day will be measurable, a magnetic "field of presence." But, even before science verifies the existence of presence, we are constantly aware of its existence in

- The store we frequent because of the unmistakable warmth we feel there.
- The great actors and actresses whose movies we never miss, so sure are we of the consistent presence and charisma they exude.
- The mentor or leader who, just by walking in a room, immediately boosts the dynamic of the environment.
- An airline responding compassionately and openly to a tragedy in the skies.

We also can see the lack of presence in

- The news anchor who is merely a news reader, adding no humanity to "today's top stories."
- The appalling staff meeting characterized by frequent interruptions, side conversations, and antagonism.

EINSTEIN'S VULNERABILITY

Although it took many years before Einstein's radical theories became a part of mainstream science, he eventually became recognized as the greatest physicist of the 20th century. At the height of his fame, a Catholic priest from the Vatican challenged a key tenet of Einstein's view of a "steady state" universe. Einstein summarily dismissed the priest, publicly branding his "mathematics poor." At that time, it was still believed that we lived in the only galaxy in the universe, but the startling pictures of the great astronomer Hubble began to present a much different picture of the cosmos. The "clouds" that scientists like Einstein believed to be part of our own galaxy, in fact, were other huge galaxies traveling away from us at unbelievably high speed. The beauty of these images took Einstein's breath away, and he publicly apologized to the priest, dramatically changing his view of cosmic reality in the process. How many leaders and visionaries are able to show the same vulnerability as Einstein—to not only publicly admit his mistake, but then to revel in the new discovery? This vulnerability and openness to truth was one of the greatest gifts Einstein gave to the world and lay powerfully beneath his understated, slightly disheveled presence.

In the future, we will seek more and more to do business with organizations where we feel presence. We will want to work only for leaders who respect presence. We will be keenly aware of our core desire to build our own presence. Presence will be an essential quality understood to determine effectiveness in whether we as people feel welcomed and understood, in the climate of an organization, and in the teams in which we work. Presence generates and increases coherence.

There is a momentum of new intelligence that cannot be stopped, even though it may appear embryonic and fragile in the face of so much chaos and pain. Organizations of the future will have to uncover the heart of the organization. Heart-based organizations will encourage and enhance the self-development and self-management of all their members. They will seek to maximize intelligence, not by aggravating people into doing more, but by nurturing, supporting, and stretching them. They will see the mental, emotional, and physical health of people in the organization as essential to productivity and long-term viability and not just an issue for those who lack hardiness. They will see communication as the flow of living information, which has the power to vitalize and regenerate. They will monitor the health and effectiveness of all communication methods, not to invade privacy but to recognize information flow as nourishment itself. They will understand and nurture the climate of the organization, not simply because it is good, or nice, or even the right thing to do; they could not conceive of doing otherwise. They will understand that the unbridled acquisition of knowledge is a pale substitute for the seasoned maturity of wisdom. Knowledge without heart is a burden; wisdom regenerates. And they will create processes that renew and revitalize both the individuals and the organization, serving the needs of all. For all this intelligent effort, they will be rewarded with unheard of breakthroughs in innovation, customer loyalty, and personal fulfillment. They will have moved from chaos to coherence.

NOTE

1. Leif Edvinsson and Michael S. Malone, *Intellectual Capital: Realizing Your Company's True Value by Finding Its Hidden Brainpower* (New York: HarperCollins, 1997), p. 49.

Appendix

Organizational Case Studies

HeartMath has provided IQM training and research programs for a large variety of corporations, government agencies, and military installations in the United States, Canada, Europe, and Asia. This appendix summarizes highlights of several such interventions. In all cases, IQM tools were provided over a several month period at the host organization. (*Full reports on these and other client interventions are available through HeartMath.*)

GLOBAL OIL COMPANY (EUROPEAN SENIOR MANAGEMENT TEAM)

Estimates of how much stress costs the U.K. economy vary from £3.7 billion to £11 billion a year. The International Labor Organization estimates that inefficiencies arising from stress cost up to 10% of the country's gross national product.

Two years ago, a joint Institute for Personnel Development (IPD)/ Institute of Occupational Health survey of nearly 2,000 personnel managers placed stress at the top of the list of occupational health research priorities. A survey of 200 personnel managers at a Sedgwick Noble Lowndes HR conference last year indicated that 66% believed that stress was an area that required special budgeting, although only 2% of respondents' companies had policies to tackle it. The Trades Union Congress (TUC), which surveyed 7,000 health and safety officers last year, found that more than two thirds said stress was their biggest concern.

In 1994, Ashridge Management College surveyed 400 managers at all levels. The results showed that 77% said that their work was a source of stress, 63% said that their work conflicted with their personal life, and nearly 50% had fears about job security, were disillusioned about the lack of career opportunities, and regularly worked more than 60 hours a week.

The Staff Council of this oil company reported increasing levels of stress within the organization. It also emphasized that stress is "very much a business issue" and a stress initiative should be a "natural extension of the company's role in protecting the safety of employees." The company's chief medical officer emphasized that line managers "have a responsibility for the health of their staff."

As a result of these statistics the oil company initiated a series of pilot studies over the last 18 months to determine what could be done to improve the health and well-being of the workforce. The seven separate studies involved over 150 employees being trained in inner quality management, led by Dr. Alan Watkins and Chris Sawicki of Hunter-Kane, Ltd.

Study Design

This study reports on the results of the IQM program attended by the European senior management team with HSE (health, safety, and environment) responsibilities. At the beginning of the IQM program all participants completed the Personal and Organizational Quality Assessment (POQA). Six weeks after the IQM program all attendees completed the POQA again.

POQA Results

The POQA has 80 items scaled to represent 12 constructs. Each question has five potential responses: almost never, rarely, occasionally, often, and most of the time; or alternatively, strongly disagree, disagree, neutral, agree, and strongly agree. The main findings are presented in Tables A–1 to A–8.

TABLE A–1   Stress Symptoms (often or most of the time)

	Baseline	*After 6 weeks*
I feel uneasy	30%	11%
I feel annoyed	10%	0%
I feel blue	10%	0%
I often feel guilty	10%	0%
I feel unhappy	0%	0%
I feel depressed	0%	0%
I feel sad	0%	0%
I feel mad	0%	0%

TABLE A–2 Physical Symptoms of Stress (often or most of the time)

	Baseline	*After 6 weeks*
I feel tense	50%	22%
I have aches and pains	50%	11%
I experience sleeplessness	30%	11%
I experience palpitations	20%	0%
I feel well	70%	89%

TABLE A–3 Positive Effects (often or most of the time)

	Baseline	*After 6 weeks*
I feel focused	70%	100%
I feel clearheaded	70%	100%
I feel cared for	50%	78%
I feel peaceful	60%	78%
I feel relaxed	50%	78%
I feel satisfied	60%	78%
I feel calm	80%	89%
I feel energetic	80%	89%
I feel lively	80%	100%
I feel healthy	90%	100%
I feel happy	70%	89%
I forgive others	80%	89%
Caring for others drains me	30%	22%

TABLE A–4 Communication (agree/strongly agree)

	Baseline	*After 6 weeks*
We listen to each other	50%	89%
We communicate well	60%	78%
Our meetings are well organized	30%	44%
I listen closely to coworkers	90%	89%
I understand others	90%	100%

TABLE A–5 Goals (agree or strongly agree)

	Baseline	*After 6 weeks*
My own and organization's goals are same	60%	78%
My work objectives are very specific	40%	44%

TABLE A–6 Productivity (agree/strongly agree)

	Baseline	*After 6 weeks*
My work produces excellent results	70%	89%
I am efficient	80%	100%
I accomplish my work objectives	80%	100%
I am creative	80%	89%

TABLE A–7   Work Satisfaction (agree/strongly agree)

	Baseline	After 6 weeks
I am satisfied with my duties	50%	89%
I like my job	60%	89%
I feel good about what I do	70%	89%
Home and work conflict	70%	56%
I feel like quitting my job	20%	11%

TABLE A–8   Decision Making (agree or strongly agree)

	Baseline	After 6 weeks
I am guided by logic	80%	100%
I am guided by intuition	60%	67%

GLOBAL TECHNOLOGY COMPANY

One of the world's largest and most profitable technology companies recognized that the value of employee retention and high productivity, especially in its engineering staff, was a critical strategy for future growth and continued leadership. Thirty engineers and support staff members, from a design group working on the development of a key next generation computer chip, participated in the three-month IQM intervention. A control group of 30 engineers and support staff members from the same division were used for comparison.

Highlights

Tables A–9 and A–10 show the percentage of respondents who answered almost never or rarely to questions on personal stress and attitude, as well as those who answered often or most of the time. The columns indicate a baseline done before training and results after training (four months later). Note in particular the dramatic shifts in the frequency of feeling calm, cheerful, exhausted, and relaxed and problems with sleeplessness.

TABLE A–9   Personal Stress and Attitude (almost never or rarely)

	Baseline	After 4 months
Mentally alert	21%	15%
Satisfied	14%	5%
Calm	28%	0%
Cheerful	11%	0%

TABLE A-10 Personal Stress and Attitude (often or most of the time)

	Baseline	*After 4 months*
Uneasy	17%	0%
Exhausted	59%	25%
Energetic	48%	61%
Relaxed	34%	60%
Depressed	17%	0%
Sleeplessness	21%	5%

Tables A–11 and A–12 on workplace effectiveness were answered by a percentage of respondents as either somewhat or strongly disagree or somewhat or strongly agree. Both baseline and posttraining data are shown. The client was particularly pleased with the improvement in responses to "Our meetings at work are well organized" and "I feel like leaving this organization." In this organization, the cost of replacing a single engineer can run $75,000–100,000 at a minimum.

TABLE A-11 Workplace Effectiveness (disagree somewhat or strongly)

	Baseline	*After 4 months*
Supervisor and I communicate well	14%	5%
I am creative at work	14%	0%
Conflict in work and personal priorities	48%	56%
Produce excellent results	10%	0%

TABLE A-12 Workplace Effectiveness (agree somewhat or strongly)

	Baseline	*After 4 months*
Our meetings at work are well organized	31%	50%
I feel like leaving this organization	28%	16%

CALIFORNIA STATE AGENCY #1

The Legal Support Services Division of a large California government agency supports the work of more than 600 lawyers statewide. Members of the Legal Support Services Division work under significant levels of stress and time pressure. California, the most populous state in the nation, carries one of the largest caseloads of civil and criminal litigation. Tens of thousands of cases at various stages of adjudication require careful research, development, planning, scheduling, tracking, and legal briefs at every step of the process. Missing, inaccurate, or incomplete documents or briefs and lack of proper procedure at any stage of the legal process can compromise the high standards for due process and due diligence and void the state's legal standing in the eyes of the court. Much of the mountain of logistical details of day to day case management and the responsibility for its timeliness and accuracy is handled by the Legal Support Services Division.

From within the Division, in Los Angeles, San Diego, San Francisco, and Sacramento, 161 people participated in an Inner Quality Management program in Fall 1997. Each participant received a one day training and a half day follow-up session about 30 days after the initial training. The Personal and Organizational Quality Assessment was administered prior to the first day of training and 30–45 days after the follow-up session.

Highlights

Statistically significant change in the feelings of the participants was seen in several areas. In addition to the areas of workplace effectiveness shown in Table A–13, other areas showed positive shifts as well. The stars indicate the level of statistical significance; the more stars, the greater the significance.

TABLE A–13   Workplace Effectiveness

Statistically significant increases	*Statistically significant decreases*
Social support ***	Sadness ***
Peacefulness ***	Fatigue ***
Happiness ***	Depression ***
Physical energy ***	Anxiety ***
Physical health **	Anger ***
Productivity *	Tension ***
Work/personal life balance *	Indigestion ***
Job satisfaction *	Body aches ***
Mental clarity *	Sleeplessness ***
Rapid heartbeats **	Overcaring **

Noteworthy Details

Tables A–14 to A–16 show the percentage of respondents who answered positively to these measures of workplace effectiveness.

TABLE A-14   Personal Attitude (often or most of the time)

	Baseline	*After 6 weeks*
Mentally alert	81%	85%
Satisfied	56%	73%
Cheerful	73%	82%
Energetic	48%	61%
Relaxed	40%	60%
Depressed	12%	3%

TABLE A-15   Productivity (agree somewhat or strongly)

	Baseline	*After 6 weeks*
I am creative at work	61%	72%
Conflict in work and personal priorities	29%	21%
Produce excellent results	80%	88%

TABLE A-16   Communication (agree somewhat or strongly)

	Baseline	*After 6 weeks*
Supervisor and I communicate well	13%	8%

CALIFORNIA STATE AGENCY #2

At another California government agency, 118 employees completed the Personal and Organizational Quality Assessment (POQA) pretest on September 9 and 12, 1997, prior to the IQM training. The employees were divided into two groups, an experimental group and a waiting control group. HeartMath conducted IQM wellness training for the experimental group in three tracks of roughly 20 people each.

Comparison with Other Employees

The POQA was completed by more than 600 employees of ten organizations, representing a sample diverse in age, gender, and job level. Scores of the agency's employees were compared to the sample group. The comparison with the norm database (norm = 50%) is just one method and option of analyzing the data.

Prior to this training, the experimental group participants were

- Higher than the norm in global negative affect, sadness, anger, distress, rapid heartbeats, fatigue, sleeplessness, anxiety, body aches, indigestion, social support, and job satisfaction.

- Lower than the norm in peacefulness, vitality, mental clarity, goal clarity, and productivity.
- At the norm in depression, positive affect, and communication effectiveness.

Prior to this training, waiting control group participants were

- Higher than the norm in global negative affect, depression, anger, distress, positive affect, communication effectiveness, sleeplessness, indigestion, and social support.
- Lower than the norm in peacefulness, goal clarity, rapid heartbeats, and productivity.
- At the norm in sadness, fatigue, vitality, mental clarity, job satisfaction, anxiety, and body aches.

Tables A–17 and A–18 show statistically significant changes that occurred following the training. (The significance levels are * indicates $p = .05$; ** indicates $p = .01$; *** indicates $p = .001$. The more stars, the greater the significance.) Other factors showed directional but not statistically significant shifts, including positive affect, mental clarity, warmheartedness, caring outlook, and work-personal life balance.

TABLE A–17   Experimental Group Posttraining Results

	Control	*Target*	*Level*
Global negative affect	-9%	-22%	***
Depression	-4%	-26%	***
Fatigue	-3%	-24%	***
Peacefulness	2%	23%	***
Sleeplessness	-5%	-24%	***
Vitality	-1%	10%	**
Anger	-10%	-20%	*
Distress	-12%	-21%	*
Sadness	-7%	-22%	*
Goal clarity	4%	9%	*
Productivity	-2%	4%	*
Anxiety	-9%	-21%	*
Rapid heartbeats	4%	-19%	*

TABLE A–18   Waiting Control Group Posttraining Results

	Result	*Level*
Global negative affect	-17%	***
Anger	-17%	***
Distress	-17%	***
Depression	-18%	***
Sadness	-14%	***
Fatigue	-12%	***
Peacefulness	9%	***
Social support	10%	***
Anxiety	-18%	***
Indigestion	-14%	***
Job satisfaction	7%	*
Goal clarity	7%	*
Sleeplessness	-13%	*
Body aches	-10%	*

Sample of Pre-, Post-, and Post-Posttraining Data

Figure A–1 shows changes in three constructs: fatigue, productivity, and peacefulness. Data were collected prior to experimental or waiting control

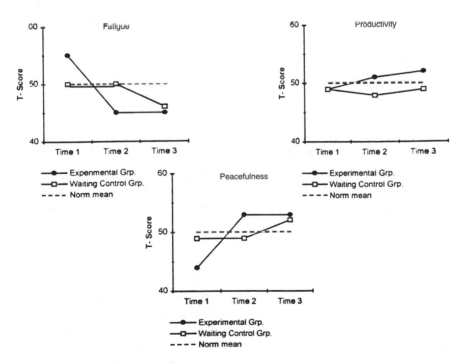

FIGURE A–1   Changes in three constructs.

group training, two weeks after the experimental group received training (the waiting control group received no training), and again nine weeks later, which was two weeks after the waiting control group received its training.

Table A–19 shows data on the experimental group collected two and nine weeks after training, showing benefits that sustain over time.

TABLE A–19   Experimental Group Posttraining Results

Construct	After 2 weeks	Level	After 9 weeks	Level
Global negative affect	-23%	*	-25%	*
Anger	-21%	*	-23%	*
Distress	-22%	*	-27%	*
Depression	-28%	*	-23%	*
Sadness	-24%	*	-26%	*
Fatigue	-26%	*	-25%	*
Positive affect	5%	*	3%	
Peacefulness	-23%	*	25%	*
Vitality	11%	*	13%	*
Social support	11%	*	11%	*
Mental clarity	3%		5%	
Job satisfaction	6%		9%	*
Goal clarity	10%	*	10%	*
Productivity	4%	*	5%	*
Communication effectiveness	6%	*	6%	*
Sleeplessness	-26%	*	-26%	*
Anxiety	-23%	*	-28%	*
Body aches	-19%	*	-22%	*
Indigestion	-15%	*	-24%	*
Rapid heartbeats	-21%	*	-18%	*

Blood Pressure Study

Among the 11 of 106 subjects who showed stage 1 hypertension in blood pressure measures, 4 of 6 individuals with high diastolic blood pressure had dropped into normal values, while 6 of 8 individuals with high systolic pressure dropped into normal values. Statistical analysis could not be performed due to the small number of subjects with high blood pressure.

GOVERNMENT CONSULTING FIRM

Fifteen participants from a large government consulting firm completed the Personal and Organizational Quality Assessment pretest on October 27, 1997, prior to the training. Participants received a two-day IQM training program and were encouraged to practice the tools and techniques for the next month. Twelve participants completed the posttest, which was received at the end of December 1997. Analysis was conducted on twelve matched pairs of pre- and posttraining data.

Prior to this training, participants were

- Lower than the norm in the following *positive aspects*: positive affect, peacefulness, goal clarity, and productivity.
- Lower than the norm in the following *negative aspects*: anger, distress, depression, sadness, fatigue, anxiety, body aches, indigestion, and rapid heartbeats.
- Higher than the norm in vitality and mental clarity.
- At the norm in social support, communication effectiveness, job satisfaction, and sleeplessness.

Table A–20 shows statistically significant (where * indicates $p = .05$ and ** indicates $p = .01$; the more stars, the greater the significance) changes after training. Other factors that showed positive directional but not statistically significant shifts included positive affect, peacefulness, anger, distress, fatigue, communication effectiveness, job satisfaction, and sleeplessness.

TABLE A–20   Results of Training

Construct	Result	Level
Depression	-19%	*
Goal clarity	18%	*
Productivity	9%	**

Positive directional changes that may have achieved statistical significance in a larger group did not reach significance in so small a sample size. Therefore, they are reflected in the tables and two-bin analysis that follow.

Two-Bin Analysis

There are a number of ways of analyzing the data. Taking a group average and seeing the pre- and posttraining change is the statistically preferred method. However, this averaging hides some of the significant changes within a group. Therefore, the data are subdivided into the top two "bins" and compared with the other three "bins." This not only makes some subgroup changes more obvious but also reflects the fact that individuals on the extremes of the scale are the ones most likely to have the greatest impact on the whole group.

Participants responded to multiple choice questions that gave five options of responses. These responses are separated into two "bins." For example, almost never, rarely, sometimes, often, and most of the time are five possible responses to the query of how often one feels fatigue. The top two bins would then be almost never and rarely, the bottom two bins would be often and most of the time.

A complete report based on this kind of analysis is provided in the reports. Tables A–21 to A–25 show a few of the highlights.

TABLE A–21   Performance (somewhat/strongly agree)

	Baseline	After training
I accomplish my objectives at work	75%	92%
I am productive at work	75%	92%
I am efficient at work	55%	83%
My work produces excellent results	67%	92%
I feel clearheaded (often/most of the time)	83%	92%
I feel focused (often/most of the time)	67%	92%

TABLE A–22   Goal Clarity (somewhat/strongly agree)

	Baseline	After training
The organization's goals are clear to me	42%	75%
I understand the priorities of my work goals	83%	100%
My work objectives are very specific	17%	58%
My goals and the organization's goals are the same	33%	58%

TABLE A–23   Relationships at Work (somewhat/strongly agree)

	Baseline	After training
We listen carefully to each other at work	33%	58%
My supervisor and I communicate well	58%	75%
People feel free to express their opinions	67%	83%
I listen closely to my coworkers	75%	100%
I communicate to higher ups when needed	92%	100%
I feel cared for	50%	58%
I feel appreciated	67%	75%

TABLE A-24   Physical Symptoms of Stress (often/most of the time)

	Baseline	*After training*
I feel exhausted	9%	0%
I feel physically fit	42%	58%
I suffer from sleeplessness	17%	8%
I suffer from body aches	33%	25%

TABLE A-25   Emotional Stress (often/most of the time)

	Baseline	*After training*
I feel unhappy	8%	0%
I feel depressed	8%	0%
I feel worried	8%	0%
I feel angry	17%	8%
I feel anxious	17%	8%
I feel peaceful	42%	67%
I feel relaxed	42%	75%
I feel cheerful	50%	75%
I feel happy	58%	75%
I feel caring	42%	58%

ORGANIZATIONAL COHERENCE SURVEY DATA FOR A LARGE U.S. GOVERNMENT AGENCY

The Organizational Coherence Survey (OCS) methodology described in Chapter Nine allows organizations to pinpoint areas of organizational incoherence and, with the assistance of IQM tools, design effective solutions. What follows are the pre- and posttraining results from a large U.S. government agency that used the OCS in conjunction with an IQM intervention. The percentage change for each question in the survey is listed in Tables A–26 through A–31.

- The baseline column represents the percentage of the respondents who felt the given item had a high priority of needing to be improved.
- The after training column represents the percentage of respondents still feeling it needed improvement.
- A negative number in the change column represents organizational improvement for that item.

TABLE A–26   Taking Care of Business

	Baseline	After training	Change
The senior management looks after its customers well	30%	0%	**−100%**
The senior management team looks after its people well	45%	25%	**−44%**
The senior management looks after the organization's financial matters well	30%	0%	**−100%**
Your manager looks after your customers well	11%	0%	**−100%**
Your manager looks after you and your team well	39%	8%	**−79%**
Your manager looks after your organization's financial matters well	25%	0%	**−100%**
My colleagues and I look after our "customer" well	10%	8%	**−20%**
My colleagues and I look after each other well	10%	17%	**70%**
My colleagues and I look after the organization's financial matters well	16%	8%	**−50%**
Your customer service (frontline) people look after their "customers" well	16%	0%	**−100%**
Your customer service (frontline) people look after your colleagues well	25%	8%	**−68%**
Your customer service (frontline) people look after the organization's financial matters well	21%	0%	**−100%**

TABLE A–27   A Sense of Well-Being at Work

	Baseline	After training	Change
Feeling you are a part of this organization	25%	17%	**−32%**
Doing work that is worthwhile	20%	8%	**−60%**
Being part of a great team	20%	0%	**−100%**
Feeling confident in your work	5%	0%	**−100%**
Feeling free to speak your mind without fear of reprisal	53%	8%	**−85%**
Feeling you can cope with the demands of your work	20%	8%	**−60%**
Feeling cared for by the organization in which you work	47%	25%	**−47%**
Feeling cared for by your manager	42%	17%	**−60%**

TABLE A–28   Relationships at Work

	Baseline	After training	Change
Your relationships with senior managers in this organization	21%	8%	–62%
Your relationship to your manager	30%	17%	–43%
Your relationship with your customer service (frontline) colleagues	15%	0%	–100%
Your relationship with your customers	15%	0%	–100%
Your relationship with colleagues in other departments	0%	0%	0%
Your relationship with your colleagues in your department or team	10%	0%	–100%
Your relationship with colleagues of the opposite sex	0%	0%	0%

TABLE A–29   Managing People

	Baseline	After training	Change
Management that treats everyone fairly	55%	33%	–40%
Management that clearly tells you what is expected of you	32%	33%	3%
Management that makes reasonable demands of you	32%	17%	–47%
Management that is interested in your welfare at work	45%	25%	–44%
Management that is interested in your welfare beyond the workplace	45%	27%	–40%
Management that honors everyone as equals, both men and women	47%	25%	–47%
Management that is receptive to your suggestions	50%	25%	–50%
Management that involves you in decisions that affect you	65%	50%	–23%
Management that appreciates your contribution	32%	33%	3%
Management that is willing to listen to any complaint you may have	45%	25%	–44%
Management that does its best for the organization	35%	25%	–29%
Management that gives you the freedom to contribute fully without interference	35%	25%	–29%
Management that trusts you	45%	45%	0%

TABLE A–30   Managing the Organization

	Baseline	After training	Change
Your salary or wages	75%	67%	−11%
The benefits you receive	30%	9%	−70%
Your physical environment at work	25%	36%	44%
Your workload	15%	18%	20%
Your career prospects	50%	45%	−10%
Your training and development opportunities	50%	33%	−34%
The social events at work	21%	25%	19%
Communication at work	47%	17%	−64%
The policies for managing people	50%	33%	−34%
The customer service procedures	20%	17%	−15%
The budgeting process	37%	33%	−11%
The appraisal process	35%	33%	−6%
The way in which good performers are recognized	65%	50%	−23%
The way in which poor performers are handled	55%	58%	5%
The resources provided to you to do your job	35%	17%	−51%
The reputation of your organization	15%	0%	−100%
Your organization's long-term prospects	20%	0%	−100%

TABLE A–31   The Working Climate

	Baseline	After training	Change
My manager supports me at work	30%	17%	−43%
My manager is very clear about the contribution he or she wants me to make	30%	8%	−73%
I know my contribution really makes a difference to my team	15%	8%	−47%
My manager readily acknowledges the contribution I make	37%	17%	−54%
My manager likes me to speak out freely at work	37%	25%	−32%
My work is challenging	26%	17%	−35%

Glossary

amygdala The key subcortical brain center that coordinates behavioral, neural, immunological, and hormonal responses to environmental threats. It also serves as the storehouse of emotional memory within the brain. Its function is to compare incoming signals from the environment with stored emotional memories. In this way, the amygdala makes instantaneous decisions about the threat level of incoming sensory information. Due to its extensive connections to the hypothalamus and other autonomic nervous system centers, the amygdala is able to activate the autonomic nervous system and emotional responses before the higher brain centers receive the sensory information.

appreciation An active emotional state in which one has clear perception or recognition of the quality or magnitude of that to be thankful for. Appreciation also leads to improved physiological balance, as measured in cardiovascular and immune system function.

asset-deficit balance sheet An IQM tool for evaluating the assets and deficits of any project, pending decision, employee performance, or for a wide variety of other uses. In conjunction with freeze-frame, the asset-deficit balance sheet can yield surprising insights and clarity on personal and professional issues.

autonomic nervous system The portion of the nervous system that regulates most of the body's involuntary functions, including mean heart rate, the movements of the gastrointestinal tract, and the secretions of many glands. Consisting of two branches (the sympathetic and parasympathetic), the autonomic nervous system regulates over 90% of the body's

---

Note: Freeze-frame, inner quality management (IQM), heart lock-in, HeartMapping, Heart-Math, and emotional virus are registered trademarks of the Institute of HeartMath.

functions. The heart, brain, immune, hormonal, respiratory, and digestive systems are all connected by this network of nerves.

balance   Stability, equilibrium, or the even distribution of weight on each side
of a vertical axis. The term also used to denote mental or emotional stability.

baroreceptor system   Nerve receptors within the heart and arteries that
are sensitive to pressure changes and transmit neural information to the
brain to help regulate short-term blood pressure. The neural signals sent
via the baroreceptor system have numerous effects on the brain and are
able to alter perception in the higher brain centers.

cardiac coherence   A mode of cardiac function in which the heart's rhythmic and electrical output is highly ordered. HeartMath research has shown
that positive emotions such as love, care, and appreciation increase the
coherence in the heart's rhythmic beating patterns. During states of cardiac
coherence, brain wave patterns have been shown to entrain with heart rate
variability patterns, nervous system balance and immune function are
enhanced, and the body functions with increased harmony and efficiency.

cardiovascular system   The system in the human body constituting the
heart and the blood vessels.

caring   This is an inner attitude or feeling of true service, with no agenda
or attachment to the outcome. Sincere caring is rejuvenating for both the
giver and receiver.

cell   The smallest structural unit of an organism that is capable of independent functioning. A complex unit of protoplasm usually with a nu-
cleus, cytoplasm, and an enclosing membrane.

cellular   Containing or consisting of cells.

cerebral cortex   The most highly developed area of the brain, which governs all higher order human capabilities such as language, creativity, and
problem solving. The cortex, like other brain centers, continues to develop
new neural circuits or networks throughout life.

chaos   Great disorder or confusion; incoherence. Comes from the Greek
word *khaos*, meaning unformed matter. The disordered state held to have
existed before the ordered universe.

coherence   Logical connectedness, internal order, or harmony among the
components of a system. The term also can refer to the tendency toward
increased order in the informational content of a system or in the information flow between systems. In physics, two or more wave forms that

are phase-locked together so that their energy is constructive are described as coherent. Coherence also can be attributed to a single wave form, in which case it denotes an ordered or constructive distribution of power content. Recently, the scientific interest in coherence in living systems has been growing. When a system is coherent, virtually no energy is wasted because of the internal synchronization among the parts. In organizations, increased coherence enables the emergence of new levels of creativity, cooperation, productivity, and quality on all levels.

coherent communication Communication between individuals that is seamless, focused, and free of inner mind static. The coherent sharing of information is a key to business effectiveness and a primary way to reduce stress. Coherent communication is Dynamic 2 of inner quality management and involves achieving understanding first, listening nonjudgmentally, listening for the essence, and authentic dialogue.

cortical inhibition A desynchronization or reduction of cortical activity, believed to result from the erratic heart rhythms and resulting neural signals transmitted from the heart to the brain during stress and negative emotional states. This condition can manifest in less efficient decision-making capability, leading to poor or shortsighted decisions, ineffective or impulsive communication, and reduced physical coordination.

cortisol A hormone produced by the adrenal glands during stressful situations, commonly known as the *stress hormone*. Excessive cortisol, while an essential hormone, has many harmful effects on the body and can destroy brain cells in the hippocampus, a region of the brain associated with learning and memory.

DHEA An essential hormone produced by the adrenal glands known as the *vitality hormone* because of its antiaging properties. As the body's natural antagonist of the glucocorticoid hormones, such as cortisol, DHEA reverses many of the unfavorable physiological effects of excessive stress. It is the precursor of the sex hormones estrogen and testosterone; and its varied functions include stimulating the immune system, lowering cholesterol levels, and promoting bone and muscle deposition. Low DHEA levels have been reported in patients with many major diseases.

DNA A complex molecule, found in every cell of the body, that carries the genetic information or blueprint determining individual hereditary characteristics. An essential component of all living matter, DNA is a nucleic acid consisting of two long chains of nucleotides twisted into a double helix and is the major constituent of chromosomes.

electromagnetic signal   In physics, the term is used to describe a wave propagated through space or matter by the oscillating electric and magnetic field generated by an oscillating electric charge. In the human body, the heart is the most powerful source of electromagnetic energy.

emotion   A strong feeling. Any of various complex reactions with both mental and physical manifestations, as love, joy, sorrow, or anger. Emotional energy is neutral, attaching itself to positive or negative thoughts to create *emotions*.

emotional virus   A metaphorical term used to describe the result of emotional mismanagement within an organization. This virus thrives in the gap between our expectations and the reality we perceive. The internal imbalances created by an emotional virus perpetuate ongoing distortion and obstacles until resolved. This concept is part of Dynamic 3, boosting the organizational climate.

entrainment   A phenomenon seen throughout nature, whereby systems or organisms exhibiting periodic behavior will fall into sync and oscillate at the same frequency and phase. A common example of this phenomenon is the synchronization of two or more pendulum clocks placed near each other. In human beings, the entrainment of different oscillating biological systems to the primary frequency of the heart rhythms often is observed during positive emotional states. This state represents a highly efficient mode of bodily function and is associated with heightened clarity, buoyancy, and inner peace. Entrained teams are those that operate with a higher degree of synchronization, efficiency, and coherent communication.

epinephrine   An adrenal hormone that stimulates the heart, increases muscular strength and endurance, constricts the blood vessels, and raises blood pressure. Also known as adrenaline.

freeze-frame   A key tool used in Dynamic 1, internal self-management, that consists of consciously disengaging one's mental and emotional reactions to either external or internal events. The center of attention then is shifted from the mind and emotions to the physical area around the heart while focus is on a positive emotion such as love or appreciation. This tool is designed to release and prevent stress through stopping inefficient reactions in the moment to provide a window of opportunity for new, intuitive perspectives. Freeze-frame has numerous applications for creative thinking, innovation, and planning, as well as improving overall health and well-being.

frequency   The number of times any action, occurrence, or event is repeated in a given period. In physics, it is the number of periodic oscillations, vibrations, or waves per unit of time, usually expressed in cycles per second. Human intelligence operates within a large bandwidth of frequencies.

heart A hollow, muscular organ in vertebrates that keeps the blood in circulation throughout the body by means of its rhythmic contractions and relaxations. It is the body's central and most powerful energy generator and rhythmic oscillator; a complex, self-organized information processing system with its own functional "little brain" that continually transmits neural, hormonal, rhythmic, and pressure messages to the brain.

heart-brain entrainment A state in which very low frequency brain waves and heart rhythms are frequency locked (entrained). This phenomenon has been associated with significant shifts in perception and heightened intuitive awareness.

heart intelligence A term coined to express the concept of the heart as an intelligent system with the power to bring both the emotional and mental systems into balance and coherence.

heart rate variability (HRV) The normally occurring beat-to-beat changes in heart rate. Analysis of HRV is an important tool used to assess the function and balance of the autonomic nervous system. HRV is considered a key indicator of aging and cardiac and overall health.

hologram A three-dimensional image made of light, created by an interference pattern of two interacting laser beams recorded on photographic film. *Holo* means complete or total. *Gram* means a writing, drawing, or record of the image.

holographic principle A unique property of a hologram is that every portion of the image contains all the information necessary to produce the whole. The holographic principle that "every part contains the whole" is mirrored in the cellular structure of the human body, whereby every cell contains the information necessary to create a duplicate of the entire organism.

hormonal system A hormone is a substance produced by living cells that circulates in the body fluids and produces a specific effect on the activity of cells remote from its point of origin. The hormonal system is made up of the many hormones that act and interact throughout the body to regulate many metabolic functions, and the cells, organs, and tissues that manufacture them.

immune system The integrated bodily system of organs, tissues, cells, and cell products, such as antibodies, that differentiates "self" from "nonself" within our body and neutralizes potentially pathogenic organisms or substances that cause disease. The organizational "immune system" is built on the core values known to enhance personal fulfillment and well-being, eliminating the emotional viruses that can permeate and destroy the effectiveness and coherence of the organization.

insight   The faculty of seeing into inner character or underlying truth and apprehending the true nature of a thing; a clear understanding or awareness.

internal coherence   A deep state of internal self-management in which one is generating increased order and harmony in the physical, mental, and emotional systems. In this state, the cardiovascular, immune, hormonal, and nervous systems function with heightened efficiency. States of internal coherence are associated with reduced emotional reactivity, greater mental clarity, creativity, adaptability, and flexibility.

internal self-management   Dynamic 1 of inner quality management, the active process of reducing and neutralizing one's automatic mental and emotional reactions to events or situations, instead of being their unwitting victim.

intuition   Intelligence and understanding that bypasses the logical, linear cognitive processes. The faculty of direct knowing as if by instinct, without conscious reasoning. Pure, untaught, inferential knowledge with a keen and quick insight; common sense.

intuitive intelligence   A type of intelligence distinct from cognitive processes, which derives from the consistent use and application of one's intuition. Research is showing that the human capacity to meet life's challenges with fluidity and grace is based not on knowledge, logic, or reason alone but also includes the ability to make intuitive decisions. HeartMath research suggests that, with training and practice, human beings can develop a high level of operational intuitive intelligence.

intuitive listening   A means of communicating that involves deeply listening to the other person while maintaining a neutral and emotionally balanced inner attitude. This communication technique enables us more readily to understand the essence of a conversation and often to perceive additional levels of subtlety within the information being communicated.

limbic system   A group of cortical and subcortical brain structures involved in emotional processing and certain aspects of memory. These structures include the hypothalamus, thalamus, hippocampus, and amygdala, among others.

nervous system　The system of cells, tissues, and organs that coordinates and regulates the body's responses to internal and external stimuli. In vertebrates, the nervous system is made up of the brain and spinal cord, nerves, ganglia, and nerve centers in receptor and effector organs.

neural circuits　Neural pathways consisting of interconnected neurons in the brain and body through which specific information is processed. Research has shown that many of these neural connections develop in early childhood, based on our experiences and the type of stimulation we receive. Likewise, even later in life, different neural circuits can either be reinforced or atrophy, depending on how frequently we use them. Specific circuits form and are reinforced through repeated behavior, and in this way both physical and emotional responses can become "hard-wired" and automatic in our system.

neuron　Any of the cells that make up the nervous system, consisting of a nucleated cell body with one or more dendrites and a single axon. Neurons are the fundamental structural and functional units of nervous tissue.

neutral　In physics, having a net electric charge of zero. With reference to machinery, it means a position in which a set of gears is disengaged. In human beings, it is a state in which we have consciously disengaged from our automatic mental and emotional reactions to a situation or issue in order to gain a wider perspective.

organizational incoherence　A state resulting from accumulated internal noise, turmoil, pressure, and conflict among the individuals that make up an organization. This state is characterized by distorted perception, high levels of emotional reactivity, and decreased efficiency, cooperation, and productivity.

overcaring　The result of caring taken to an inefficient extreme and crossing the line into anxiety and worry. Overcaring is one of the greatest inhibitors of personal and organizational resilience. It has become so natural that people often do not know they are experiencing it, because it postures itself as caring. As individuals learn to identify and plug the leaks in their own personal systems caused by overcaring, they stop draining energy and effectiveness, personally and organizationally.

parasympathetic　The branch of the autonomic nervous system that slows or relaxes bodily functions. This part of the nervous system is analogous to the brakes in a car. Many known diseases and disorders are associated with diminished parasympathetic function.

perception   The act or faculty of apprehending by means of the senses; the way in which an individual views a situation or event. How we perceive an event or an issue underlies how we think, feel, and react to that event or issue. Our level of awareness determines our initial perception of an event and our ability to extract meaning from the available data. Research is showing that when the mind's logic and intellect are harmoniously integrated with the heart's intuitive intelligence, our perception of situations can change significantly, offering wider perspectives and new possibilities.

quantum theory   A mathematical theory that describes the behavior of physical systems. It is particularly useful in studying the energetic characteristics of matter at the subatomic level. One of the key principles of quantum theory is that we are not merely observing reality but participating in the way we create our reality.

solar plexus   The large network of nerves located in the area of the belly just below the sternum, named for the raylike patterns of its nerve fibers. This neural network is distributed throughout the tissue lining the esophagus, stomach, small intestine, and colon, sometimes called the *enteric nervous system* or *gut brain*.

stress   Pressure, strain, or a sense of inner turmoil resulting from our perceptions and reactions to events or conditions. A state of negative emotional arousal, usually associated with feelings of discomfort or anxiety that we attribute to our circumstances or situation.

sympathetic   The branch of the autonomic nervous system that speeds up bodily functions, preparing us for mobilization and action. The fight or flight response to stress activates the sympathetic nervous system and causes the contraction of blood vessels and a rise in heart rate and many other bodily responses. This part of the nervous system is analogous to the gas pedal in a car.

time shift   Used here to describe the time saved when we are able to disengage from an inefficient mental or emotional reaction and make a more efficient choice. Time shifting stops a chain-link reaction of time and energy waste and catapults people into a new domain of time management, where there is greater energy efficiency and fulfillment.

Selected Reading

Autry, James A. *Love and Profit: The Art of Caring Leadership*. New York: William Morrow and Company, 1991.

Block, Peter. *Stewardship: Choosing Service over Self-Interest*. San Francisco: Berrett-Koehler Publishers, 1993.

Bracey, Hyler, Jack Rosenblum, Aubrey Sanford, and Roy Trueblood. *Managing from the Heart*. New York: Dell, 1995.

Champy, James. *Reengineering Management: The Mandate for New Leadership*. New York: HarperCollins, 1995.

Childre, Doc. *Self-Empowerment: The Heart Approach to Stress Management*. Boulder Creek, CA: Planetary Publications, 1992.

Childre, Doc. *Freeze-Frame: One-Minute Stress Management*. Boulder Creek, CA: Planetary Publications, 1994; Revised edition, 1998.

Childre, Doc, and Sara Paddison. *HeartMath Discovery Program: Daily Readings and Self-Discovery Exercises for Creating a More Rewarding Life*. Boulder Creek, CA: Planetary Publications, 1998.

Collins, James C., and Jerry I. Porras. *Built to Last: Successful Habits of Visionary Companies*. New York: HarperBusiness, 1994.

Conner, Daryl R. *Managing at the Speed of Change: How Resilient Managers Succeed and Prosper Where Others Fail*. New York: Villard Books, 1993.

Cooper, Robert, and Ayman Sawaf. *Executive EQ: Emotional Intelligence in Leadership and Organizations*. New York: Grosset/Putnam, 1997.

Corbin, Carolyn. *Conquering Corporate Codependence: Lifeskills for Making It Within or Without the Corporation*. Englewood Cliffs, NJ: Prentice-Hall, 1993.

Covey, Stephen R. *The Seven Habits of Highly Effective People: Powerful Lessons in Personal Change*. New York: Simon and Schuster, 1989.

Cox, Allan. *Straight Talk for Monday Morning: Creating Values, Vision, and Vitality at Work*. New York: John Wiley and Sons, 1990.

Cox, Allan, and Julie Liesse. *Redefining Corporate Soul: Linking Purpose and People*. Chicago: Irwin Professional Publishing, 1996.

DePree, Max. *Leadership Is an Art*. New York: Dell, 1989.

DePree, Max. *Leadership Jazz*. New York: Dell, 1992.

Edvinsson, Leif, and Michael S. Malone. *Intellectual Capital: Realizing Your Company's True Value by Finding Its Hidden Brainpower*. New York: Harper-Collins, 1997.

Farkas, Charles M., and Philippe DeBacker. *Maximum Leadership: The World's Leading CEOs Share Their Five Strategies for Success*. New York: Henry Holt and Company, 1996.

Frankl, Victor. *Man's Search for Meaning*. New York: Simon and Schuster, 1970.

Galvin, Robert W. *The Idea of Ideas*. Schaumburg, IL: Motorola University Press, 1991.

Gerzon, Mark. *A House Divided: Six Belief Systems Struggling for America's Soul*. New York: Putnam Books, 1996.

Gibson, Rowan, ed. *Rethinking the Future*. London: Nicholas Brealey Publishing, 1997.

Goleman, Daniel. *Emotional Intelligence: Why It Can Matter More than IQ*. New York: Bantam Books, 1995.

Hammond, Sue Annis. *Appreciative Inquiry*. Plano, TX: Kodiak Consulting, 1996.

Hawley, Jack. *Reawakening the Spirit of Work: The Power of Dharmic Management*. San Francisco: Berrett-Koehler Publishers, 1993.

Helgesen, Sally. *The Web of Inclusion*. New York: Doubleday, 1995.

Heskett, James L., W. Earl Sasser, Jr., and Leonard A. Schlesinger. *The Service-Profit Chain: How Leading Companies Link Profit and Growth to Loyalty, Satisfaction, and Value*. New York: The Free Press, 1997.

Hesselbein, Frances, Marshall Goldsmith, and Richard Beckhard. *The Leader of the Future*. San Francisco: Jossey-Bass, 1996.

Jaworski, Joseph. *Synchronicity: The Inner Path of Leadership*. San Francisco: Berrett-Koehler, 1996.

Johansen, Robert, and Rob Swigart. *Upsizing the Individual in the Downsized Organization: Managing in the Wake of Reengineering, Globalization, and Overwhelming Technological Change*. Reading, MA: Addison-Wesley Publishing, 1996.

Land, George, and Beth Jarman. *Breakpoint and Beyond: Mastering the Future Today*. New York: HarperBusiness, 1992.

Lebow, Rob. *A Journey into the Heroic Environment: Eight Principles That Lead to Greater Productivity, Quality, Job Satisfaction, and Profits*. Rocklin, CA: Prima Publishing, 1996.

McMaster, Michael D. *The Intelligence Advantage: Organising for Complexity*. Isle of Man, United Kingdom: Knowledge Based Development Company, Ltd., 1995.

O'Hara-Devereaux, Mary, and Robert Johansen. *Global Work: Bridging Distance, Culture and Time*. San Francisco: Jossey-Bass, 1994.

Osborne, David, and Ted Gaebler. *Reinventing Government: How the Entrepreneurial Spirit Is Transforming the Public Sector*. New York: Penguin Books, 1993.

O'Shea, James, and Charles Madigan. *Dangerous Company: The Consulting Powerhouses and the Businesses They Save and Ruin*. New York: Random House, 1997.

Paddison, Sara. *The Hidden Power of the Heart: Discovering an Unlimited Source of Intelligence*. Boulder Creek, CA: Planetary Publications, 1992.

Pearce, Joseph Chilton. *Evolution's End*. San Francisco: HarperCollins, 1992.

Peters, Tom. *Thriving on Chaos*. New York: Harper and Row, 1987.

Peters, Tom. *The Pursuit of Wow: Every Person's Guide to Topsy-Turvy Times*. New York: Vintage Books, 1994.

Popcorn, Faith, and Lys Marigold. *Clicking: Sixteen Trends to Future Fit Your Life, Your Work, and Your Business*. New York: HarperCollins, 1996.

Rechtschaffen, Stephan. *Time Shifting: Creating More Time to Enjoy Your Life*. New York: Doubleday, 1997.

Schultz, Howard, and Dori Jones Yang. *Pour Your Heart into It: How Starbucks Built a Company One Cup at a Time.* New York: Hyperion, 1997.

Srivastva, Suresh, David L. Cooperrider, and Associates. *Appreciative Management and Leadership: The Power of Positive Thought and Action in Organizations.* San Francisco: Jossey-Bass, 1990.

Taylor, Jim, and Watts Wacker, with Howard Means. *The 500 Year Delta: What Happens After What Comes Next.* New York: HarperCollins, 1997.

Tiller, William A. *Science and Human Transformation: Subtle Energies, Intentionality and Consciousness.* Walnut Creek, CA: Pavior Publishing, 1997.

Treacy, Michael, and Fred Wiersema. *The Discipline of Market Leaders: Choose Your Customers, Narrow Your Focus, Dominate Your Market.* Reading, MA: Addison-Wesley, 1995.

Ulrich, William M., and Ian S. Hayes. *The Year 2000 Software Crisis: Challenge of the Century.* Upper Saddle River, NJ: Prentice-Hall PTR, 1997.

Watkins, Alan. *Mind-Body Medicine: A Clinician's Guide to Psychoneuroimmunology.* London: Churchill Livingstone, 1997.

Wheatley, Margaret J. *Leadership and the New Science: Learning about Organization from an Orderly Universe.* San Francisco: Berrett-Koehler, 1992.

Wheatley, Margaret J., and Myron Kellner-Rogers. *A Simpler Way.* San Francisco: Berrett-Koehler Publishers, 1996.

Wylie, Janet C. *Chances and Choices: How Women Can Succeed in Today's Knowledge-Based Businesses.* Vienna, VA: EBW Press, 1996.

Index

Adaptability, of organizations, 127–128
Amygdala
  description of, 32
  effect on cardiovascular system, 38
  effect on perception, 32
  learning and, 38–39
Appreciation, of teams, 162–163
Asset-deficit balance sheet, 65–66
Atrial natriuretic factor, 142–143
Attention, 179
Authentic communication
  description of, 81
  elements of, 81
  requirements for, 82–83
Autonomic nervous system
  divisions of, 33, 34f
  stress and, 33–35

Balance
  description of, 77–78
  examples of, 78
  heart, 147
Body. *See* Human body
Body language, 83
Brain
  communication with heart, 36
  desynchronization of, 38
  first, 30, 30f
  functions of, based on anatomy, 30–32

gender differences, 140–141
  second, 31
  third, 31
Brain natriuretic factor, 142–143
Brown and Leigh study, of organizational climate, 112–114, 113f
Burnout, 54, 112

Capital
  human, 102–103
  intellectual, 101–102
Cardiac coherence
  definition of, 9
  description of, 37–38
  effect of heart coherence, 37–38
Care
  equation for, 129–130
  organizational benefits of, 130–131
  sincere, 131–132
Caregivers, 131–132
Change, in organization, 16
Climate, of organization
  boosting of, 109
  definition of, 111
  description of, 4
  ignoring of, 114–115
  principles of, 5
  productivity and, relationship between, 112–114
  viruses that attack. *See* Emotional virus

Page references followed by "t" denote tables; "f" denote figures.

Coaching, operationalized, 165–167
Coherence
  benefits of, 9
  biomedical measurement of, 9
  business success and, 41, 72–73
  cardiac
    definition of, 9
    description of, 37–38
    effect of heart coherence, 37–38
  daily experience with, 8–9
  effect of negative thoughts on, 9
  effect of perception on, 18
  entrainment and, 159
  importance for children, 40
  influence on quantum future, 177
  military, 167–168
  organizational. *See* Organizational
      coherence
  progressive nature of, 9–10
  scientific example of, 8
  self-care and, 135–136
Coherent communication
  description of, 81
  elements of, 79
  principles of, 4, 6
Common sense
  description of, 44
  as form of intuition, 44
Communication
  authentic
    description of, 81
    elements of, 81
    requirements for, 82–83
  barriers to, 86–87
  by body language, 83
  coherent. *See* Coherent
      communication
  electronic forms, 95
  e-mail. *See* E-mail
  gender differences in, 144
  voice mail, 106
Compassion, 59
Computers
  business capital spent on, 97
  productivity effects, 101
Core values
  description of, 126
  as intelligence, 127

  as organizational foundation,
      126–127
  types of, 126
Cortical inhibition, 38
Cortisol
  gender differences, 142–143
  release of, effect of stress on, 33

Decoding, 86
DHEA
  description of, 35
  maladaptation effects on, 52–53
DNA, 24

Efficiency
  effect of listening on, 90–91
  energy, from freeze-frame, 64–65
Ego drive, 149–150
E-mail
  organizational incoherence from, 96
  reading strategies for, 105
Emotional hijacking, 33
Emotional intelligence
  biological origins of, 29–30
  definition of, 28
  gender differences, 143
  in men, 143
  studies of, 28
  in women, 143
Emotional virus
  description of, 115–117
  elimination of, 117–118
  globalization of, 119
  how to spot, 120–122, 121f
  individuals responsible for, 118–119
  methods of attacking, 115–116
  strengthening of organizational
      immune system to prevent,
      119–120
  symptoms of, 120–121
Emotions
  business success and, 29
  coherence of, 41
  drain of, 55–56
  function of, 27
  gender and, 141–142
  heart and, relationship between,
      26–27, 54–55

immune health and, 53–54
mismanaged, 29, 56
processing of, 27
reciprocity of, 40
second brain processing of, 31
stress and, 33, 35
Encoding, 86
Energy
accumulation of, 56
drain sources
description of, 70
judgmental, 76–77
unmet expectations, 75
efficient use of, 64–65
Entrainment
coherence and, 159
concept of, 11f
definition of, 10, 159
examples of, 11
for teamwork success, 159–160
Expectations
reality and, 74
sales, 75–76
unmet
destructive effects of, 73–74
energy expenditure for, 75

Female-male issues
balance of, 148–149
competitiveness, 149–150
future considerations, 150–151
gender-based differences
biological, 139–140
communication styles, 144
emotional intelligence, 143
emotions, 141–142
global perspective of, 144–145
language, 141
neurological, 140–141
Freeze-frame
for coherence, 161
description of, 58–59
effect on information, 104
elements of, 61
energy efficiency from, 64–65
heart intelligence, 60–61, 66
for overcaring, 134
reasons why it works, 60–61

for reducing expectations, 76
steps, 59–60
Frequency
definition of, 42
of intelligence, 42–43

Global Oil Company, 183–184, 184t–186t
Global Technology Company, 186–187
Gut brain, 26

Health
effect of genetics on, 53
productivity and, relationship
between, 13–14
stress and, 14
Heart
communication with brain, 36, 41
cultural interpretations of, 36, 37f
emotions and, 26–27
entrainment of, 11–12
hormones produced by, 142
intrinsic nervous system in, 26–27
intuition and, 26–27
rhythmic changes in, 41
stress effects on, 54–55
survival of, 54–55
Heart balance, 147–149
Heart intelligence
definition of, 41, 43, 46
description of, 36
for discriminating significance of
events, 128–129
freeze-frame access to, 60–61, 66
information technology and, 98–100
listening to, 85–86
principles of, 42
for women, 146
Heart lock-in, 136–137
HeartMapping
applications, 171–173
description of, 168–169
schematic representation, 172f–173f
teamwork improvements using,
169–171
HeartMath
founding of, 2–3
heart intelligence definition, 43
mental intelligence definition, 43

Heart stand, 147–148
Hormones, 142–143. *See also specific hormones*
Human body
    caring for, 45–46
    resilience of, 27–28
Human capital, 102–103

Illness, in workplace, 114–115
Immune system
    emotions and, 53–54
    of organization, strengthening to
        prevent emotional virus,
        119–120
Immunoglobulin A, 120f
Incoherence, organizational
    causes of, 76
    consequences of, 29
    effect on individual coherence, 39
    e-mail and, 96
    example of, 39
Information
    sharing of, intuitive intelligence
        effects on, 103–104
    value-added, 104
Information overload phenomenon,
    96
Information technology. *See also*
    Technology
    future of, 104–107
    heart intelligence response to,
        98–100
    productivity enhancements
        through, 100–101
    sources of, 97
Inner quality management
    case studies
        California State Agency #1,
            187–188, 188t–189t
        California State Agency #2,
            189–192
        Global Oil Company, 183–184,
            184t–186t
        Global Technology Company,
            186–187
        government consulting firm,
            192–194, 193t–195t
    results of, 13–15, 91, 160, 164–167

development of, 3
dynamics of
    coherent communication, 6
    internal self-management. *See*
        Internal self-management
    organizational climate. *See*
        Climate, of organization
    overview, 3–4, 4f
    renewal. *See* Renewal, of
        organization
    overview, 179–180
    stress reductions, 160–161
Intellectual capital, 101–102
Intelligence
    computing developments and, sim-
        ilarities between, 24
    definition of, 23–24
    distributed, 24–26
    distribution in human system, 3
    frequencies of, 42–43
    intuitive, 44–45
    mental, 43
    neural pathways of, 24–25
    scientific view of, 23–24
    values as, 127
Internal self-management
    case study of, 66–68
    dynamics of intelligence. *See* Intelli-
        gence stress. *See* Stress
    freeze-frame. *See* Freeze-frame
    principles of, 4–5
    schematic of, 21f
    well-being improvements, 67
Intuition
    common sense as form of, 44
    compassion and, 43
    heart and, relationship between,
        26–27
    of women, 145–147
Intuitive intelligence
    description of, 44–45, 85
    information sharing enhancements
        using, 103–104
    significance of events and, 128
Intuitive listening
    description of, 87–88
    elements of, 88
    example of, 89–90

organizational applications for,
91–92
for team entrainment, 161
IQM. *See* Inner quality management

Judgmental
causes for, 76
energy drain from being, 76–77

Learning
amygdala and, 38–39
coherence and, 39–40
Listening
effect on efficiency, 90–91
to heart intelligence, 85–86
importance of, 85
intuitive, 86–90, 161
levels of, 87

Maladaptation
description of, 50–51
hormonal, 52–53
to stress, 50–51
Male-female issues
balance of, 148–149
competitiveness, 149–150
future considerations, 150–151
gender-based differences
biological, 139–140
communication styles, 144
emotional intelligence, 143
emotions, 141–142
global perspective of, 144–145
language, 141
neurological, 140–141
Management
key skills for, 158–161
overcaring by, 135
quantum, 177–179
service-profit chain approach, 157
supportive types of, 113
Medulla, 49
Memory
amygdala's role in, 32
automaticity of, 49
Military coherence, 167–168
MindMapping, 168–169, 172f
Mind stances, 147

Neutral
benefits of, 63
definition of, 61
importance of, 63
for negative reactions, 64
workplace use of, 62

Organizational coherence
case study of, 12
effect of individual coherence on,
10
measurement of, 10
survey to assess
case study of, 195, 196t–198t
description of, 122–125
Organizational incoherence
causes of, 76
consequences of, 29
effect on individual coherence,
39
e-mail and, 96
example of, 39
Organizations
adaptability of, 127–128
changes in, 15–16
chaos in, 2
climate of. *See* Climate, of
organization
composition of, 4–5
criteria for success, 141
intuitive listening application to,
91–92
Overachieving, 163–164
Overcare
definition of, 132
draining effects of, 132–133
effect on effectiveness, 134–135
examples of, 132
freeze-frame for, 134
identification of, 133–135
in management style, 135
self-care for reducing, 135–136
Oxytocin, 142

Perception
amygdala's role in, 32
effect on coherence, 18
effect on stress-related emotions, 35

Perception *continued*
  of organization climate and productivity, relationship between, 112–114
Presence, 180–181
Productivity
  effect of computers on, 101
  of employees
    effect of organizational change on, 16
    health and, relationship between, 13–14
  information technology-based enhancement of, 100–101
  organizational climate and, relationship between, 112–114
Pruning, 40

Quantum future, 175–177
Quantum management, 177–179

Ratios, 75–76
Renewal, of organization
  description of, 4
  principles of, 6–7
  schematic representation of, 153f
  service-profit chain, 156–158
Resilience, of human body and spirit, 27–28

Self-care
  balanced, 135
  coherence and, 135–136
  description of, 135
Self-management. *See* Internal self-management
Self-security, 178
Service-profit chain, 156–158
Significance, of events, 128–129
Sincerity, 131–132, 162
State-specific feelings, 28
Strategy, 155
Stress
  annual costs associated with, 16
  cortisol release and, 33
  effect on cortical brain regions, 32
  emotion and, 33, 35
  feelings associated with, 33

freeze-frame. *See* Freeze-frame
  globalization of, 16–17
  health and, 14
  inner quality management reductions, 160–161
  maladaptation to, 50–51
  physiologic effects of, 52–53
  physiology of, 33–36
  prevention of, 63–64
  word origin of, 51
  in workplace, 16, 114–115
Supportive management, 113

Teams
  appreciation of, 162–163
  coherence of, freeze-frame for, 161
  energizing of, 161
  HeartMapping use. *See* Heart-Mapping
  overachieving of, 163–164
Technology. *See also* Information technology
  changing forms of, 96–97
  consumers and, relationship between, 98
  data increases, 95–96
  growths in, 94
  information quality increases from, 99
Time
  convenience, 73
  experts in use of, 72–73
  management of, 70–71
  problem resolution after expenditure of, 71–72
  unmanageable state of, 73
Time shift, 71–72
Tone of voice, 83
Touch, electricity transferred during, 83, 84f

Underachievers, 164

Value-added information, 104
Virus, emotional
  description of, 115–117
  elimination of, 117–118
  globalization of, 119

how to spot, 120–122, 121f
individuals responsible for, 118–119
methods of attacking, 115–116
strengthening of organizational
    immune system to prevent,
    119–120
symptoms of, 120–121
Voice mail, 106
Vulnerability, 181–182

Women
    intuition of, 145–147
    men and
        balance of, 148–149
        competitiveness, 149–150

future considerations, 150–151
gender-based differences
    biological, 139–140
    communication styles, 144
    emotional intelligence, 143
    emotions, 141–142
    global perspective of, 144–145
    language, 141
    neurological, 140–141

Year 2000 computer problem, 94–95,
    97

Butterworth-Heinemann Business Books . . .
for Transforming Business

5th Generation Management, Co-creating Through Virtual Enterprising, Dynamic Teaming, and Knowledge Networking, Revised Edition,
Charles M. Savage, 0-7506-9701-6

Beyond Strategic Vision: Effective Corporate Action with Hoshin Planning,
Michael Cowley and Ellen Domb, 0-7506-9843-8

Beyond Time Management: Business with Purpose,
Robert A. Wright, 0-7506-9799-7

The Breakdown of Hierarchy: Communicating in the Evolving Workplace,
Eugene Marlow and Patricia O'Connor Wilson, 0-7056-9746-6

Business and the Feminine Principle: The Untapped Resource,
Carol R. Frenier, 0-7506-9829-2

Cultivating Common Ground: Releasing the Power of Relationships at Work,
Daniel S. Hanson, 0-7506-9832-2

Flight of the Phoenix: Soaring to Success in the 21st Century,
John Whiteside and Sandra Egli, 0-7506-9798-9

Getting a Grip on Tomorrow: Your Guide to Survival and Success in the Changed World of Work,
Mike Johnson, 0-7506-9758-X

Innovation Strategy for the Knowledge Economy: The Ken Awakening,
Debra M. Amidon, 0-7506-9841-1

The Intelligence Advantage: Organizing for Complexity,
Michael D. McMaster, 0-7506-9792-X

The Knowledge Evolution: Expanding Organizational Intelligence,
Verna Allee, 0-7506-9842-X

Leadership in a Challenging World: A Sacred Journey,
Barbara Shipka, 0-7506-9750-4

Leading from the Heart: Choosing Courage over Fear in the Workplace,
Kay Gilley, 0-7506-9835-7

Learning to Read the Signs: Reclaiming Pragmatism in Business,
F. Byron Nahser, 0-7506-9901-9

Marketing Plans that Work: Targeting Growth and Profitability,
   Malcolm H.B. McDonald and Warren J. Keegan, 0-7506-9828-4

A Place to Shine: Emerging from the Shadows at Work,
   Daniel S. Hanson, 0-7506-9738-5

Power Partnering: A Strategy for Business Excellence in the 21st Century
   Sean Gadman, 0-7506-9809-8

Resources for the Knowledge-Based Economy Series

   Knowledge Management and Organizational Design,
      Paul S. Myers, 0-7506-9749-0

   Knowledge Management Tools,
      Rudy L. Ruggles, III, 0-7506-9849-7

   Knowledge in Organizations,
      Laurence Prusak, 0-7506-9718-0

   The Strategic Management of Intellectual Capital,
      David A. Klein, 0-7506-9850-0

Setting the PACE® in Product Development: A Guide to Product
And Cycle-time Excellence,
   Michael E. McGrath, 0-7506-9789-X

Time to Take Control: The Impact of Change on Corporate Computer Systems,
   Tony Johnson, 0-7506-9863-2

The Transformation of Management,
   Mike Davidson, 0-7506-9814-4

Who We Could Be at Work, Revised Edition,
   Margaret A. Lulic, 0-7506-9739-3

To purchase a copy of any Butterworth-Heinemann Business title, please visit your
local bookstore or call 1-800-366-2665.

DOC CHILDRE

In 1991 Doc founded the Institute of HeartMath (IHM), a nonprofit research and training organization dedicated to researching the role of the heart in the human system, and putting the heart back into social systems. He assembled a talented team of research scientists, professional educators, and businesspeople who care deeply about the stresses people face today. HeartMath tools help people systematically learn how to utilize "heart intelligence" for greater health, well-being, improved communication skills, and job satisfaction.

Doc consults to presidents and leaders in organizations in how to create profound shifts in decision-making effectiveness, time use, and productivity, while dramatically enhancing personal balance and well-being. HeartMath provides individuals and organizations with practical, scientifically-validated technology that Doc developed to release stress in the moment and find inner peace of mind and new hope. In 1998 IHM licensed all of its training and business consulting activities to HeartMath LLC, of which Doc is President and CEO.

The HeartMath system has been featured in *USA Today, US News & World Report,* CNN, NBC's "Today Show," "CBS This Morning," *Psychology Today, Industry Week, Army Times, New York Times, Los Angeles Times, San Francisco Chronicle, Truckers' USA,* and numerous other publications that span many facets of society.

Doc is the author of seven other books that explore applications of the HeartMath system:

- *The How to Book of Teen Self-Discovery* (approved as a textbook in California)
- *Self-Empowerment: The Heart Approach to Stress Management*
- *Freeze-Frame: One-Minute Stress Management* (new edition 1998)
- *A Parenting Manual: Heart Hope for the Family*
- *Cut-Thru: How to Care Without Becoming a Victim*
- *Teaching Children to Love: Raising Balanced Kids in Unbalanced Times*
- *The HeartMath Solution* (May 1999)

Doc is also an acclaimed composer whose concept of "designer music" became internationally recognized through his first album, *Heart Zones.* His latest album, *Speed of Balance,* is described as "a musical adventure for emotional and mental regeneration."

BRUCE CRYER

Bruce brings more than 20 years of experience in business management, human performance training, and organizational change to the position of Vice President, Global Business Development, HeartMath LLC. Bruce helped launch the Institute of HeartMath and is one of the key architects of the Inner Quality Management (IQM) training programs. IQM incorporates the Institute's innovative biomedical research into practical tools and strategies to enhance organizational effectiveness, creativity, innovation, and increased productivity.

Bruce successfully guided HeartMath programs into the global corporate arena, with significant projects at clients such as Motorola, Hewlett-Packard, CIBC (Canadian Imperial Bank of Commerce), Royal Dutch Shell, LifeScan (a Johnson & Johnson company), and Cathay Pacific Airways. He also has trained trainers who are now delivering HeartMath programs for Fortune 500 companies, the U.S. military, and public and private sector organizations in Canada, Europe, and Asia.

Bruce has edited more than 25 books on human performance, stress reduction, and education, including *Freeze-Frame: One-Minute Stress Management* (now in its fourth printing), and is contributing editor for *A Parenting Manual*. For eight years, Bruce served as Vice President for a biotech company, where his broad-based, senior-level experience was in the areas of marketing, training, distribution, project planning, logistics, and implementation.

Bruce is on the faculty of the Stanford Executive Program, has lectured at the Stanford Sloan Program, the University of California at Berkeley Haas Business School, the Santa Clara University Leavey School of Business, the Wharton Club of Northern California, and the Nanyang Polytechnic University School of Business Management in Singapore. His views on developing a more coherent, effective workforce have been presented to business audiences such as Young President's Organization (YPO), The Executive Committee (TEC), Council of Growing Companies, The Leadership Network, Women for Women (WOW) in Singapore, Institute for the Future's Organization to Organism Conference, the 1996 Business Process and Workflow Conference, the 1997 Giga World IT Forum, the 1998 Systems Thinking in Action Conference, the 1998 Year 2000 Conference in New York, and the LPGA (Ladies Professional Golf Association). He has also been interviewed in or written for such publications as *New York Times, Christian Science Monitor, Industry Week, Computerworld, CIO, Customer Service Professional, California Business, At Work, Entrepreneur Magazine, Advance,* and *Executive Directions.* He has been a guest on hundreds of television and radio programs nationwide. A former actor and singer on Broadway, Bruce brings a warm, engaging style to all his work.

The HeartMath Experience

HeartMath training programs are specifically designed to provide tools to increase productivity through enhanced job satisfaction, goal clarity and improved health by reducing tension, burnout, physical symptoms of stress and negative moods. The tools and techniques are for practical use in the midst of life's fast-paced situations, information overload and often unpredictable stresses.

HeartMath provides retreats, seminars and off-site programs to help individuals and organizations discover and sustain the use of the HeartMath System. Inner Quality Management (IQM) is the flagship organizational program and has a modular design so it can be customized to fit an organization's specific business objectives.

For more information on trainings and seminars

call 1-800-450-9111

or write to:

HEARTMATH®

14700 West Park Avenue
Boulder Creek, CA 95006
Visit our web site: http://www.heartmath.com

Continue the HeartMath Experience with Books, Tapes and Learning Programs

The HeartMath System, developed by Doc Childre, provides simple, proven techniques to help people manage mental and emotional responses to life through the natural common-sense intelligence of their own hearts. Explore and experience more of the HeartMath System with books, music, audio tapes and learning programs.

HeartMath products can be used by individuals, small groups or organizations to learn and sustain the skills necessary to function at a higher level of personal and organizational quality.

For a free catalog of our complete HeartMath product line or for information on volume discounts

Call 1-800-372-3100

or request through:

info@planetarypub.com

or write to:

PLANETARY
Publishers of the HeartMath® System

PO Box 66
Boulder Creek, CA   95006
Visit our web site: http://www.planetarypub.com

Support the HeartMath Experience

The Institute of HeartMath (IHM) is a nonprofit research organization that is revolutionizing our understanding of human intelligence and what role the heart plays. IHM scientific studies showing how the heart affects perception, information processing, hormonal and immune system balance have been published in major medical journals such as *The American Journal of Cardiology*, *Stress Medicine* and the *Journal of Advancement in Medicine*.

In addition, IHM is constructing a wellness clinic, conducts capital campaigns to support the research and administrates the HeartMath Hub program—a network of small study groups for developing heart intelligence.

For information on
- *Participating in or starting a Hub group in your area*
- *Contributing to Capital Campaigns*
- *IHM research and case studies*
- *Volunteer programs*

Call 831-338-8500

or email us at:

info@heartmath.org

or write to:

INSTITUTE OF HEARTMATH®
A NONPROFIT CORPORATION

PO Box 1463
Boulder Creek, CA 95006
Visit our web site: http://www.heartmath.org